GLAMOUR: A WORLD PROBLEM

BOOKS BY ALICE A. BAILEY

Initiation, Human and Solar
Letters on Occult Meditation
The Consciousness of the Atom
A Treatise on Cosmic Fire
The Light of the Soul
The Soul and its Mechanism
From Intellect to Intuition
A Treatise on White Magic
From Bethlehem to Calvary
Discipleship in the New Age–Vol. I
Discipleship in the New Age–Vol. II
Problems of Humanity
The Reappearance of the Christ
The Destiny of the Nations
Glamour: A World Problem
Telepathy and the Etheric Vehicle
The Unfinished Autobiography
Education in the New Age
The Externalisation of the Hierarchy
A Treatise on the Seven Rays:
Vol. I–Esoteric Psychology
Vol. II–Esoteric Psychology
Vol. III–Esoteric Astrology
Vol. IV–Esoteric Healing
Vol. V–Rays and Initiations

GLAMOUR:
A WORLD PROBLEM

by

ALICE A. BAILEY

LUCIS PUBLISHING COMPANY
New York

LUCIS PRESS LIMITED
London

COPYRIGHT © 1950 BY LUCIS TRUST
COPYRIGHT © RENEWED 1978 BY LUCIS TRUST

First Printing, 1950

Fourth Printing, 1971 (First Paperback Edition)

Eleventh Printing, 2014

ISBN No. 978-085330-109-7
0-85330-109-3

Library of Congress Catalogue Card Number: 50-14189

All rights reserved. No part of this book may be reproduced or utilised in any form or by any means, electronic or mechanical, including photocopying, recording, or by any information storage and retrieval system, without permission in writing from the publisher.

The publication of this book is financed by the Tibetan Book Fund which is established for the perpetuation of the teachings of the Tibetan and Alice A. Bailey.

This Fund is controlled by the Lucis Trust, a tax-exempt, religious, educational corporation.

The Lucis Publishing Company is a non-profit organisation owned by the Lucis Trust. No royalties are paid on this book.

This title is also available in eBook,
Audiobook and Clothbound editions.

This book has been translated into Croatian, Danish, Dutch, French, German, Greek, Hungarian, Italian, Japanese, Portuguese, Russian, Spanish and Swedish. Translation into other languages is proceeding.

LUCIS PUBLISHING COMPANY
120 Wall Street, New York, NY 10005

LUCIS PRESS LIMITED
Suite 54, 3 Whitehall Court, London SW1A 2EF
www.lucistrust.org

EXTRACT FROM A STATEMENT BY THE TIBETAN

Suffice it to say, that I am a Tibetan disciple of a certain degree, and this tells you but little, for all are disciples from the humblest aspirant up to, and beyond, the Christ Himself. I live in a physical body like other men, on the borders of Tibet, and at times (from the exoteric standpoint) preside over a large group of Tibetan lamas, when my other duties permit. It is this fact that has caused it to be reported that I am an abbot of this particular lamasery. Those associated with me in the work of the Hierarchy (and all true disciples are associated in this work) know me by still another name and office. A.A.B. knows who I am and recognises me by two of my names.

I am a brother of yours, who has travelled a little longer upon the Path than has the average student, and has therefore incurred greater responsibilities. I am one who has wrestled and fought his way into a greater measure of light than has the aspirant who will read this article, and I must therefore act as a transmitter of the light, no matter what the cost. I am not an old man, as age counts among the teachers, yet I am not young or inexperienced. My work is to teach and spread the knowledge of the Ageless Wisdom wherever I can find a response, and I have been doing this for many years. I seek also to help the Master M. and the Master K.H. whenever opportunity offers, for I have been long connected with Them and with Their work. In all the above, I have told you much; yet at the same time I have told you nothing which would lead you to offer me that blind obedience and the foolish devotion which the emotional aspirant offers to the Guru and Master Whom he is as yet unable to contact. Nor will he make that desired contact until he has transmuted emotional devotion into unselfish service to humanity,—not to the Master.

The books that I have written are sent out with no claim for their acceptance. They may, or may not, be correct, true and useful. It is for you to ascertain their truth by right practice and by the exercise of the intuition. Neither I nor A.A.B. is the least interested in having them acclaimed as inspired writings, or in having anyone speak of them (with bated breath) as being the work of one of the Masters. If they present truth in such a way that it follows sequentially upon that already offered in the world teachings, if the information given raises the aspiration and the will-to-serve from the plane of the emotions to that of the mind (the plane whereon the Masters *can* be found) then they will have served their purpose. If the teaching conveyed calls forth a response from the illumined mind of the worker in the world, and brings a flashing forth of his intuition, then let that teaching be accepted. But not otherwise. If the statements meet with eventual corroboration, or are deemed true under the test of the Law of Correspondences, then that is well and good. But should this not be so, let not the student accept what is said.

AUGUST 1934

THE GREAT INVOCATION

From the point of Light within the Mind of God
   Let light stream forth into the minds of men.
   Let Light descend on Earth.

From the point of Love within the Heart of God
   Let love stream forth into the hearts of men.
   May Christ return to Earth.

From the centre where the Will of God is known
   Let purpose guide the little wills of men—
     The purpose which the Masters know and serve.

From the centre which we call the race of men
   Let the Plan of Love and Light work out.
   And may it seal the door where evil dwells.

Let Light and Love and Power restore the Plan on Earth.

"The above Invocation or Prayer does not belong to any person or group but to all Humanity. The beauty and the strength of this Invocation lies in its simplicity, and in its expression of certain central truths which all men, innately and normally, accept—the truth of the existence of a basic Intelligence to Whom we vaguely give the name of God; the truth that behind all outer seeming, the motivating power of the universe is Love; the truth that a great Individuality came to earth, called by Christians, the Christ, and embodied that love so that we could understand; the truth that both love and intelligence are effects of what is called the Will of God; and finally the self-evident truth that only through *humanity* itself can the Divine Plan work out."

ALICE A. BAILEY

TABLE OF CONTENTS

		PAGE
CERTAIN PRELIMINARY CLARIFICATIONS		1
I.	THE NATURE OF GLAMOUR	26
	1. Glamour upon the Mental Plane—Illusion	53
	2. Glamour upon the Astral Plane—Glamour	69
	3. Glamour upon the Etheric Levels—Maya	84
	4. Glamour upon the Higher Mental Planes—The Dweller on the Threshold	90
II.	THE CAUSES OF GLAMOUR	94
	1. The Racial and Individual Growth of Glamour	94
	2. The Causes Producing World Glamour	104
	3. The Contrast between Higher and Lower Glamours	125
	a. Illusion and Intuition	128
	b. Glamour and Illumination	139
	c. Maya and Inspiration	148
	d. The Dweller on the Threshold and the Angel of the Presence	152
III.	THE ENDING OF GLAMOUR	161
	1. Outline of the Technique of the Presence	172
	a. The Intuition Dispels Individual Illusion	177
	b. Group Intuition Dispels World Illusion	184

2. Outline of the Technique of Light	190
a. Individual Glamour	202
b. Group Glamour and World Glamour	212
3. Outline of the Technique of Indifference	241
a. Force Distribution and Manipulation upon the Etheric Plane	246
b. The Use of the Science of the Breath	253
c. The Technique of Indifference	260
IV. THE TECHNIQUE OF FUSION.	266
INDEX	275

PUBLISHER'S STATEMENT

In *Discipleship in the New Age, Volumes I and II*, certain personal instructions given by the Tibetan to a group of disciples were made public. These instructions together with certain esoteric teaching were first published by Alice A. Bailey, with the consent of the disciples involved, in 1944.

Unpublished manuscripts containing additional instructions and esoteric teachings as completed by Mrs. Bailey are now available. This text was written from time to time over a period of nine years from 1935 to 1944.

In various places in the text of *Glamour: A World Problem* references are made to the same discipleship group.

In the present volume certain forms of group work in meditation are included because of their informative value and because they illustrate the practical value of the teaching given. The reader, however, should recognise that meditations suitable for special group purposes are not in general as effective when used as an individual exercise.

The potency of an integrated group composed of disciples who have a common vision and an established group purpose is very great, and can be a real service to mankind. The newer Aquarian techniques include such group endeavours. The published writings by the Tibetan and Alice A. Bailey provide information for wise and useful experimentation in group work which is undertaken as a spiritual world service and not as a means of spiritual unfoldment of the individual aspirant.

Such group action, voluntarily entered into, when not dominated by autocratic leadership control, and if undertaken with due humility and caution, is greatly to be desired at the present time. Such action should be recognized as being pioneering experimental ventures.

Groups of this sort have already appeared in various parts of the world and may well contribute to the success of the work of the New Group of World Servers. Information about this worldwide group of servers is given in *A Treatise on White Magic* and in *A Treatise on the Seven Rays, Vol. II.*

FOSTER BAILEY

July 1950

CERTAIN PRELIMINARY CLARIFICATIONS

All groups involved in esoteric work have their own dharma or duty and all have their peculiar objective. In order that you may clearly vision what you, as aspirants to discipleship have to do, and so intelligently cooperate, I will concisely state the purpose:

Dharma means duty, or obligation, and it is your definite and specific obligation to develop the intuition. The means or methods whereby this development is to be brought about, can be by the study of symbols.

I would ask you to note that generalities concerning the intuition, and attempts to define it are very common, but that a real appreciation of it is rare.

We are told by physicians and scientists that thousands of cells in the human brain are still dormant and, consequently, that the average human being uses only a small part of his equipment. The area of the brain which is found around the pineal gland is that connected with the intuition, and it is these cells which must be roused into activity before there can be any real intuitive perception which, when aroused, will manifest soul control, spiritual illumination, true psychological understanding of one's fellowmen, and a development of the true esoteric sense, which is the objective before you at this time.

I would like to divide what I have to say into three parts, and I plead for a close study of my words:

I. I seek to define for you the intuition.

II. I shall deal with its mode of development through the study of symbology.

III. I shall close by giving some specific instructions as to a useful mode of procedure.

Should you, therefore, find these articles hard to understand and your reaction slow, you must bear in mind that this indicates your need for this study and corroborates what I am telling you. If you will seriously consider with me what the intuition is *not*, I think my words will find in you an inner response.

I. Definition of the Intuition

The intuition is not a welling forth of love to people and, therefore, an understanding of them. Much that is called the intuition is recognition of similarities and the possession of a clear analytical mind. Intelligent people who have lived in the world for some time and who have experienced much and who have contacted many other people can usually sum up with facility the problems and dispositions of others, provided they are interested. This they must not, however, confound with the intuition.

The intuition has no relation to psychism, either higher or lower; the seeing of a vision, the hearing of the Voice of the Silence, a pleased reaction to teaching of any kind does not infer the functioning of the intuition. It is not only the seeing of symbols, for that is a special sort of perception and the capacity to tune in on the Universal Mind upon that layer of Its activity which produces the pattern-forms on which all etheric bodies are based. It is not intelligent psychology, and a loving desire to help. That emanates from the interplay of a personality, governed by a strong soul orientation, and the group-conscious soul.

Intuition is the synthetic understanding which is the prerogative of the soul and it only becomes possible when the soul, on its own level, is reaching in two directions: towards the

Certain Preliminary Clarifications

Monad, and towards the integrated and, perhaps (even if only temporarily) coordinated and at-oned personality. It is the first indication of a deeply subjective unification which will find its consummation at the third initiation.

Intuition is a comprehensive grip of the principle of universality, and when it is functioning there is, momentarily at least, a complete loss of the sense of separateness. At its highest point, it is known as that Universal Love which has no relation to sentiment or to the affectional reaction but is, predominantly, in the nature of an identification with all beings. Then is true compassion known; then does criticism become impossible; then, only, is the divine germ seen as latent in all forms.

Intuition is light itself, and when it is functioning, the world is seen as light and the light bodies of all forms become gradually apparent. This brings with it the ability to contact the light centre in all forms, and thus again an essential relationship is established and the sense of superiority and separateness recedes into the background.

Intuition, therefore, brings with its appearance three qualities:

Illumination. By illumination I do not mean the light in the head. That is incidental and phenomenal, and many truly intuitive people are entirely unaware of this light. The light to which I refer is that which irradiates the Way. It is "the light of the intellect," which really means that which illumines the mind and which can reflect itself in that mental apparatus which is held "steady in the light." This is the "Light of the World," a Reality which is eternally existent, but which can be discovered only when the individual interior light is recognised as such. This is the "Light of the Ages," which shineth ever more until the Day be with us. The intuition is therefore the recognition in oneself, not theoretically but as a fact in one's experience, of one's complete identification with the Universal Mind, of one's constituting a part of the great World Life, and of one's participation in the eternal persisting Existence.

Understanding. This must be appreciated in its literal sense as that which "stands under" the totality of forms. It connotes the power of recession or the capacity to withdraw from one's agelong identification with form life. I would like to point out that this withdrawal is comparatively easy for those who have much of the first ray quality in them. The problem is to withdraw in the esoteric sense, but to avoid at the same time the sense of separateness, of isolation and of superiority. It is easy for first ray people to resist the tendency to identify themselves with others. To have true understanding involves an increased ability to love all beings and yet, at the same time, to preserve personality detachment. This detachment can be so easily founded on an inability to love, in a selfish concern for one's own comfort—physical, mental or spiritual, and above all, emotional. First ray people dread emotion and despise it, but sometimes they have to swing into an emotional condition before they can use emotional sensitivity in the right manner.

Understanding involves contact with life as an integrated personality, plus egoic reaction to the group purposes and plans. It connotes personality-soul unification, wide experience, and a rapid activity of the indwelling Christ principle. Intuitional understanding is always spontaneous. Where the reasoning *to* an understanding enters, it is not the activity of the intuition.

Love. As earlier said, this is not affectionate sentiment, or the possession of a loving disposition; these two later aspects are incidental and sequential. When the intuition is developed, both affection and the possession of a spirit of

Certain Preliminary Clarifications

loving outgo will, necessarily, in their pure form, be demonstrated, but that which produces these is something much more deep and comprehensive. It is that synthetic, inclusive grasp of the life and needs of all beings (I have chosen these two words with intent!) which it is the high prerogative of a divine Son of God to operate. It negates all that builds barriers, makes criticism, and produces separation. It sees no distinction, even when it appreciates *need,* and it produces in one who loves as a soul immediate identification with that which is loved.

These three words sum up the three qualities or aspects of the intuition and can be covered by the word, universality, or the sense of universal Oneness.

Is that not something which all aspirants aim to achieve? And is it not something that each of you, as individuals, needs in a peculiar sense? Where it is present, there is an immediate decentralisation of the dramatic "I," of that capacity always to relate all happenings, all phenomena, all group work to oneself as the centre.

I cannot enlarge further upon the subject of Intuition. It is too vast a matter, and too abstruse. All I can do is to put before you its three aspects and then to urge upon you the need to submit to that training and to apply to yourselves that discipline which will work out in your life as love, light and understanding. When the theory is grasped and the right adjustments are made and when the needed work is done, the personality then becomes magnetic, whilst the brain cells around the pineal gland, which have hitherto been dormant, become awakened and vibrant. The nucleus of every cell in the body is a point of light, and when the light of the intuition is sensed, it is this cell-light which will immediately respond. The continuance of the inflow of the light of the intuition will draw forth, esoterically speaking, into the light of day every cell which is so constituted that it will respond.

II. THE MODE OF AWAKENING THE INTUITION

There are many ways in which the intuition can be drawn into activity, and one of the most useful and potent is the study and interpretation of symbols.

Symbols are the outer and visible forms of the inner spiritual realities, and when facility in discovering the reality behind any specific form has been gained, that very fact will indicate the awakening of the intuition.

First ray people belong to what is called the "Destroyer Ray" and the power of the first aspect, which is the power to bring to an end, flows through them. They will have a tendency to destroy, as they build, through a wrong direction of energy, through overemphasis of energy in some particular direction, or through misuse of energy in work with themselves or others. Many first ray people have the tendency to pride themselves on this and hide behind a plea that, being upon the first ray, a destructive tendency is unavoidable. Such is not the case. Builders, such as second ray people always are, have to learn to destroy, when prompted by group love and acting under the Will or first ray aspect. Destroyers have to learn to build, acting ever under the impulse of group love and utilising the power of attachment in a detached manner. Both groups, builders and destroyers, must ever work from the standpoint of reality, from the inner nucleus of truth and must "take their stand at the centre."

The study of symbols tends to bring this about and when carried out with faithfulness and diligence, will produce three effects:

1. It trains in the power to penetrate behind the form and to arrive at the subjective reality.

2. It tends to bring about a close integration between soul-mind-brain, and when that is brought about, the inflow of the intuition and, consequently, of illumination and truth becomes more rapidly possible.

3. It will put a strain upon certain unawakened areas in the brain and arouse into activity the brain cells there found, and this is the first stage in the experience of the aspirant. With the majority of true aspirants, the centre between the eyebrows is awakened, whilst the centre at the top of the head is vibrating very gently, but is not in full functioning activity. This higher centre must be awakened more fully before aspirants can measure up to their full opportunity.

In the study of symbols, I would urge upon you the necessity always to put before yourselves the goal of arriving at the underlying concept of any symbol studied. This concept will ever be synthetic. It will not be detailed and in sections. You may have to arrive at this concept through a study of detail and through arriving at the significance of various sections or parts of the symbol under consideration. When, however, your analysis is completed, you must not rest satisfied until you have summed up the meaning of the symbol in some synthetic idea, concept, meaning or name.

Symbols have to be studied in three ways:

a. *Exoterically.* This involves study of its form as a whole, of its lines, and therefore of its numerical significance, and also study of its sectional forms—by which I mean its arrangements, for instance, of cubes, triangles and of stars and their mutual inter-relation.

b. *Conceptually.* This involves arriving at its underlying idea, which may be expressed in its name; at its meaning as that emerges in the consciousness through meditation; and at its significance as a whole or in part. You should, when doing this, bear in mind that the idea connotes the higher or abstract intent; that the meaning is that intent expressed in terms of the concrete mind; and that its significance has in it more of an emotional quality and might be expressed as the type of desire it arouses in you.

c. *Esoterically.* This would cover the effect of the force or energy upon you and of the quality of the vibration it may arouse in you perhaps in some centre, perhaps in your astral body, or perhaps only in your mind.

This study, rightly undertaken, would lead to the unfoldment of the intuition, with its consequent manifestation on the physical plane as illumination, understanding and love.

In the first instance, the objective of the study of symbolism is to enable the student to sense its quality and to contact that vibrant something which lies behind that aggregate of line, colour and form of which the symbol is composed.

To some types of people this study is relatively easy; to the majority it is not easy at all, thereby indicating a lack that must be supplied by the use of those faculties at the present dormant. It is always distasteful to arouse the latent faculties and requires an effort and a determination not to be swayed by personality reactions. To many it is not easily apparent how the penetration into the meaning of a symbol can provide a means whereby the dormant buddhic or intuitional faculty can be brought into functioning activity. It is a delicate art, this art of symbol reading, of "spiritual reading," as our ancient master, Patanjali, calls it. This power to

Certain Preliminary Clarifications

interpret symbols ever precedes true revelation. The comprehension of a truth for which a line or a series of lines composing a symbolic form may stand is not all that has to be done. A good memory may remind you that a series of lines forming a triangle or a series of triangles signifies the Trinity, or any series of triplicates within the macrocosmic or microcosmic manifestation. But that activity and accuracy of the memory will do naught to awaken the dormant brain cells or call into play the intuition. It must be remembered (and here becomes evident the value of a certain amount of technical or academic occultism) that the plane whereon the intuition manifests and where the intuitional state of consciousness is active is that of the buddhic or intuitional plane. This plane is the higher correspondence of the astral or emotional plane, the plane of sensitive awareness through a felt identification with the object of attention or attraction. It becomes evident therefore that if the intuitional faculty is to be brought into activity through the study of symbols, the student must feel with, or be in some way identified with, the qualitative nature of the symbol, with the nature of that reality which the symbolic form veils. It is this aspect of symbolic reading that you are asked to study.

Students should ascertain, therefore, after due study of the form aspect, what the symbol is doing to them, what feeling it evokes, what aspirations it arouses, and what dreams, illusions, and reactions are consciously registered. This stage is an intermediate one between the exoteric reading of a symbol and the conceptual understanding. There is later another intermediate stage between conceptual understanding and esoteric comprehension and application. This latter stage is called "synthetic recognition." Having studied the form and become aware of its emotional significance, you pass to the stage of grasping the basic idea of the symbol, and from thence to a synthetic comprehension of its purpose. This leads to true esotericism which is the practical application of its living synthetic power to the springs of individual life and action.

I would ask you to render not only an intelligent interpretation of the symbol, but also a recognition of the more subtle reaction of your sensitive feeling nature to the symbol as a whole. Study a total of four symbols a year. First, approach the symbol from its form aspect and seek to familiarise yourself with its outer aspect, with the sum total of lines, triangles, squares, circles, crosses and other forms of which it is composed, and as you do this endeavour to comprehend it from the standpoint of the intellect, using your memory and what knowledge you have, to understand it exoterically.

Then as soon as the symbol is truly familiar to you and can be recalled to mind with little effort, endeavour to sense its quality, to contact its vibration and to note its emotional effect upon you. This may vary from day to day or it may always be the same. Be simply honest in your noting this astral reaction to the symbol and see where such reactions lead you, remembering always that they are not intuitional but are reactions to the feeling or astral body.

Finally, take note of what you have found to be, for you, the basic quality of the symbol and then (as in meditation work) lift the whole subject into the mental realm by bringing the focussed attentive mind to bear upon it. This will lead you into the realm of concepts.

We have consequently the following stages in the analysis of a symbol:

1. Its exoteric consideration: line, form and colour.
2. A comprehension in the astral or emotional body of its

quality, the reaction of a sensitive response to the impact of its qualitative nature.

3. A conceptual consideration of its underlying idea, of what it is intended to teach, of the intellectual meaning it is intended to convey.

4. The stage of the synthetic grasp of the purpose of a symbol, of its place in an ordered manifesting plan, of its true unified intent.

5. Identification with the quality and purpose of the symbol as it is illuminated by the mind "held steady in the light." This final stage brings into activity the brain as well as the mind.

The study of symbols viewed as a whole, involves three stages:

First, the investigation of a symbol, and the consequent progress of the analyst from one progressive stage of awareness to another, to a gradual inclusion of the entire field covered by the symbol.

Secondly, an intuitive perception of the symbols to be seen everywhere in the divine manifestation.

Third, the use of symbols on the physical plane, and their right adaptation to a seen and recognised purpose, leading to the subsequent magnetisation of the symbol with the needed quality through which the idea can make its presence felt, in order that the intuited qualified idea may find proper form on the physical plane.

Deal, therefore, with the symbols in a wide generalisation, exoteric, conceptual and esoteric, but add to that an analysis of your sensitivity and response to the quality of the symbol.

Let me recapitulate for a moment. First of all it is valuable to remember that the study of the symbol *exoterically* involves the use of the brain and the memory. You endeavour to study line and form, number and general external aspects, knowing that each line has significance, all numbers have their interpretation and all forms are symbols of an inner quality and life.

The study of symbols *conceptually* carries you inward from the brain to the mind, into the realm of ideas. It sweeps into focussed activity the mental apparatus. You then become aware of the concept or idea which the sign or symbol embodies. You comprehend its meaning and for what it stands. You grasp the purpose for which the form has been brought into manifestation. Your study of number and of line has given you a rich background of knowledge upon the objective plane—a richness in this case dependent upon your own personal reading, mental equipment and knowledge. Your capacity to read a "meaning" into a symbol will be dependent also upon the richness of the meaning you ascribe to the events of your daily life, and your ability to really meditate.

I would like to make clear to you that there is no set interpretation of any symbol, and that for each human being that symbol—whatever it may be—will convey unique meaning. A lack of interest in symbols presupposes usually a lack of interest in the due interpretation of life forms and their meaning. Also, too much *academic* interest in symbols may presuppose a tortuous and intricate mind which loves design and line and form and numerical relationships, but which misses entirely the significance of meaning. The balancing in the mind of form and concept, of expression and quality, of sign and meaning is vital to the growth of the disciple and the aspirant.

The great need for most students is to arrive at *meaning* and to work with ideas and concepts. This activity will necessitate the use of the mind to understand, to grasp and to interpret. It requires the development of that mental sensitivity which will enable its possessor to respond to the vibrations of what we call the Universal Mind, the Mind of God, the Instigator of the Plan. It presupposes a certain ability to interpret and the power to express the idea underlying the symbol so that others may share it with you. *This thought of service and of growth in usefulness must be steadily borne in mind.*

Can you not see how this power to study, to interpret and to penetrate to *meaning* will further your growth spiritually? Can you believe that through the use of this method you may learn to work more intelligently with the Plan and become a better helper of your fellowman?

What is there in this objective world that is not the inadequate symbol of a divine idea? What have we in our outer manifestation but the visible sign (at some stage of the evolving purpose) of the plan of the creating Deity? What are you yourself but the outer expression of a divine idea? We must learn to see symbols all around us and then to penetrate behind the symbol to the idea which it should express.

There is however a technique of study which may be of service to you as you attempt to arrive at an idea and thus study conceptually the many symbols by which we are surrounded. It is largely the technique for which meditation should have prepared you. The difference between this technique and meditation work is mainly one of polarisation and goal. In the study of symbols conceptually, the consciousness is polarised in the mental body, and no attempt is definitely made to contact or involve the soul or ego. Herein lies the distinction between this second stage of symbol interpretation and ordinary meditation. You have exhausted the method of familiarising yourself with the form aspect of the symbol, and you know well its outer contour and externalisation. You know too that a peculiar series of lines (such as, for instance, the three lines forming a triangle) represent such and such an idea or truth or teaching. This is recorded in your brain, drawing on the resources of your memory. The registering of old information and knowledge anent the figures in a symbol serves to pull your consciousness up on to the mental plane and to focus it there in the world of ideas or of concepts. The concepts exist already upon the concrete levels of the mental plane. They are your mental and racial heritage and are ancient mental forms which you can now employ in order to arrive at meaning and significance.

It is an ancient statement of fact, which Plutarch expresses for us in the familiar words, that "An idea is a Being incorporeal, which has no subsistence of itself, but gives figure and form unto shapeless matter and becomes the cause of the manifestation." The figure and form you have registered with your brain and memorised, and likewise its activity in time and space, along with its innate capacity to build the form and express through that form a concept or idea. As you work inwards, you are also becoming aware of the nature of the motivating idea through the study of its form and its demonstrated activity, and you are discovering the field of ideas of analogous nature in which the idea embodied in the symbol finds itself. This field of ideas, inter-related and mutually explanatory, is now open to you and you will increasingly find yourself in a position to move in this world of concepts with freedom. To work and live in the world of ideas now becomes your objective and main effort. You train yourself in the recognition of ideas and concepts as they lie behind every form; you begin to think clearly about them and to see the direction in which they lead you and where, within the Eternal Plan, they fit.

Certain Preliminary Clarifications

If aspirants will do three things:

    a. Develop the power to visualise,

    b. Train the mind to intuit reality,

    c. Rightly interpret that which is seen,

they can provide a demonstrating laboratory for the trained Observers of the world.

One of the things which the developed intuition can do is to break the glamour and illusion which invade the life. One of the things that a group of aspirants, whose intuitional interplay is established, can accomplish, is to aid in the work of smashing world glamour. Such work can be done when you have awakened the intuition, and when your inter-related understanding is firm and true. The Hierarchy will be able to use the world aspirants as an instrument for the breaking of group glamour wherever it may be found. I refer to this possibility in order to incite you all to more rapid and steady growth and effort.

You have been told that one of the needs lying before all aspirants is to arrive at that intuitional knowledge and that intelligent understanding of glamour, both individual and planetary, which will enable them most definitely to work at its dispelling. That understanding will necessarily be only relative, but in the course of the next few years, your knowledge of the subject and of the methods whereby glamour can be dissipated can be materially increased. This *must* happen if you work at the problem consciously in your own lives, and attempt to grasp the underlying theory also.

Very little has been written or taught hitherto anent the subject of glamour, and it may mean much of value if we undertake the consideration of this subject, of its causes, and its effects, and also deal with the technique whereby it can be dissipated and dispelled. It is obvious that I cannot deal with the subject adequately in one instruction, and we will take the next two or three years, therefore, to discuss and study this important matter growing out of the need of the present time and the increased sensitivity of humanity to subtler impressions. It has not been possible for me to do this up till now, as the group was incomplete and the inner cohesion needed strengthening. Now I can do so, as the group members are functioning together with a much increased inner relationship, and a "spirit of love" has been shed abroad among you through the group reaction to each other's need in the recent period of glamour.

It is my intention, therefore, to change your work somewhat, retaining the symbolic phrases as an exercise for your intuitional insight, but dropping the consideration of the more formal and visual symbols. You have not gained from these symbolic forms what has been hoped, for the concrete mind of the majority of the group members simply increased the form aspect, and the remainder needed not this method of instruction and development. We shall change the focus of attention to a deep study of glamour. Herein will lie your service, for as you think truly and use your illumined intelligence (if you can achieve this, my brothers) you can help in time to do two things:

1. Clarify the group mind on this subject. I refer not here to your particular group, but to the world consciousness.

2. Help shatter the great illusion which has held, and still holds, the sons of men in thrall.

I ask, therefore, for your service along these lines, and I request also that you give increased attention at the time of your full moon contact with myself. This group should have a special aptitude for work along the line of dispelling glamour at the period of the full moon. Contact is made on the different planes according to the focus of the subtle bodies of the personnel of the group, and this group makes its contact with me on the higher levels of the astral plane. Hence the clarity of their reactions and the wealth of their detailed records. Also, herein will lie eventually their service, for they can later (but not for some long time yet) utilise the days of contact and the "moment of entrance" (as it is sometimes called) for definite work in dispelling some of the world illusion. First must come, however, aptitude in dispelling it in the personal life of each one of you.

Another group makes its contact with me on mental levels and therein will lie their field of service. Still other groups are only as yet in an embryonic stage. Their personnel is incomplete and the group integration only in process of being set up.

I will, therefore, ask you to intensify your effort each month at the full moon period, and seek to strengthen your tie with myself and with your fellow group members. One word of warning only will I give. Success along this line will bring both its rewards and also its difficulties. You will have to watch with care for the undue stimulation of your astral or emotional nature, with consequent and subsequent glamour. You will have to exercise the deepest watchfulness in the endeavour to work thus on the astral plane, holding simultaneously the attitude of the Observer on the high plane of the soul. No constructive work and no service of vital importance can be rendered in this difficult sphere of activity unless there is this detached and liberated attitude. You are to work in one of the most difficult spheres of activity—perhaps the most difficult to which a disciple can be called—and hence the advisability of working there in group formation. I cannot emphasise too strongly that you are to work as a group and not as individuals.

Three great events are immanent in the world consciousness today:

1. The growth and understanding of telepathic work.
2. A comprehension and scientific investigation of illusion and world glamour.
3. An increase in the right methods of healing.

If this is so, you can see how groups of disciples can constitute a contribution to the emerging revelation and how useful our consecrated service can be. I say "our" advisedly, brother of old, as I am working definitely towards these three ends as a part of my ordained (self-ordained) service. I ask for your cooperation and assistance. *The steady impact of right thought on the human consciousness by trained groups of thinkers* is the method that can be most successfully applied at this time, and here these groups can help profoundly.

One of the things which will emerge most definitely during the next three or four decades is the work that groups can do on levels other than the physical. Group service and united effort towards group welfare has for two centuries been seen on Earth in all fields of human endeavour—political, philanthropic and educational. Group service on the astral plane has been started also since 1875, but united effort to dispel the world glamour is only now in process of organising and this group can be a part of the corporate effort towards this end, and swell the number of those so engaged. Train yourselves, therefore, and learn how to work. Telepathic sensitivity is necessarily the objective of all groups of disciples, but it is the main objective of that group which we might call the Telepathic Communica-

Certain Preliminary Clarifications

tors; here they can render potent service. Groups of sensitives of this order can constitute a working, mediating body, and transmit the new knowledge and teaching for the race; they can mould public opinion and change the current of men's thoughts. All small groups of people, naturally and inevitably, arrive at a telepathic relation between themselves, and between the personnel of similar groups, and this is to be desired and fostered and should rightly and steadily increase. But, as your telepathic sensitivity is increased, see to it that you are not deflected from your main group objective, which is to study and understand the significance of glamour and the laws for its dissipation. Record and note all telepathic activity and phenomena and learn to work this way, but regard it as a secondary issue for you at this time.

One of the outstanding characteristics of the work done at the time of the full moon will be the mass of phenomena noted. This is to be expected as this service calls you to work on the astral plane. But it will provide you with a field for the wise use of the faculty of discrimination. It is too early as yet for you to work at the problem of separating the real from the unreal; your task at first will be *recording.* Keep detailed records. Preserve the scientific attitude of detachment and of recognition and write down all that is sensed, seen or contacted. These records will serve as the basis of analysis if all goes well, and from that analysis we may gather much of value.

What I have to say to you as regards the subject of Glamour falls into certain broad generalisations such as:

      I. The Nature of Glamour.
      II. The Causes of Glamour.
      III. The Dissipation of Glamour.

As we proceed we shall divide our subject up into greater detail, but in this instruction I only seek to get certain broad outlines into your minds so that the theme may fall into right places in your thoughts.

There are four phrases which have for long been bandied about among so-called occultists and esotericists. They are: *glamour, illusion, maya* and the expression, *the dweller on the threshold*. They all stand for the same general concept or some differentiation of that concept. Speaking generally, the interpretations have been as follows, and they are only partial interpretations, and are almost in the nature of distortions of the real truth, owing to the limitations of the human consciousness.

Glamour has oft been regarded as a curious attempt of what are called the "black forces" to deceive and hoodwink well-meaning aspirants. Many fine people are almost flattered when they are "up against" some aspect of glamour, feeling that their demonstration of discipline has been so good that the black forces are interested sufficiently to attempt to hinder their fine work by submerging them in clouds of glamour. Nothing could be further from the truth. That idea is itself part of the glamour of the present time, and has its roots in human pride and satisfaction.

Maya is oft regarded as being of the same nature as the concept promulgated by the Christian Scientist that there is no such thing as matter. We are asked to regard the entire world phenomena as maya and to believe that its existence is simply an error of mortal mind, and a form of auto-suggestion or self-hypnotism. Through this induced belief we force ourselves into a state of mind which recognises that the tangible and the objective are only figments of man's imaginative mind. This, in its turn, is likewise a travesty of reality.

Illusion is regarded rather the same way, only (as we define it) we lay the emphasis upon the finiteness of man's mind. The world of phenomena is not denied, but we regard the mind as misinterpreting it and as refusing to see it as it is in reality. We consider this misinterpretation as constituting the Great Illusion.

The Dweller on the Threshold is usually regarded as presenting the final test of man's courage, and as being in the nature of a gigantic thoughtform or factor which has to be dissipated, prior to taking initiation. Just what this thoughtform is, few people know, but their definition includes the idea of a huge elemental form which bars the way to the sacred portal, or the idea of a fabricated form, constructed sometimes by the disciple's Master to test his sincerity. Some regard it as the sum total of a man's faults, his evil nature, which hinders his being recognised as fit to tread the Path of Holiness. None of these definitions, however, give a true idea of the reality.

I would point out here that (generally speaking) these four expressions are four aspects of a universal condition that is the result of the activity—in time and space—of the human mind. The activity of MINDS! Ponder on this phrase for it gives you a clue to the truth.

The Problem of Illusion lies in the fact that it is a soul activity, and the result of the mind aspect of all the souls in manifestation. It is the soul which is submerged in the illusion and the soul that fails to see with clarity until such time as it has learnt to pour the light of the soul through into the mind and the brain.

The Problem of Glamour is found when the mental illusion is intensified by desire. What the Theosophist calls "kama-manas" produces glamour. It is illusion on the astral plane.

The Problem of Maya is really the same as the above, plus the intense activity produced when both glamour and illusion are realised on etheric levels. It is that vital unthinking emotional MESS (yes, brother of old, that is the word I seek to use) in which the majority of human beings seem always to live.

The Dweller on the Threshold is illusion-glamour-maya, as realised by the physical brain and recognised as that which must be overcome. It is the bewildering thoughtform with which the disciple is confronted, when he seeks to pierce through the accumulated glamour of the ages and find his true home in the place of light.

The above are necessarily only generalisations, and the result also of the activity of the analytical mind, but they serve to embody a part of the problem in words and to convey to your minds a definite thoughtform of what we shall later discuss in detail.

As to the causes of this world condition, what can I say, brother of mine, which will convey meaning to your minds? The cause lies far back in the consciousness of the "imperfect Gods." Does that sentence really mean aught to you? But little, I fear. We must descend into the realm of greater practicality and only deal with the matter as far as it concerns humanity. Planetary illusion will later be briefly dealt with, but the immediate problem before man and the significant contribution of the disciple is the dissipation of much of the glamour in which mankind is immersed and which, during the coming Aquarian Age, will largely disappear in connection with the astral life of the race. The point I would here make is to call attention to the fact that it is in meditation and in the technique of mind control that the thinkers of the world will begin to rid the world of illusion. Hence the increasing interest in meditation as the weight of the world glamour is increasingly realised, and hence the vital necessity for right understanding of the way of mind control.

Another point which should be noted is that in the crystallisation of this material age comes the great opportunity to strike a deadly blow on the planetary Dweller on the Threshold. The reaction at this time, through the stress of circumstances, is bringing about a more spiritual understanding and a reorganisation of human values, and this is part of the process whereby a vital part of the world glamour may be dissipated—if only all men of goodwill within the world aura adhere to their appointed task.

When the Buddha was on Earth and achieved illumination, He "let in" a flood of light upon the world problem through His enunciation of the Four Noble Truths. His body of disciples and His nine hundred arhats formulated those four great truths into a structure of dogma and doctrine that—by the power of collective thought—has greatly helped in the attack upon the world illusion. Today the Christ is carrying forward the same great task and in the spiritual significance of His imminent Coming (and in the language of symbolism) He and His nine thousand arhats will strike a second blow at the world glamour. It is for this that we prepare. Only the intuition can dispel illusion and hence the need of training intuitives. Hence the service you can render to this general cause by offering yourselves for this training. If you can overcome glamour in your own lives and if you can, therefore, comprehend the nature of illusion you will help in

a. The destruction of the dweller on the threshold,

b. The devitalising of the general maya,

c. The dissipation of glamour,

d. The dispelling of illusion.

This you have to do in your own lives and in the group relation. Then your more general contribution will help in the wider human issues. The acuteness of the intellect, and the illumination of the mind, plus love and intention will accomplish much. To this service, I reiterate my call.

During the next few months I would suggest that you do three things:

1. Define in your own words and as the result of meditation, your understanding of the four expressions with which I have been dealing. I ask for a real analysis and not just four sentences of definition. Before I enlarge upon this subject I would like you to organise your minds on the matter, using definitions as a guide to your thought, yet stating the problem as you see it, and seeking to see the differences existing between these four aspects of the world glamour.

2. Say each day, with care and thought, a very familiar prayer, The Lord's Prayer. It has many meanings and the trite and usual Christian significance is not for you. Ponder on this most ancient formula of truth and interpret it entirely in terms of a formula for the dissipation of illusion. Write an exegesis on it from this angle, taking it phrase by phrase and regarding it as giving us seven keys to the secret of the elimination of glamour. The formula (which is not essentially a prayer) can be divided as follows:

   a. Invocation to the solar Lord.
   b. Seven sentences, embodying seven keys for the dissipation of illusion.
   c. A final affirmation of divinity.

Use your intuition and apply these all to the subject of glamour and see at what knowledge you will arrive.

Then write it down in the form of an interpretation or article and we may arrive at much value.

3. Keep a copy of your full moon record and, at the close of six months, subject it to a careful analysis and see what is the sum total of gain. Divide your analysis into the following heads and express your understanding of the phenomena:

    a. As to any real contact.
    b. As to any colour contact or phenomena.
    c. As to any other phenomena sensed, or seen or heard.

That we may all go forward into greater light and understanding, and that the light may shine upon *the vertical Way* of the disciple is my prayer and aspiration for you.

SECTION ONE

THE NATURE OF GLAMOUR

In the preceding pages we dealt with certain definitions of the words (frequently used interchangeably) dealing with illusion and glamour. We found that:

1. *Illusion* is primarily of a mental quality and was characteristic of the attitude of mind of those people who are more intellectual than emotional. They have outgrown glamour as usually understood. It is the misunderstanding of ideas and thoughtforms of which they are guilty, and of misinterpretations.

2. *Glamour* is astral in character, and is far more potent at this time than illusion, owing to the enormous majority of people who function astrally always.

3. *Maya* is vital in character and is a quality of force. It is essentially the energy of the human being as it swings into activity through the subjective influence of the mental illusion or astral glamour or of both in combination.

4. *The Dweller on the Threshold*, always present, swings however into activity only on the Path of Discipleship, when the aspirant becomes occultly aware of himself, of the conditions induced within him as a result of his interior illusion, his astral glamour and the maya surrounding his entire life. Being now an integrated personality (and no one is a disciple, my brother, unless he is mental as well as emotional, which is a point the

The Nature of Glamour

devotee oft forgets) these three conditions (with the preponderance of the effect in one or other of the bodies) are seen as a whole, and to this whole the term the "Dweller on the Threshold" is applied. It is in reality a vitalised thoughtform—embodying mental force, astral force and vital energy.

The problem, therefore, before all of you in this group is to learn first of all:

1. To distinguish between these three inner illusory aspects.
2. To discover what conditions in the environment or in the individual constitution induce these situations of difficulty.
3. To find out what methods are effective in inducing a cessation of the bewildering deceiving conditions.

It must be remembered also that these distorting conditions, found in all of you, are the medium whereby you are tuned in on the world glamour and illusion. The emphasis has been laid in esoteric teaching on the training and liberation of the individual aspirant. This is, of course, necessary, for the mass is made up of the individuals, and in the steady release from the control of these inner delusions will come the eventual clarification of humanity. Therefore each of you in this group must of necessity work separately and apart with himself, and learn to induce those conditions of clarity and truth which will overcome the ancient rhythms and deep-seated habits and thus steadily purify the aura. But this has now to be done *as a group,* and this group constitutes one of the first of the exoteric groups with which it is intended to work in the new age. Through the activity of such groups, the world glamour will be dissipated, but first of all the aspirant must learn to deal with individual and group glamour. It is necessary to remember the following three things. I am going to be brief and technical in teaching this group, for my time is short and you have an adequate technical knowledge with which to understand that whereof I speak.

First, the united auras of the group members ever determine the group condition, the group activity, usefulness, problem and glamour. Hence emerges individual group responsibility and individual usefulness. Each of you either hinders or aids the group, according to his auric condition, which is either in a state of glamour or illusion or is kept relatively free from these conditions.

Second, that the first job that each of you has to do is to determine his own peculiar problem. In giving you your individual instructions, I will take up with you in this instruction where the particular tendency in this direction of each of you lies, and whether it is glamour, illusion or maya to which you habitually succumb. I will deal with directness, for I have tested your sincerity and believe in your willingness to be told the truth. Once you have each determined the specific nature of your peculiar problem, you can then work with deliberation towards its solution—with deliberation, brother of old, and with no speed, but with due care and caution and with right understanding.

Thirdly, you must remember that as I look at the individual in any of these groups, I can at the same time gauge the quality of the group itself as a whole. The amount of inner light that can shine through and make its presence felt in your auras can be seen by me and indicate to me the strength and the efficiency and also the potency of your individual group influence, for the positive auras subordinate the negative auras. What is required is a combination of positive auras, deliberately subordinated to group

The Nature of Glamour

work. As you deal with illusion and as you free your minds from its effects, and as you dissipate the astral glamour in which you are all more or less immersed, you will enter into a greater freedom of living and usefulness. As the maya of distorted energy currents ceases to swing you into lines of undesirable activity, the light that is in you will shine forth with greater clarity. Incidentally the Dweller on the Threshold will slowly and surely disintegrate and leave your way, to the door of Initiation, free and unimpeded.

Strongly *mental* types are subject to illusion. This illusion is in reality a condition wherein the aspirant is being definitely controlled by:

1. A thoughtform of such potency that it does two things:

   a. Controls the life activity or output.
   b. Tunes the aspirant in on the mass thoughtforms, which are of a similar nature, and which are built by others under the dominance of a similar illusion.

This, in its worst aspect, produces mental insanity or *idée fixe,* but in its least dangerous and normal result produces the fanatic. The fanatic is usually—even if he realises it not—a bewildered man, who has a potent idea of some kind or another, but who finds it quite impossible to integrate it into the world picture; to make those needed, and often divinely directed, compromises which profoundly help humanity; to find the time or place for the realities which are within his natural grasp.

2. When a man is highly developed, the mental illusion is built around a definite intuition and this intuition is concretised by the mind until its appearance is so real that the man believes he sees so clearly that which should be done or given to the world that he spends his time endeavouring in a

fanatical manner to make others see it too. Thus his life slips away on the wings of illusion and his incarnation is a relatively profitless one. In a few rare cases, this combination of intuition and mental activity produces the genius in some field or another; but then there is no illusion, but clear thinking, coupled with a trained equipment in that particular field or enterprise

3. The weaker and more average mental types of people succumb to the general field of illusion and of mass illusion. The mental plane manifests a different sort of distortion to that of the astral plane or the etheric. The faculty of discrimination which is being developed has produced sharper lines of demarcation, and instead of the dense fogs and mists of the astral plane or the swirling tides and currents of energy of the etheric plane, we have on the mental plane masses of sharply indicated thoughtforms of a particular quality and note and tone, around which are grouped lesser thoughtforms, created by those who respond to these forms, and to their note, quality and tone. Similarities are then seen to exist which constitute channels or avenues for the magnetic drawing power of the more potent thoughtforms. Ancient theologies in modern garb, fixed presentations of half truth, the wild thinking of various world groups, and many similar emanating sources have—down the ages—produced the world of illusion and those mental states which have held humanity prisoner to wrong concepts and thoughts. So many are these thought producing illusions that the effect in the world today has been to cause a general division of the human race into varying schools of thought (philosophy, science, religion, sociology, etc., etc.), into many parties and groups, all of them coloured by an analogous idea, into groups of idealists fighting each other on behalf of their pet concepts,

The Nature of Glamour

and into tens of thousands of participants in group mental activity. These are today producing the world literature, through which the world platforms are coloured; by their means the world leaders are inspired; and they are responsible at this time for the mass of experiments in the field of government, of education, and of religion which are producing so much of the world unrest, and consequently so much of the world illusion.

What is needed therefore at this time, are thinkers who are training themselves in that mental attitude and one-pointedness which is divorced from the danger of a negative receptivity and is responsive, at the same time, to the higher intuitional inspiration. *It is mediating interpreters of ideas that are needed and not mediums.*

The *emotional* types respond with facility to world glamour and to their own individual inherited and self-induced glamour. The bulk of the people are purely emotional with occasional flashes of real mental understanding—very occasional, my brother, and usually entirely absent. Glamour has been likened to a mist or fog in which the aspirant wanders and which distorts all that he sees and contacts, preventing him from ever seeing life truly or clearly or the conditions surrounding him as they essentially are. When he is a somewhat advanced aspirant, he is aware of the glamour and occasionally sees in a flash in what direction truth for him may lie. But then again the glamour settles down upon him and he is rendered powerless to release himself or to do anything constructive. His problem becomes further complicated by his consequent distress and his deep disgust with himself. He walks ever in a fog and sees naught as it truly exists. He is deceived by the appearance and forgets that which the appearance veils. The emanatory astral reactions which each human being initiates ever surround him and through this mist and fog he looks out upon a distorted world. These reactions and the surrounding aura which they constitute blend and merge with the world glamour and fog and form part of the miasmas and unhealthy emanations for which the masses of men, for millions of years, are responsible.

I would point out to you that, in Lemurian days, glamour and illusion were relatively unknown from the human standpoint. There were no mental reactions and but little emotional response to environment. Men were largely instinctual animals. Glamour began to be found in Atlantean days, and since that time has steadily precipitated, until today when the Hierarchy looks at humanity it appears to be walking in a deep and constantly changing density of currents which hide and distort, and which swirl around the sons of men and prevent their seeing the LIGHT as it is. This is all the more obvious when it is remembered that the other kingdoms of nature are relatively free from glamour and illusion. In our race, the Aryan, the world illusion is gathering weight and slowly emerging into recognition in the human consciousness and this is a real point gained, for that which is recognised can then be intelligently handled, if the will to do so exists. Today illusion is so potent, that few people whose minds are in any way developed but are controlled by these vast illusory thoughtforms, which have their roots and draw their life from the lower personality life and desire nature of the masses of men. It is interesting to remember also in connection with our Aryan race that these thoughtforms draw their vitality also from *the realm of ideas*, but of ideas wrongly intuited and grasped and forced to serve the selfish purposes of men. Their forms have been brought into activity by the steadily growing creative power of mankind, and have been subordinated to the wishes of men, through the

The Nature of Glamour

use of language with its power to limit and distort. The illusion is also precipitated more potently than would otherwise be the case by the effort of many devoted idealistic men to impose these distorted thoughtforms upon the mental bodies of the masses. This constitutes one of the major problems with which the Hierarchy today has to concern itself; it is also one of the first factors which a Master has to consider in connection with any aspirant and disciple.

Glamour, as we have seen, is of more ancient standing and of earlier emergence than is illusion. It has little in it of the mental quality and is the major factor controlling the majority. The objective of all training given on the Path of Discipleship and up to the third initiation is to induce that clear thinking which will render the disciple free from illusion and give to him that emotional stability and poise which gives no room for the entrance of any of the world glamour. This freedom becomes possible when there is in the aspirant no personal glamour, and no deliberately self-induced response to the determining factors which have produced glamour down the ages. With these factors we will later deal.

Maya is the result of both glamour and illusion. It connotes, when present, an integrated personality and therefore the capacity to tune in on mental illusion and astral glamour. Where this condition is found, the problem of the disciple is one of the greatest in the world. What constitutes the prime difficulty of any disciple is the fact that the battleground of his life involves every aspect of his nature. The whole man is involved. Technically, the word MAYA should only be used in two cases:

1. In reference to the united glamour-illusion to which a man who is an integrated personality responds.

2. In speaking of the limitations of the planetary Logos of our planet.

In the above remarks I have given you much food for thought—not only as regards your own personal problems (for all of you are subject to these conditions), but I have also indicated to you what is the nature of glamour. The word is used in all esoteric books and teaching to cover the conditions which are differentiated under the words maya, illusion and glamour itself. Later I will give you some teaching upon the causes of glamour and the methods of its dissipation. But I have given you here enough for the present, for it is my desire that you ponder upon these ideas during the next few months and learn somewhat of the significance of these words which you so lightly use. Watch yourselves and your daily life with discrimination, so that you learn to distinguish between glamour, illusion and maya. See whether you can discover the form which your individual Dweller upon the Threshold is likely to assume as you come into conflict with it; and if you do the same for your group brothers and the immediate world need, you will lose no time in the work of your astral clarification and mental release.

I would ask you to study these instructions with peculiar care, for I am taking the time and trouble these busy days to meet your need and to bring as much light as I can, without infringing your free will, to meet your need and clear your course to service.

I would suggest also that you find out all that you can anent the much misunderstood subject of the *aura*: search out what is said in my books and in the writings extant in any good occult library. I seek no copying out of paragraphs but a formulation of your knowledge so that you can answer

The Nature of Glamour

clearly questions which might be asked. The following three questions are basic:

1. What is the aura and how does it come into existence?
2. How can the aura be made the medium of light, and the light which should shine through it be intensified?
3. Have you noticed what is the effect which your own individual aura is making upon your environment and how can you improve that effect?

This will enable you to make practical application of that which I seek to teach you. Forget not that as you look out upon the world and your immediate environment, that you look out through your aura and have, therefore, to deal with glamour and illusion.

There are three further questions which you might put to yourself, facing the issue in the light of your soul:

1. Do I suffer primarily from glamour or from illusion?
2. Do I know which quality or characteristic in my nature facilitates my tuning in on the world glamour or the world illusion?
3. Have I reached the point where I can recognise my peculiar Dweller on the Threshold, and can I state what form it takes?

That you may indeed as individuals and also as a group learn the meaning of true self-knowledge and so learn to stand in spiritual being, increasingly free from glamour and illusion, is the prayer of your friend and brother who has fought his way through to a greater measure of light . . .

During the past six months, four members of this group of students have been fighting glamour in their own individual lives, and for the most part successfully. I make reference to this because in an experimental group such as this, it is well to anticipate such a situation; such wrestling will naturally occur, because only that which is experimentally known becomes a true content of the equipment of the disciple. Earlier I referred to the fact that part of the plan of the Hierarchy embraces the starting of small groups such as this one which would have the definite objective of providing the active means whereby the world glamour—today so potent and deep—can be dissipated.

The time has not yet come for dealing with the world illusion on a large scale, for the race is not adequately mental nor has the illusion (which is, as I have stated, pre-eminently the result of the misinterpretation of ideas) reached its height. But the hour *has* struck for the first steps to be taken in the dissipation of glamour, and the hold of glamour upon the race should be appreciably lessened in the future. Hence the practical training now being given in this group in their own lives; hence also the intended teaching later to be given to the group—if they measure up to the opportunity—which will enable them to aid in the concerted and planned attack upon the world glamour. Wrestle therefore with your personal problems along these lines, my brothers, for in this way you will gain facility in discernment, in clear precise action, and in strengthened understanding.

In the process of dissipating glamour, the way of the greatest potency is to realise the necessity to act purely as a channel for the energy of the soul. If the disciple can make right alignment and consequent contact with his soul, the results show as *increased light.* This light pours down and irradiates not only the mind, but the brain consciousness as

The Nature of Glamour

well. He sees the situation more clearly: he realises the facts of the case as against his "vain imaginings"; and so the "light shines upon his way." He is not yet able to see truly in the larger sweeps of consciousness; the group glamour and, of course, the world glamour remain to him as yet a binding and bewildering mystery, but his own immediate way begins to clear, and he stands relatively free from the fog of his ancient and distorting emotional miasmas. Alignment, contact with his soul, and then steadfastness, are the keynotes to success.

It will therefore be apparent to you that small groups such as this, if established in different countries and cities and if successful in their personal activities, could play a most useful part. Such groups would have two aspects to their endeavour. They would have to wrestle with group glamour which creeps inevitably into group life through the instrumentality of the group members. Their united personal glamours provide the open door through which group glamour can enter. An instance of this can be seen in this group, when glamour entered in through the medium of L.T.S-K., and swept I.B.S. into its vortex of force. It was overcome, fortunately, leaving you all the richer and more united on account of the strong stand in love taken by the other group members. May I remind L.T.S-K. and I.B.S. of their deep indebtedness to the love of their brothers. The group love protected them. I.B.S. has gone a long way in freeing herself from certain aspects of glamour. L.T.S-K. is also freer than he was, but still has much to do. It is always difficult for the third ray person to cultivate the intuition. The *apparently* profound wisdom of the manipulative and devious science of the intelligence inherent in matter prevents oft the entrance of the true wisdom of the illumined mind. Six months ago I felt that it was probably impossible for L.T.S-K. to free himself from the glamour in which he habitually walked. Today a little more light shines upon his way and he may, if he frees himself still further from his self-generated thoughtforms, make the needed grade.

When group glamour has been somewhat dissipated and the group can walk in the "lighted Way" with freedom, then will come the time when the group can be trained in *group alignment, group contact* and *group steadfastness.* It can then begin the definite and scientific task of attacking the world glamour. It is of interest in this particular group to be reminded that this is part of the activity now being undertaken by certain people in the New Group of World Servers. Through the emphasis in the world of certain basic ideas such as goodwill and mutual inter-dependence, much is being done to dissipate the glamour in which the people of the world are walking. It is not the function of every server to form part of the massed attack upon the world glamour which is now getting under way. Everyone has to deal with glamour in his own personal life, but functions and activities differ. Yours is the work of the trained observers, and that training takes much time. At present, many of you do not recognise glamour when it meets you, and envelops you. It is only by its effects that you eventually know it for what it is. The time must come when your processes of observation are so keen that you will recognise it in its true nature before it immerses and engulfs you and produces those conditions which enable you to say later: "Why did I allow myself to be glamoured? Why was I so deluded?"

At this point I desire to do two things: I seek to outline a little more carefully this discussion or short treatise on glamour, so that our ideas may be clearly formulated and you will have a textbook for future reference which will serve to guide your group and analogous groups in the way of right activity. Secondly, I wish to recapitulate somewhat those things which I have already stated so as to enrich your understanding of the various phases of the world glamour. This world glamour, the analytical mind has to differentiate into distinctive phases, calling them Illusion, Glamour, Maya and that synthetic thoughtform, found on the Path of Discipleship, which is called by some schools of esotericism the Dweller on the Threshold.

As you will see from this, my brothers, we have set ourselves a large theme, which must be very carefully handled. My task is a difficult one, because I write for those who are still held by the varying aspects of glamour, and usually by the secondary glamour and maya. Illusion does not yet fully play its part and the Dweller is seldom adequately realised. I would here remind you of a stupendous occult fact and will ask you to endeavour to understand that whereof I speak. The Dweller on the Threshold does not emerge out of the fog of illusion and of glamour until the disciple is nearing the Gates of Life. Only when he can catch dim glimpses of the Portal of Initiation and an occasional flash of light from the Angel of the Presence Who stands waiting beside that door, can he come to grips with the principle of *duality,* which is embodied for him in the Dweller and the Angel. Do you comprehend that whereof I speak? As yet, my words embody for you symbolically a future condition and event. The day will surely come, however, when you will stand in full awareness between these symbols of the pairs of opposites, with the Angel on the right and the Dweller on the left. May strength then be given to you to drive straight forward between these two opponents, who have for long ages waged warfare in the field of your life, and so may you enter into that Presence where the two are seen as one, and naught is known but life and deity.

In summarising some of the information I have given to you concerning the four aspects of glamour, I would offer the following tabulation for your careful consideration.

Note:

1. A dawning sense of *maya* arose in Lemurian days, but there was no real glamour and illusion.

2. *Glamour* arose in early Atlantean times.

3. *Illusion* arose among advanced human beings in later Atlantean days and will be a controlling factor in our Aryan race.

4. *The Dweller on the Threshold* arrives at full potency at the end of this race, the Aryan, and in the lives of all initiates prior to taking the third initiation.

5. The subhuman kingdoms in nature are free from glamour and illusion, but are immersed in the world maya.

6. The Buddha and His 900 arhats struck the first blow at the world glamour when He promulgated His Four Noble Truths. The Christ struck the second blow with His teaching of the nature of individual responsibility and of brotherhood. The next blow will be struck by the New Group of World Servers, acting under the direction of Christ and His disciples, symbolically described as "Christ and His 9000 initiates."

7. The Four Keynotes to the solution of the problem of glamour are:

Intuition . . . . Illumination . . . . .Inspiration
 . . . . . . The Angel of the Presence.

THE ASPECTS OF GLAMOUR

Name	Plane	Opposite	Objective	Battleground	Technique
Illusion	Mental	Intuition Spiritual perception	Dispelling	Path of Initiation World of Ideas	Contemplation by soul
Glamour	Astral	Illumination Lucidity Vision	Dissipation	Path of Discipleship	Meditation Holding mind steady in the light
Maya	Etheric	Inspiration	Devitalisation	Path of Probation Purification	Occultism Force Manipulation
Dweller on the Threshold	Physical Brain consciousness	Angel of the Presence	Discrimination	Integrated personality	At-one-ment. End of duality

I would call your attention to the fact that the whole problem concerns itself with the use or misuse of force or energy, and that much will clear up in your minds if you will realise three things:

1. That average man, in everyday life, and the aspirant upon the Path of Probation or Purification, works with the forces of life on the three planes of human endeavour, plus the principle of life itself.
2. That the disciple begins to discriminate between the forces and energy. Upon the Path of Discipleship he begins to work with soul-energy. This eventually dominates the forces.
3. That the initiate works, upon the Path of Initiation, with energy and learns to distinguish between the energy of life, the energies of the soul, and the forces of the phenomenal world.

Another point also should be emphasised here and that is that the nature of these forces and energies, and their use and control have always to be realised and worked out in full consciousness upon the physical plane. Theory must become fact, and the battles which take place on the subtler levels of the astral and mental planes *must* be realised in the brain consciousness. It is there that the application is made. As these realisations and inner activities become practical parts of the disciple's life and their consequences become clear to his perception in waking consciousness, they form in time part of his *quality equipment*. He is in reality integrating and synthesising experience in the three worlds and becoming a Master through conscious mastering. He grasps the fact that all that appears and all that happens is due to the circulation and constant mutation of force. He discovers then how these forces interplay in his own experiences

The Nature of Glamour

and nature, and grasps then the fundamental fact that only those forces which he himself can use and master in his own life as an individual can be employed by him in group activity and be used in the dispelling of the world glamour. It might be expressed in illustration thus:

1. Through alignment and subsequent contact, the intuition is evoked, awakened and used. This is the great dispelling agency, and pours down from the plane of the intuition (the plane of buddhi) through the soul and the brain to the heart of the disciple.

2. Through alignment and subsequent contact, the energy of the soul is evoked, awakened and used. This is the great dissipating agency, and pours down from soul levels (the higher levels of the mental plane) through the mind to the brain of the disciple carrying illumination to the astral plane.

3. These two types of spiritual energy work differently upon the forces of the personality, and their purpose and activity have to be realised in the brain consciousness of the disciple as he works upon the physical plane.

4. Then and only then can the light of the intuition and the light of the soul return to the astral plane through the conscious effort and the dynamic intelligent will of the serving disciple.

Ponder on these points for they outline your way and your service. . . .

I have organised somewhat our ideas and outlined the plan under which we would approach this theme. I gave you certain basic concepts and a skeleton outline of the subject as a whole. (See the Table of Contents.) Today we will begin with our real discussion. As you know, it is not my intention to write a long and ponderous thesis on this subject. The books which will be compiled from the instructions offered to these groups of disciples, will not be heavy treatises as are those on *Cosmic Fire* and *White Magic*. They will constitute a series of relatively short volumes, and must therefore be packed with information, and not discursive in style.

Above everything else, my brothers, these instructions must be of a definitely practical value and must leave the student with the realisation that he understands better the subtle world of thought currents and of forces in which he dwells; and that he knows better the means he must employ and the technique he must follow if he is to clear his path from darkness and confusion and follow on to light and harmony. Our study must be comparative also, and the reader must bear in mind that he will not be able to distinguish the truth or isolate that aspect of the teaching which is for him of paramount importance unless he *applies* that which is helpful, and ascertains clearly whether he is the victim of illusion or of glamour. In the last analysis, he must know where he stands before he can take his next needed step forward. The disciple is the victim and, let us hope, the dissipator of both glamour and illusion, and hence the complexity of his problem and the subtlety of his difficulties. He must bear in mind also (for his strengthening and cheer) that every bit of glamour dissipated and every illusion recognised and overcome "clears the way" for those who follow after, and makes easier the path of his fellow disciples. This is par excellence, the Great Service, and it is to this aspect of it that I call your attention. Hence my attempts in these instructions to clarify this issue.

One of the problems which confronts the aspirant is the problem of duly recognising glamour when it arises, and of being aware of the glamours which beset his path and the illusions which build a wall between him and the light. It is much that you have recognised that glamour and illusion exist. The majority of people are unaware of their presence. Many good people today see this not; they deify their glamours and regard their illusions as their prized and hard won possessions.

The very recognition, in its turn however, carries with it its own problems, so unable is the average disciple to free himself from the glamour-making faculties developed in the past, and so hard does he find it to preserve a due proportion and a proper sense of values in regard to the truths of the mental plane. A hard won truth and a principle of reality can be grasped, and then around it the disciple can build the easily formed illusions of the mind which is just beginning to find itself. The glamours of an emotional nature can emerge and gather about the ideal, for that is as yet unclarified and is prone to attract to itself that which—emotionally and sensitively—it believes itself to be and have.

Let us illustrate my point from two angles, both of which are entirely in the realm of discipleship, or encountered upon the Path of Probation. We will call them the "illusion of power" and the "glamour of authority." This form of words will show you that one is to be encountered upon the astral plane and the other upon the mental.

The Glamour of Authority is a mass glamour in most cases. It has its roots in mass psychology and is one of the indications that humanity is at the nursery stage as yet, wherein men are safeguarded from themselves by the imposition of some rule, some set of laws, some authoritative dictum, emanating from state control, from the rule of an oligarchy, or from the dictatorship of some individual. It reduces mankind, as far as one can judge, to set forms and standardises men's activities, regimenting their lives and work. It is imposed and ordered through catering to the fear complex, rampant in humanity at this time; and this fear is one of the most fruitful sources of glamour which we have. We might perhaps and with reason regard it as the seed of all glamour upon our planet. Fear has been the incentive to those conditions which have brought about the glamour of the astral plane, though not the illusions of the mental levels of consciousness.

When the glamour of authority transfers itself into the spiritual consciousness of man, we have such a state of affairs as the period of the Inquisition in its worst forms, of Church authority, with the emphasis upon organisation, government and penalties, or the unquestioned rule of some teacher. In its highest forms we have the recognition of the right of the solar Angel, of the soul or ego, to rule. Between these two extremes, which express the infancy of the race and the freedom which comes when mankind achieves its majority and the freedom of the soul, lie all the many types and kinds of intermediate reactions. In illustration of our point, and thus emphasising the glamour aspect as it affects the disciple and the problem which he faces, what do we find? The disciple has freed himself somewhat from the imposed control of an orthodox teaching and from the rule of a teacher. He stands (as far as he can tell) free from such control. Knowing however his essential weakness and the lure of the personality, he is on guard against himself, and against the ancient rules of control and learns steadily to stand on his own feet, to come to his own decisions, to distinguish truth for himself. He learns to choose his way. But, like all persons who have not taken some of the higher initiations, he can (in due time) become enamoured of his freedom, and automatically then swing into the glamour of *his* ideal of freedom,—an ideal which he has created. He becomes the prisoner of freedom. He rejects all rule except that which he calls the "rule of his own soul," forgetting that his contact with his soul is still intermittent. He demands the right to stand alone. He revels in his new found freedom. He forgets that, having given up the authority of a teaching and of a teacher, he has to learn to accept the authority of the soul and of the group of souls with which he is affiliated through his karma, his ray type, his choice, and the inevitability of the effects of the at-one-ment. Having relinquished the guidance of another person upon the Path, and having his eyes partially opened, he now seeks to tread that Path to the goal, forgetting however that he treads the Path *in unison with others*, and that there are certain "Rules of the Road" which he must master, and which he must master in unison with others. He has exchanged the individual law for the group law, but does not yet know that group law as it should be known. He marches on as best he can alone, glorying in the freedom from authority which he has succeeded in achieving. He promises himself that he will brook no authority or guidance.

Those of us who are considering him and looking on at him from the clearer heights of attainment see him gradually becoming obscured by wisps of fog and by a glamour which is gradually growing up around him as he becomes a "prisoner of the fog of freedom" and revels in what he deems the fact of his independence. When his sight has cleared, and when his mental aspect is more developed and unfolded, he will know that the Law of the Group must, and will, impose itself upon him, and that the rule of the lower nature has only to be exchanged for the rule of the soul. This is group rule and works under the law of the group. He has struggled out of the mass of seekers of the Road on to the Road itself. He is, therefore, ahead of the masses but he is not alone, even if he thinks that he is. He will discover many others who are travelling the same way with him, and their numbers will steadily increase as he progresses. The rule of interplay, of travel, and of group recognition and work and service will impose themselves upon him until he finds that he is a member of the New Group of World Servers, working under the conditions which are the rules governing their activities. As he learns to travel with them upon the Road, their governing incentives and the techniques of their chosen service will penetrate his consciousness, and automatically and naturally he will begin to obey the higher rhythm and give his assent to the laws which control group life and group consciousness. Finally, he will find himself entering into the silent places where the Masters of the Wisdom dwell, and will work in group rhythm with Them, obeying thus the laws of the spiritual realm, which are the subjective laws of God.

Time and again, along the Road, he will revolt from control and will fall back into the glamour of his supposed freedom. There *is* freedom from the control of the personality. There *is* freedom from the control of personalities. But there is never any freedom from the Law of Service, and from the constant interplay between man and man, and soul and soul. To stand really free is to stand in the clear unimpeded light of the soul, which is basically and intrinsically group consciousness.

Therefore, when one of you is beset by uncertainty and unrest, desiring and demanding to walk free and that no authority be imposed upon you, see that you are not submitting to the glamour of a desire to be freed from your group impacts, and make sure that you are not seeking—as a sensitive soul—a way of escape. I am using this phrase in the modern psychological sense. Be sure to ask yourself the question: Is your comfort and your peace of mind of such definite importance to yourself and to others that it warrants your sacrificing the group integrity in order to have it? Does

The Nature of Glamour

your own interior satisfaction provide an adequate excuse for delaying the planned group purpose? For delay it, it certainly will. Whatever you decide will constitute, in its turn, an authoritative decision with all the consequent reactions upon the group . . . .

What is this occult obedience, my brothers, about which we hear so much? Not what many occult groups make it out to be. It is not the control of an external organisation, dedicated to so-called occult work. It is not the imposed conditions of any teacher of any rank. It is not the exchange of the prison of one set of ideas for those of another set with perhaps a larger range or import. A prison is a prison, whether it is a tiny cell or an isolated island of vast extent, from which escape is impossible.

The authority to which we, the teachers on the inner side, respond is twofold in nature, and to it you are just beginning (as units in a group) to respond. To what do you respond?

1. To the slowly emerging realisation of the "light beyond," using that phrase as a symbol. This light is different *in its appeal* to the individual. Yet it is ONE LIGHT. But its recognition reveals new laws, new responsibilities, new duties and obligations, and new relations to others. These constitute an authoritative control. None can escape this authority, but can disobey it in time and space and for a temporary period.

2. To the authority of the *Rules of the Road* which are imposed upon one as one passes from the Path of Probation on to the Path of Discipleship. Yet it is ONE ROAD. Upon this "narrow, razor-edged path," one learns to walk with discipline and discretion

and with the desirelessness which one experiences in unison with one's fellow disciples.

What, briefly and succinctly, are these rules of the Road? Let me give you six of the simplest rules, begging you to remember that they are not authoritatively imposed by an arbitrary Board of Directors, such as a group teacher or teachers (of whom I might, of course, be one) but are the outcome of the conditions to be found upon the Path itself. They carry the warrant of a man's own soul and are the result of the experience of millions of travellers upon that Path.

I will give you these six rules (even as I gave them to another aspirant*) in ancient and symbolic form, translating them as well as I can from the ancient records, stored in the Hall of Wisdom, and available to all earnest disciples,—such as you.

The Six Rules of the Path

(Rules of the Road)

I. The Road is trodden in the full light of day, thrown upon the Path by Those Who know and lead. Naught can then be hidden, and at each turn, a man must face himself.

II. Upon the Road the hidden stands revealed. Each sees and knows the villainy of each. (I can find no other word, my brother, to translate the ancient word which designates the unrevealed stupidity, the vileness and crass ignorance, and the self-interest which are distinguishing characteristics of the average aspirant.) And yet there is, with that great revelation, no turning back, no spurning of each other,

---

* *Discipleship in the New Age*, Vol. I, pp. 583-584.

The Nature of Glamour

and no shakiness upon the Road. The Road goes forward into day.

III. Upon that Road one wanders not alone. There is no rush, no hurry. And yet there is no time to lose. Each Pilgrim, knowing this, presses his footsteps forward, and finds himself surrounded by his fellowmen. Some move ahead; he follows after. Some move behind; he sets the pace. He travels *not* alone.

IV. Three things the Pilgrim must avoid. The wearing of a hood, the veil which hides his face from others; the carrying of a water pot which only holds enough for his own wants; the shouldering of a staff without a crook to hold.

V. Each Pilgrim on the Road must carry with him what he needs: a pot of fire, to warm his fellowmen; a lamp, to cast its rays upon his heart and show his fellowmen the nature of his hidden life; a purse of gold, which he scatters not upon the Road but shares with others; a sealed vase, wherein he carries all his aspiration to cast before the feet of Him Who waits to greet him at the gate—a sealed vase.

VI. The Pilgrim, as he walks upon the Road, must have the open ear, the giving hand, the silent tongue, the chastened heart, the golden voice, the rapid foot, and the open eye which sees the light. He knows he travels not alone.

The Illusion of Power is perhaps one of the first and most serious tests which comes to an aspirant. It is also one of the best examples of this "great mistake," and I therefore bring it to your attention as being one against which I beg you most carefully to guard yourself. It is rare indeed for any disciple to escape the effects of this error of illusion for it is, curiously, based upon right success and right motive. Hence the specious nature of the problem. It might be expressed thus:

An aspirant succeeds in contacting his soul or ego through right effort. Through meditation, good intention, and correct technique, plus the desire to serve and to love, he achieves alignment. He becomes then aware of the results of his successful work. His mind is illumined. A sense of power flows through his vehicles. He is, temporarily at least, made aware of the Plan. The need of the world and the capacity of the soul to meet that need flood his consciousness. His dedication, consecration and right purpose enhance the directed inflow of spiritual energy. He knows. He loves. He seeks to serve, and does all three more or less successfully. The result of all this is that he becomes more engrossed with the sense of power, and with the part he is to play in aiding humanity, than he is with the realisation of a due and proper sense of proportion and of spiritual values. He over-estimates his experience and himself. Instead of redoubling his efforts and thus establishing a closer contact with the kingdom of souls and loving all beings more deeply, he begins to call attention to himself, to the mission he is to develop, and to the confidence that the Master and even the planetary Logos apparently have in him. He talks about himself; he gestures and attracts notice, demanding recognition. As he does so, his alignment is steadily impaired; his contact lessens and he joins the ranks of the many who have succumbed to the illusion of sensed power. This form of illusion is becoming increasingly prevalent among disciples and those who have taken the first two initiations. There are today many people in the world who have taken the first initiation in a previous life. At some period in the present life cycle, recurring and recapitulating as it does the events of an earlier development, they again reach a point in their realisation which they earlier reached. The significance of their attainment pours in upon them, and the sense of their responsibility and their knowledge. Again they over-estimate themselves, regarding their missions and themselves as unique among the sons of men, and their esoteric and subjective demand for recognition enters in and spoils what might otherwise have been a fruitful service. Any emphasis upon the personality can distort most easily the pure light of the soul as it seeks to pour through the lower self. Any effort to call attention to the mission or task which the personality has undertaken detracts from that mission and handicaps the man in his task; it leads to the deferring of its fulfilment until such time when the disciple can be naught but a channel through which love can pour, and light can shine. This pouring through and shining forth has to be a spontaneous happening, and contain no self-reference.

These two illustrations of glamour and of illusion will show you not only the subtlety of the problem, but also the urgent need for its recognition. There are today so many manifesting these two qualities of the lower nature.

1. Glamour on the Mental Plane . . . . *Illusion.*

In this section of our discussion we shall give less time to the consideration of illusion than we shall to that of glamour, or of maya. Illusion is not met squarely, faced and overcome until a man has:

      a. Shifted the focus of his consciousness on to the mental plane.

      b. Worked definitely at the task of intelligent service.

c. Made his soul alignment consciously and easily, and firmly established his technique of contact.
   d. Taken the first initiation.

The word *illusion* is frequently lightly used to signify lack of knowledge, unsettled opinions, glamour, misunderstandings, psychic bewilderment, the dominance of the lower psychic powers, and many other forms of the world illusion. But the time has come when the word must be used with a developed discriminating sense, and when the disciple must know clearly and comprehend the nature of that phenomenal miasma in which humanity moves. For the purposes of clarity and in order to distinguish more definitely and effectively between the forms of illusion in which the soul moves, and from which it must liberate itself, it will be necessary for us to separate the Great Illusion (in its various aspects) into its component parts in time and space, and this I attempted partially to do when I defined for you the words Maya, Glamour, Illusion, and the Dweller on the Threshold. I want you to keep very clearly in your mind these distinctions, and to study with care the tabulation earlier given you.

Illusion, for our purposes, can be understood to signify the reaction of the undisciplined mind to the newly contacted world of ideas. This contact opens up from the moment a man has aligned himself and brought the lower nature into touch with the higher. Ideas come to us from the plane of the intuition. The soul illumines the plane of the mind and the plane of the intuition so that they stand revealed to each other and their mutual relationship becomes then apparent. The mind of the man (which is slowly becoming the centre of his consciousness and the major reality in his existence) becomes aware of this new and undiscovered world of ideas and he seizes upon some idea or group

The Nature of Glamour

of ideas and endeavours to make them his own. At first, with the majority of people and especially with the average mystical type, the appreciation of ideas is vague and nebulous, and frequently is arrived at from a second-hand angle. The illumination, coming through the medium of the feebly established soul contact, seems to the unaccustomed neophyte to be of a supreme wonder and of vital moment. The ideas contacted appear to him of great marvel, and superbly unusual, and vitally needed by humanity.

But the mind is still self-centred, the contact feeble and the alignment uncertain. The ideas are therefore only dimly sensed. But the *uniqueness* of the experience in the realised content of the mind of the disciple leads him deep into the realm of illusion. The idea, or ideas, which he has contacted are, if he could realise, only a fragment of a far greater Whole. That which he brings to their interpretation is inadequate. The idea which has emerged in his consciousness, through the partial awakening of his intuition, will be distorted in its descent to his brain consciousness in several ways. That which he brings to the materialising of the idea and to its transformation into a practical working scheme is as yet wholly unsuitable. The equipment does not suffice for accuracy. The ways in which this distortion and this stepping down of the idea take place might be outlined for you as follows:—*The passage of an idea from the plane of the intuition to the brain.*

I. The idea is seen by the mind, "held steady in the light of the soul."

II. It descends to the higher levels of the mental plane and there clothes itself with the substance of those levels. It remains still an abstraction, from the angle of the lower mind. This point should be carefully noted by the would-be intuitive.

III. The soul throws its light upward and outward, and the idea, nebulous and faint, emerges into the consciousness of the man. It stands revealed, much as an object stands revealed when the bright beam of a powerful searchlight is thrown upon it. The mind, endeavouring to remain in constant steady conscious contact with the soul, seeing into the higher world through the medium of the "soul's wide-opened eye," registers the idea with increasing clarity.

IV. The idea, revealed, becomes then an ideal to the attentive mind and eventually something to be desired and materialised. The thoughtform-making faculty of the mind then comes into play; the "mind-stuff" becomes actuated by the energy of the idea, vitalised by the recognition of the soul, and the idea then takes its first real step towards embodiment. An ideal is only an embodied idea.

These are the first steps towards materialisation. Embodiment becomes possible. Thus illusion is produced.

V. Distortion now sets in. This is brought about by various causes. These might be enumerated as follows:

1. The ray type of the ego colours the man's interpretation of the idea. It colours the emerging thoughtform. Symbolically speaking, the pure light is changed into coloured light. The idea is then "clothed with colour, and thereby the first veil descends."

2. The point in evolution which the man has reached has also its effect, plus the quality of the in-

The Nature of Glamour

tegration existing between the three aspects of the personality, and the alignment established between soul-mind-brain. This, being necessarily imperfect, produces indefiniteness of outline and consequently of the final form. Therefore we have:

    a. Imperfect integration of the personality.
    b. Indefiniteness of the proposed thoughtform.
    c. The wrong material consequently attracted for the building of the thoughtform.
    d. A shifting focus of attention, owing to the dimness of the seen ideal.
    e. The rapport of the mind, with the sensed idea, is not stable.

3. The quality of the development of the mental body of the disciple produces the next "veiling" of the idea, as it is called. The idea has become changed through the ray colouring of the soul, and now a still more distorting change is brought about by the ray type of the mental body itself, which may be, and usually is, different to that of the soul ray.

These are the second steps towards materialisation. The form of the embodiment is qualified. Thus illusion is produced.

VI. This illusion demonstrates in seven ways usually:

1. *Through wrong perception of an idea.* The disciple cannot distinguish between an idea and an ideal, between an idea and a thoughtform, or between an intuitive and a mental concept. This is one of the ways of producing illusion found most commonly among aspirants. The mental atmosphere in which we all dwell is one of illusion.

It is also an atmosphere or area of conscious contact wherein thoughtforms of all kinds are to be found. Some of them are placed there by the Hierarchy for man's finding; some of them are men's thoughtforms, built around ideas; some of them are very ancient ideals and have been discarded, but still persist as thoughtforms; some of them are entirely new, and therefore are not yet potent, but most attractive. All of them have been created by man at some stage or another of his individual and racial development. Many of them are the shells of long exploded concepts; still others are embryonic; some of them are static and stable; many are in process of descent from intuitional levels; a few are still illumined by the clear light of the soul and are ready for embodiment. A large number of other thoughtforms are in process of disintegration. Some of these forms or embodied ideas are of a destructive nature, owing to the type of matter of which they are formed. Others are constructive. All of them are coloured by some ray energy. A large number of these forms are necessarily built through the activity of the world of personality; others are in process of construction through the agency of the soul, as well as through the joint activity of both these manifestations. Right perception is therefore essential for each mind, functioning correctly. Aspirants must learn to distinguish between:

    a. An idea and an ideal.
    b. Between that which is embodied, that which is in process of being embodied, and that which is awaiting disintegration.

The Nature of Glamour

c. Between that which is constructive and that which is destructive.
d. Between the old and the new forms and ideas.
e. Between the ray ideas and forms as they colour the higher presentations.
f. Between ideas and thoughtforms, and between those which are purposely created by the Hierarchy and those which are created by humanity.
g. Between racial thoughtforms and group ideas.

I could list many more differentiations, but the above will suffice to show the need for right perceptions, and to indicate the roots of the prevalence of the world illusion, brought about by wrong perception.

The *cause* is an untrained, unillumined mind.

The *cure* is training in the technique of Raja Yoga.

This results in the ability to hold the mind steady in the light, to perceive correctly, to achieve a right outlook, and to attain a right mental attitude. It was these right attitudes with which the Buddha was dealing when He outlined the Noble Eightfold Path. It involves the reaching of a right mental altitude. Yes, I said altitude, my brothers, and not attitude.

2. *Through wrong interpretation.* The idea, a vital entity or a germ of living potency, is seen through the medium of a partial view, distorted through the inadequacy of the mental equipment, and frequently stepped down into futility. The

mechanism for right understanding is lacking, and though the man may be giving his highest and his best, and though he may be able in some measure to hold his mind steady in the light, yet what he is offering to the idea is but a poor thing at the best. This leads to illusion through misinterpretation.

The *cause* is an over-estimation of one's mental powers. The sin, par excellence, of the mental type is pride, and that colours all activities in the early stages.

The *cure* is the development of a cautious spirit.

3. *Through wrong appropriation of ideas.* Misappropriation of an idea is based upon the drama-making faculty and tendency of the personality to the self-assertion of the little self. These lead a man to appropriate an idea as his own, to credit himself with its formulation, and to give therefore undue importance to it, because he regards it as his. He proceeds to build *his* life around *his* idea, and to make *his* aims and *his* objectives of major importance, expecting others to recognise his proprietorship of the idea. He forgets that no one idea belongs to anyone but, coming as ideas do, from the plane of the intuition, they are a universal gift and possession, and the property of no one mind. His life, as a personality also, becomes subordinated to his idea of an idea, and his ideal of an idea. The idea becomes the dramatic agent of his self-imposed life purpose, driving him from one extreme to another. This leads to illusion through misappropriation.

The Nature of Glamour

> The *cause* is over-estimation of personality and undue impress of personality reactions upon the sensed idea and upon all who attempt to contact the same idea.
>
> The *cure* is a steady attempt to decentralise the life from the personality, and to centre it in the soul.

One point I would like to make clear at this point. Ideas very seldom come into the world consciousness and into the human mind direct from the intuitional levels. The stage of human development today does not yet permit this. They can come from the intuitional levels only when there is a very highly developed soul contact, a potent mind control, a trained intelligence, a purified emotional body, and a good glandular equipment, as the result of the above requirements. Ponder upon this thought.

Most ideas, when of a very high order, are stepped down into the consciousness of a disciple by his Master and are imparted to him through mental telepathy, and as a result of his sensitivity to the "psychic gift waves," as the Tibetan teaching calls them. Ideas are also sensed in the interplay between disciples. Frequently, when disciples meet together and thus stimulate each others' minds and centralise each others' focussed attention, they can unitedly make a contact with the world of ideas which would otherwise be impossible, and bring through the newer concepts into being. Again, certain great ideas are to be found existing as currents of energy upon the mental plane, and can there be contacted and forced into embodiment through the trained attention of disciples. These currents of mental energy, coloured by a basic idea, are placed there by the Hierarchy. When thus contacted and discovered, the neophyte is apt to regard his achievement in a personal way and attribute the idea to his own wisdom and power. You will note therefore the great need for right understanding of that which is contacted as well as for right interpretation.

4. *Through wrong direction of ideas.* This is due to the fact that, as yet, the disciple does not see the picture as it is. His horizon is limited, his vision myopic. A fraction or a fragment of some basic idea impinges upon his consciousness and he interprets it as belonging to a range of activities with which it may have absolutely no relation at all. He therefore starts to work with the idea, distributing it in directions where it is entirely useless; he begins to clothe it in form from an utterly wrong angle, embodying it in such a way that its usefulness is negated. Thus, from the very first moment of contact, the disciple has been suffering from illusion and as long as this is persisted in, the general illusion is strengthened. This is one of the most ordinary forms of illusion, and is one of the first ways in which the mental pride of the disciple can be broken. It is illusion through an initial misapplication, leading to a wrong use or wrong direction of the idea.

Its *cause* is a small and non-inclusive mind.

Its *cure* is the training of the mind to be inclusive, well-stocked and well developed from the angle of modern intelligence.

5. *Through wrong integration of an idea.* Every disciple has a life plan, and some chosen field of service. If he has not such a field, he is not a disciple. It may be the home or the school or a larger

The Nature of Glamour

field, but it is a definite place wherein he expresses that which is in him. In his meditation life and through his contact with his fellow disciples, he touches some idea of importance, perhaps, to the world. Immediately he seizes upon it and seeks to integrate it into his life purpose and life plan. It may have for him no definite use, and is not an idea with which he should be working. The over-activity of his mind is probably responsible for his so seizing upon this idea. All ideas sensed and contacted need not necessarily be ideas with which every disciple should work. This the disciple does not always realise. He therefore seizes upon the idea and attempts to integrate it into his plans, and tries to work with energies for which he is not temperamentally suited. He imposes an energy current upon his mental body with which he cannot cope and disaster follows. Many good disciples demonstrate this over-fertile, over-active mind, and arrive at no good constructive objectives, or life activity. They seize upon every idea that comes their way, and use no discrimination of any kind. This is illusion, through acquisitiveness.

> Its *cause* is selfish grasping for the little self, even if this is unrealised and the disciple is glamoured by the idea of his own selfless interests.
>
> Its *cure* is a humble spirit.

6. *Through wrong embodiment of ideas.* This refers primarily to the difficulties encountered by those developed souls who do touch the world of the intuition, who do intuit the great spiritual ideas, and

whose responsibility it is to embody them in some form, automatically and spontaneously, through a trained and rhythmic activity of the soul and mind, working always in the closest collaboration. The idea is contacted, but is wrongly clothed in mental matter and therefore wrongly started on its way to materialisation. It finds itself, for instance, integrated into a group thoughtform of a colouring, keynote and substance which is entirely unsuited to its right expression. This happens far more often than you might think. It concerns the higher interpretations of the Hindu aphorism: Better one's own dharma than the dharma of another.

This is illusion through wrong discrimination where substance is concerned.

> Its *cause* is lack of esoteric training in creative activity.
> Its *cure* is the application of fifth ray methods, which are the methods of the mental plane.

This form of error seldom applies to the average aspirant and concerns an illusion which is the testing applied to many initiates of fairly high degree. The ordinary disciple, such as you and others in this group, seldom touch a pure idea, and hence seldom need to embody it.

7. *Through wrong application of ideas.* How often does this form of illusion descend upon a disciple! He contacts an idea intuitively and also intelligently (note the distinction here expressed) and misapplies it. This is perhaps an aspect of the synthetic illusion or the illusion

The Nature of Glamour

of the whole of the mental plane, as modern man contacts it. Illusion varies from age to age, according to what the Hierarchy is attempting to do, or according to the general trend of men's thoughts. The disciple can therefore be swept into a wrong activity and a wrong application of ideas because the general illusion (growing out of the six types of illusion to which I have referred above) is over-dominant in his mind.

I could continue enlarging on the ways whereby illusion traps the unwary disciple but this will suffice to awaken in you that constructive analysis which leads from knowledge to wisdom. We have noted that the seven major ways of illusion are as follows:

1. The way of wrong perception.
2. The way of wrong interpretation.
3. The way of wrong appropriation.
4. The way of wrong direction.
5. The way of wrong integration.
6. The way of wrong embodiment.
7. The way of wrong application.

These are the third steps towards expression. The form of the expression is also qualified. Thus the seven ways of illusion are produced.

I have here outlined for you the causes and the various types of illusion to which the disciple is prone. In its pure form, this illusion has to be met and some day surmounted; it has to be isolated and dispelled by the initiate. It was the final successful effort to do this that led Jesus upon the Cross to cry out in words of apparent distress. He then finally dissipated the illusion of the personal, objective Deity. At that moment, He entered fully into the consciousness that He was Himself God, and naught else; that the theory of unity outlined by Him in the Gospel of St. John, chapter XVII, was indeed and in truth a fact in His Own consciousness, established unalterably. Yet, nevertheless, in this infinite and supreme realisation, there entered for a moment a sense of loss and of negation, forcing from His dying Personality that tremendous utterance which has bewildered, and at the same time comforted, so many. This signified the surmounting of the final synthetic illusion. When that has been dispelled, illusion, as it can be understood in the human family, disappears. The man stands free. The illusion of the mental plane can no longer deceive him. His mind is a pure instrument for the reflection of light and of truth. The glamours of the astral plane have no further hold over him, and the astral body itself fades out.

You will remember that I hinted to you in *A Treatise on White Magic* that the astral body itself was an illusion. It is the definition of the illusory mind upon the mental plane of that which we call the sum total of the desires of the man in incarnation. When illusion and glamour have both been overcome, the astral body fades out in the human consciousness. There is no desire left for the separated self. Kama-manas disappears, and man is then regarded as consisting essentially of soul-mind-brain, within the body nature. This is a great mystery, and its significance can only be understood when a man has controlled his personality and eliminated all aspects of glamour and of illusion. This is accomplished by accomplishing. This mastery is achieved by mastering. This elimination of desire is brought about by conscious eliminating. Get therefore to work, my brothers, and clarification of the problem must inevitably ensue.

The Nature of Glamour

That which is the opposite pole of illusion is, as you well know, the intuition. The intuition is that recognition of reality which becomes possible as glamour and illusion disappear. An intuitive reaction to truth will take place when—along a particular line of approach to truth—the disciple has succeeded in quieting the thoughtform-making propensities of the mind, so that light can flow directly, and without any deviation, from the higher spiritual worlds. The intuition can begin to make its presence felt when glamour no longer grips the lower man, and a man's low or high desires, interpreted emotionally or self-centredly, can no longer come between his brain consciousness and the soul. Fleeting moments of this high freedom come to all true aspirants at times, during their life struggle. They have then an intuitive flash of understanding. The outline of the future and the nature of truth sweeps momentarily through their consciousness, and life is never again exactly the same thing. They have had their guarantee that all struggle is warranted and will evoke its adequate reward.

As pointed out in the tabulation (See page 41), that which dispels illusion and substitutes for it a true spiritual and infallible perception is contemplation,—a contemplation necessarily carried on by the soul. Perhaps some grasp of the sequence of development can be arrived at, if you realise that the entire meditation process (in its three major divisions) can be divided as follows:

1. The Aspirant .. Probationary Path .... Concentration .... Maya.
2. The Disciple .. Path of Discipleship ... Meditation .... Glamour.
3. The Initiate ... Path of Initiation ..... Contemplation .... Illusion.

The above tabulation will suffice to show the connection between the meditation process as outlined and taught in the Arcane School, and the problem which all of you have to face.

The technique of the dispelling of illusion, as used by the initiate, is that of contemplation. But of what use is it for me to discuss this with you, if you are not initiate? Would it profit you at all, or would it only satisfy your curiosity, if I outlined for you the peculiar processes, employed by a soul in contemplation for penetrating and (through an act of the trained will and through some first ray formulas) for dispelling it? Naught that I can imagine.

I shall therefore conclude my remarks on this point concerning illusion from the angle of your evolutionary status. Glamour is your problem, as it is the problem of the world, at this time. Some of you, whose mental bodies are in process of organising, may suffer somewhat from illusion, but your major problem—as a group and as individuals—is one of glamour. Your field of living experience is on the higher levels of the astral plane. Your task is to overcome glamour, each in your individual lives, and, as a group, later to approach the arduous task of aiding in the dispelling of the world glamour. This you may later be able to do, if you submit to training and, as individuals, understand and master your personal glamours. Just as soon as you have begun to do this, I can begin to use you, *as a group*. But before you can work as a group, and before you can assist in the dissipation of the world glamour, you have to understand better and master more definitely the glamours and illusions of your personality. The time has now come for me to help you deal more drastically with this problem of glamour, with the view to your destined group service and not with a view of your personal release . . . .

I ask you to set to work, therefore, with fresh courage and determination and with fresh understanding, and to carry on for another year. Will you bend your effort to the task? For task it is.

The Nature of Glamour

2. *Glamour on the Astral Plane* . . . . *Glamour*

I have dealt with the problem of illusion or glamour on the mental plane. I dealt with it succinctly and briefly, pointing out that it is not primarily the major problem of this group of aspirants but that they—along with the world aspirant, humanity—are primarily occupied with glamour. Those aspirants who stand in the forefront of humanity and whose task it is to confront the world glamour and forge a way through it, have the task of releasing soul energy and mind potency. Among these pioneering souls you should take your stand, realising the magnitude of the opportunity and the imminence of the hour of release.

You stand on the verge of accepted discipleship. This means that you will shortly have to add to your battle with glamour that of the battle with illusion. Are you strong enough for this? Forget not, that a disciple who is dealing with the aspiration of his nature and who is also wrestling with the problems that result from mental polarisation and awareness, and with the energies which become active through soul contact, is rapidly becoming an integrated personality. His task is not therefore easy and calls for the focussed activity of his best self. By that phrase, I mean the soul and the aspirational personality.

Already you are battling somewhat with the illusion of ideas with which I dealt in my last instruction. You are thus beginning to develop that discrimination which will lead to right choice of life themes. In this instruction I seek to cast some light upon the glamour which confronts the disciple as an individual and also consider the aspect of glamour with which he must deal as a world server in training.

Speaking symbolically, I would say that the planetary astral body (viewing it from soul levels) is lost in the depths of a surrounding fog. When at night you look out at some clear sky, you see the stars and suns and planets shining with a clear cold brilliancy and with a twinkling blazing light which penetrates for many millions of miles (or light years as they are called) until the human eye registers them and records the existence of these shining stars. Looking, however, at the astral body of the planet, could you but do so, you would see no such clear shining but simply a murky ball of seeming steam and mist and fog. This fog is of a density and thickness which would indicate not only impenetrability but also those conditions which are unfavourable to life. Yet we pass and come and go, we the Teachers on the inner side; and in that fog—seeing all things misshapen and distorted—labour the sons of men. Some are so habituated to the fog and the density that they remain oblivious of its existence, regarding it as right and good and the unchangeable place of their daily life. Others have caught faint glimpses of a clearer world wherein more perfect forms and shapes can be seen and where the fog hides not a dimly sensed reality—though what that reality may be they know not. Still others, such as yourselves, see before you an open path leading to the clear light of day. You know not yet, however, that as you tread the path you must, on the Path itself, work actively and intelligently with the surrounding glamour, following a trail blazed by those who have liberated themselves from the environing mists and passed on into a world of clear horizons. So much of the time spent by disciples on the Path is a process of almost cyclic immersion in glamour and fog, alternating with hours of clarity and vision.

There are four things which you who seek to work with glamour need to grasp; four basic recognitions which, when

The Nature of Glamour

understood, will serve to clear and lighten, and therefore straighten your way:

1. Each human being stands in an environing world of glamour which is the result of:

> a. His own past, with its wrong thinking, selfish desires, and misinterpretation of the purposes of life. There is, or has been, no comprehension of the intended life purpose as visioned by the soul and there cannot be until there is some definite organisation of the mental body.
>
> b. His family "desire life," both past and present. This becomes increasingly potent as evolution proceeds and the desire life of the family unit becomes comes marked and emphasised, constituting then inherited and demonstrated psychological tendencies and characteristics.
>
> c. National glamour, which is the sum total of the desire life, plus the illusions, of any nation. These we term national characteristics and they are so persistent and marked that they are usually recognised as embodying national psychological traits. These are, of course, based on ray tendencies, past history, and world interrelations but constitute in themselves a glamorous condition out of which every nation must work as it marches on towards the realisation of (and identification with) reality.
>
> d. An extension of the above idea into what we call racial glamour, using the word race to mean the human race. This constitutes a very ancient glamour or almost a series of glamours, of entrenched desires, potent aspirations of some kind and definitely human-made forms which—fluidic, enveloping and pulsating with dynamic life—seek

to hold the consciousness of humanity upon the astral plane. Such a glamorous concept is that of money and its materialistic value. This glamorous desire is like a dense widely distributed fog, cutting off the vision of truth, and distorting a very large number of human values.

2. This fog, this glamour which envelops humanity at this time must be realised as a definite substantial thing, and must be dealt with as such. The disciple or aspirant who is seeking to dispel glamour, either in his own life or as a service rendered to the world, must recognise that he is working with substance, with the breaking up of the forms which it has assumed, and with the dissipation of a material all-enveloping substance—material in the same sense as thoughtforms are substantial things but (and here is a point of importance) of a less substantial nature than the forms of glamour found upon the astral plane. We are quite willing to remember that "thoughts are things" and that they have a form life and a purpose of their own. But they have a more unique and separative existence, and more clearly defined and more definite outlines. The forms of glamour on the astral plane are even more substantial but are less clearly defined. Thoughtforms are dynamic, penetrating, clear cut and outlined. Glamours are smothering, vague, and enveloping. In them, a person is immersed as in the ocean or in a "sea of fog." With thoughtforms, he is confronted or faced, but not immersed. It might almost be said that the astral body of a person comes into being as a part of the general world glamour; it is difficult for him to differentiate between his own astral body and the glamours which affect and sway and submerge him. His problem upon the mental plane is more clearly defined, even if it is equally difficult.

The Nature of Glamour

3. Astral glamour is a form of energy and an energy of great potency, owing to three factors:

a. It is of such an ancient rhythm, being inherent in astral substance itself, that it is most difficult for a human being to become aware of it or to understand it; it is the result of the age-long activity of human desire.

b. It is a corporate part of a man's own energy nature, and therefore constitutes for him the line of least resistance; it is part of a great world process and therefore a part of the individual life process also, and is, in itself, not wrong but an aspect of reality. This realisation necessarily complicates man's thought about it.

c. It is likewise definitely Atlantean in nature, being brought to a very high point of development in that race. It can therefore only be finally dissipated by the Aryan race using the right technique. The individual who is learning to dissipate glamour has to do two things:

1. Stand in spiritual being.
2. Keep the mind steady in the light.

From this it will be apparent that the energy of the astral plane as it expresses itself in the sentient desire life of the race, produces the major glamours of humanity, and can only be dissipated, dispersed and dispelled by the bringing in of the higher energy of the mind, motivated by the soul.

4. The glamours which hold humanity in thrall are:

a. The glamour of materiality.
b. The glamour of sentiment.
c. The glamour of devotion.

    d. The glamour of the pairs of opposites.
    e. The glamours of the Path.

Let me now elucidate these glamours for you a little more in detail.

The glamour of materiality is the cause of all the present world distress, for what we call the economic problem is simply the result of this particular glamour. Down the ages, this glamour has held the race increasingly interested, until today the entire world has been swept into the rhythm of money interest. A rhythm emanating from soul levels has always existed, being established by Those Who have freed Themselves from the control of material requirements, from the thraldom of money and the love of possessions. Today that higher rhythm is commensurate with the lower rhythmic glamour, and hence the whole world is thinking in terms of the way out from this present material impasse. Those souls who stand in the light to be found upon the mountain top of liberation and those who are advancing upward out of the fogs of materiality are now sufficient in numbers to do some definite work in connection with the dissipation of this glamour. The influence of their thoughts and words and lives can and will bring about a readjustment of values, and a new standard of living for the race, based upon clear vision, a correct sense of proportion and a realisation of the true nature of the relationship existing between soul and form, between spirit and matter. That which will meet a need that is vital and real ever exists within the divine plan. That which is unnecessary to the right expression of divinity and to a full and rich life can be gained and can be possessed, but only through the loss of the more real and the negation of the essential.

    Students, however, need to remember that that which is necessary varies according to the stage of evolution which

The Nature of Glamour

has been reached by an individual. For some people, for instance, the possession of that which is material may be as great a spiritual experience and as potent a teacher in life expression as the more elevated and less material requirements of the mystic or hermit. We are rated as regards action and point of view by our place upon the ladder of evolution. We are rated really by our point of view and not by our demand upon life. The spiritually minded man and the man who has set his feet upon the Path of Probation and who fails to attempt the expression of that which he believes, will be judged as caustically and pay as high a price as does the pure materialist—the man whose desires centre around substantial effects. Bear this in mind and sit not in the seat of the judge or the scornful.

Today the glamour of materiality is lessening perceptibly. The peoples of the world are entering the wilderness experience, and will find in the wilderness how little is required for full living, true experience and real happiness. The gluttonous desire for possessions is not regarded as so reputable a desire as formerly, and a desire for riches is not producing the clutching hands as earlier in racial history. Things and possessions are slipping out of the hands which have hitherto tightly held them, and only when men stand with empty hands and a realised new standard of values do they again acquire the right to own and to possess. When desire is absent and the man seeks nothing for the separated self, the responsibility of material wealth can again be handed back to man, but his point of view will then be free from that particular glamour, and the fogs of astral desire will be lessened. Illusion in many forms may still hold sway but the glamour of materiality will be gone. It is the first destined to disappear. Students would do well to remember that all forms of possessions and all material objects, whether it is money, or a house, a picture or an automobile, have an intrinsic life of their own, an emanation of their own, and an activity which is essentially that of their own inherent atomic structures (for an atom is a unit of active energy). This produces counterparts in the world of etheric and astral life, though not in the mental world. These subtler forms and distinctive emanations swell the potency of the world desire; they contribute to the world glamour and form part of a great and powerful miasmic world, which is on the involutionary arc but in which humanity, upon the upward arc, is nevertheless immersed. Therefore the Guides of the Race have felt the necessity of standing by whilst the forces set up by man himself proceed to strip him and thus release him to walk in the wilderness. There, in what is called straightened circumstances, he can readjust his life and change his way of living, thus discovering that freedom from material things carries with it its own beauty and reward, its own joy and glory. Thus he is liberated to live the life of the mind.

The glamour of sentiment holds the good people of the world in thrall, and in a dense fog of emotional reactions. The race has reached a point wherein the men of good intention, of some real understanding and owning a measure of freedom from the love of gold (symbolic way of speaking of the glamour of materiality) are turning their desire to their duty, their responsibilities, their effects upon others, and to their sentimental understanding of the nature of love. Love, for many people, for the majority indeed, is not really love but a mixture of the desire to love and the desire to be loved, plus a willingness to do anything to show and evoke this sentiment, and consequently to be more comfortable in one's own interior life. The selfishness of the people who are desirous of being unselfish is great. So many contributing sentiments gather around the sentiment or desire to show those amiable and pleasant characteristics which will evoke a corresponding reciprocation towards the would-be lover or server who is still completely surrounded by the glamour of sentiment.

It is this pseudo-love, based primarily on a theory of love and service, which characterises so many human relationships such as those existing, for instance, between husband and wife, parents and their children. Glamoured by their sentiment for them and knowing little of the love of the soul which is free itself and leaves others free also, they wander in a dense fog, often dragging with them the ones they desire to serve in order to draw forth a responsive affection. Study the word "affection," my brother, and see its true meaning. Affection is not love. It is that desire which we express through an exertion of the astral body and this activity affects our contacts; it is not the spontaneous desirelessness of the soul which asks nothing for the separated self. This glamour of sentiment imprisons and bewilders all the nice people in the world, imposing upon them obligations which do not exist, and producing a glamour which must eventually be dissipated by the pouring in of true and selfless love.

I am but touching with brevity upon these glamours for each of you can elaborate them for yourselves, and in so doing will discover where you stand in the world of fog and glamour. Thus, with knowledge, you can begin to free yourselves from the glamour of the world.

The glamour of devotion causes many probationary disciples to wander circuitously around in the world of desire. This is primarily a glamour which affects sixth ray persons and is particularly potent at this time owing to the age-long activity of the sixth Ray of Devotion during the rapidly passing Piscean Age. It is today one of the potent glamours of the really devoted aspirant. They are devoted to a cause, to a teacher, to a creed, to a person, to a duty, or to a responsibility. Ponder on this. This harmless desire along some line of idealism which confronts them becomes definitely harmful both to themselves and to others, because through this glamour of devotion they swing into the rhythm of the world glamour which is essentially the fog of desire. Potent desire along any line, when it obliterates the wider vision and shuts a man within a tiny circle of his own desire to satisfy his sentiment of devotion, is just as hampering as any of the other glamours, and is even more dangerous because of the beautiful colouring which the resultant fog takes on. A man gets lost in a rapturous mist of his own making, which emanates from his astral body and which is composed of the sentimentalising of his own nature about his own desire and devotion to the object of his attracted attention.

With all true aspirants, owing to the increased potency of their vibrations, this devotional sentiment can be particularly difficult and bring about a lengthy imprisonment. One illustration of this is the sentiment of devotion poured out in a glamorous ecstasy by probationary disciples upon the Masters of the Wisdom. Around the names of the Members of the Hierarchy and around Their work, and the work of the initiates and the disciplined disciples (mark that phrase) a rich glamour is created which prevents Them ever reaching the disciple or his reaching Them. It is not possible to penetrate the dense glamour of devotion, vibrating with dynamic ecstatic life, which emanates from the concentrated energy of the disciple, working still through the solar plexus centre.

For this glamour there are some age-old rules: Contact the greater Self through the medium of the higher Self and thus lose sight of the little self, its reactions, its desires, and intentions. Or: The pure love of the soul which is not personalised in any way and which seeks no recognition can then pour into the world of glamour which surrounds the

The Nature of Glamour

devotee, and the mists of his devotion (upon which he prides himself) will melt away.

Upon the Probationary Path there comes the swing, consciously registered, between the pairs of opposites until the middle way is sighted and emerges. This activity produces the *glamour of the pairs of opposites,* which is of a dense and foggy nature, sometimes coloured with joy and bliss and sometimes coloured with gloom and depression as the disciple swings back and forth between the dualities. This condition persists just as long as the emphasis is laid upon *feeling*—which feeling will run the gamut between a potent joyfulness as the man seeks to identify himself with the object of his devotion or aspiration, or fails to do so and therefore succumbs to the blackest despair and sense of failure. All this is, however, astral in nature and sensuous in quality and is not of the soul at all. Aspirants remain for many years and sometimes for many lives imprisoned by this glamour. Release from the world of feeling and the polarising of the disciple in the world of the illumined mind will dissipate this glamour which is part of the great heresy of separateness. The moment a man differentiates his life into triplicities (as he inevitably must as he deals with the pairs of opposites and identifies himself with one of them) he succumbs to the glamour of separation. Perhaps this point of view may aid or perhaps it will remain a mystery, for the secret of world glamour lies hid in the thought that this triple differentiation veils the secret of creation. God Himself produced the pairs of opposites—spirit and matter—and also produced the middle way which is that of the consciousness aspect or the soul aspect. Ponder deeply on this thought.

The triplicity of the pairs of opposites and of the narrow way of balance between them, the noble middle path, is the reflection on the astral plane of the activity of spirit, soul and body; of life, consciousness and form, the three aspects of divinity—all of them equally divine.

As the aspirant learns to free himself from the glamours upon which we have touched, he discovers another world of fog and mist through which the Path seems to run and through which he must penetrate and thus free himself from *the glamours of the Path*. What are these glamours, my brothers? Study the three temptations of Jesus, if you would know clearly what they are. Study the effect that the affirmation schools which emphasise divinity (materially employed) have upon the thought of the world; study the failures of disciples through pride, the world saviour complex, the service complex, and all the various distortions of reality which a man encounters upon the Path, which hinder his progress and which spoils the service to others which he should be rendering. Emphasise in your own minds the spontaneity of the life of the soul and spoil it not with the glamour of high aspiration selfishly interpreted, self-centredness, self-immolation, self-aggressiveness, self-assertiveness in spiritual work—such are some of the glamours of the Path.

Next, we will consider glamour on the etheric plane and the theme of the Dweller upon the Threshold, and thus complete the brief outline of our problem which the first part of this teaching was intended to convey.

Before taking up this subject in some detail, I would like to add something to our previous consideration of the problem of glamour. In your last instruction, I elaborated somewhat upon the subject of the various types of glamour and left with you the concept of their great importance in your individual lives. The battlefield (for the man who is nearing accepted discipleship or who is upon the path of discipleship, in the academic sense) is primarily that of

The Nature of Glamour

glamour. That is the major problem and its solution is imminent and urgent for all disciples and senior aspirants. It will be apparent, therefore, to you why the emphasis has been put, during the Aryan age, upon the necessity for the study of Raja Yoga, and the cultivation of submission to its discipline. Only through Raja Yoga can a man stand steady in the light, and only through illumination and the achievement of clear vision can the fogs and miasmas of glamour be finally dissipated. Only as the disciple learns to hold his mind "steady in the light," and as the rays of pure light stream forth from the soul, can the glamour be discovered, discerned, recognised for what it essentially is and thus be made to disappear, as the mists of earth dissolve in the rays of the rising sun. Therefore I would counsel you to pay more adequate attention to your meditation, cultivating ever the ability to reflect and to assume the attitude of reflection—held steady throughout the day.

You would find it of real value to ponder deeply upon the purposes for which the intuition must be cultivated and the illumined mind developed, asking yourselves if those purposes are identical in objective and synchronous in time. You would then discover that their objectives differ, and the effects of their pronounced unfoldment upon the personality life are likewise different. Glamour is not dispelled through the means of the intuition nor is illusion overcome by the use of the illumined mind.

The intuition is a higher power than is the mind, and is a faculty latent in the Spiritual Triad; it is the power of pure reason, an expression of the buddhic principle, and lies beyond the world of the ego and of form. Only when a man is an initiate can the exercise of the true intuition become normally possible. By that I mean that the intuition will then be as easily operative as is the mind principle in the case of an actively intelligent person. The intuition, however, will make its presence felt much earlier in extremity or on urgent demand.

It is *illumination* that the majority of aspirants, such as are found in this group, must seek; and they must cultivate the power to use the mind as a reflector of soul light, turning it upon the levels of glamour, and therefore dissipating it. The difficulty, my brothers, is to do so when in the midst of the agonies and deceptions of glamour. It requires a quiet withdrawing in mind and thought and desire from the world in which the personality habitually works, and the centering of the consciousness in the world of the soul, there silently and patiently to await developments, knowing that the light will shine forth, and illumination eventually take place.

A deep distrust of one's reactions to life and circumstance, when such reactions awaken and call forth *criticism, separativeness* or *pride*, is of value. The qualities enumerated above are definitely breeders of glamour. They are occultly "the glamorous characteristics." Ponder on this. If a man can free himself from these three characteristics, he is well on the way to the relinquishing and the dissipation of all glamour. I am choosing my words with care in an effort to arrest your attention.

Illusion is dispelled, rejected, and thrust away through the conscious use of the intuition. The initiate *insulates* himself from the world of illusion and of illusory forms and from the attractive urges of a personality nature and thereby—through the medium of isolation—comes into touch with the reality in all forms, hidden hitherto by the veil of illusion. This is one of the paradoxes of the Path. Insulation and isolation of the right kind lead to the right relationships and the correct contacts with the real. They produce eventual identification with reality, through insulation of oneself against the unreal. It is this idea which lies

The Nature of Glamour

behind the teaching given in the last book in the Yoga Sutras of Patanjali. These have often been misinterpreted and their meaning twisted into a plea for the wrong kind of isolation by those with separative tendencies and for selfish ends.

It is the soul itself which dispels illusion, through the use of the faculty of the intuition. It is the illumined mind which dissipates glamour.

I would like here to point out that many well-meaning aspirants fail at this point, due to two errors.

1. They omit to discriminate between illusion and glamour.
2. They endeavour to dispel glamour through what they believe to be right method,—by calling in the soul, whereas they really need to use the mind correctly.

When one is in the midst of fogs and glamours, however, it is much easier to sit down and hypnotise oneself into the belief that one is "calling in the soul" than it is to subject one's astral and emotional nature to the effect of hard straight thinking, using the mind as the instrument whereby glamour can be dispelled. Strange as it may seem, the "calling in of the soul" to deal directly with glamour may (and frequently does) lead to an intensification of the difficulty. The mind is the means whereby light can be brought to bear on all conditions of glamour, and students would do well to bear this thought constantly in their consciousness. The process is one of linking up the mind with the soul and then focussing oneself consciously and with precision in the mind nature or in the mental body, and not in the soul nature or the egoic form. Then, through analysis, discrimination and right thought one proceeds to deal with the problem of glamour. The trouble is that disciples often do not recognise the condition as one of glamour and it is difficult to give a clear and infallible rule whereby that recognition can come. It might be stated, however, that glamour can always be found where there exists:

1. Criticism, when careful analysis would show that no criticism is really warranted.
2. Criticism, where there is no personal responsibility involved. By that I mean, where it is not the place or the duty of the man to criticise.
3. Pride in achievement or satisfaction that one is a disciple.
4. Any sense of superiority or separative tendency.

Many other clues to a right recognition of glamour might be given, but if all of you would pay close attention to the above four suggestions, you would release your lives most perceptibly from the influence of glamour and be of greater service consequently to your fellowmen. I have endeavoured to give you here some practical assistance in this difficult battle between the pairs of opposites, which is the major cause of glamour.

3. Glamour Upon Etheric Levels . . . . *Maya*

We come now to a consideration of the ways and means whereby *maya* can be ended and the disciple stand free from *the influence of physical plane force.* In the above statement the whole story of maya can be found. It might be added also (perhaps not wholly correctly but nevertheless with sufficient truth to warrant the statement) that maya, as a recognised effect, is only experienced when one is upon the Path, beginning with the Path of Probation or Purification. One is always in the midst of forces. But maya (as a problem) only

The Nature of Glamour

becomes so when recognised, and this recognition is not possible in the early stages of evolution. Upon the Path, one begins to watch for and to discover the effects of force; one finds oneself consciously the victim of force currents; one is swept into activity of some kind by uncontrolled forces, and the world of force becomes a consciously sensed reality to the struggling aspirant. It is for this reason that I have stated that maya is predominantly a difficulty of the etheric body, for in relation to maya we are dealing with the forces pouring through the seven centres of the body (in all or in some), producing reactions and effects that are desirable or disastrous.

It is naturally necessary to realise that all manifestation on all levels is an expression of force, but the forces to which I refer here under the term maya are those uncontrolled energies, those undirected impulses which emanate from the world of prana and from the latent force of matter itself. These sweep a man into wrong activity and surround him with a whirlpool of effects and of conditions in which he is entirely helpless. He is the victim of mass force, hidden in the animal nature or in the world and the environing circumstances in which he finds himself. When to the power of maya is added the condition of glamour and also the illusions of the advanced disciple, it will be seen how necessary it is that there should be quiet differentiation between the three types of deception. It should he remembered that when we use the term "deception," we mean deception from the angle of the soul. The aspirant has to learn to stand free from illusion, glamour, and maya, and to do this he must understand the means to freedom which are: Intuition, Illumination and Inspiration.

The problem of maya is complicated by the fact that upon the physical plane (as upon the astral plane, though this is as yet little realised) you have the battle of a pair of opposites. These are of a different nature in some respects to those found upon the astral plane. On the physical plane (and by that I mean upon the etheric levels of the physical plane whereon the deceptive power of maya is experienced) there is the meeting of the forces of the subjective world of the personality and the ancient energies of matter itself, brought over as latent seeds from an earlier solar system.

It might perhaps become clearer to your perception if I worded the truth about maya as follows:

The latent impulses of the personality life, when divorced from and not under soul control, are blended with the pranic fluids within the periphery of the personality sphere of influence, and then become potent directed streams of force, seeking emergence into physical manifestation through the medium of the seven centres in the physical body. These forces or impulses, plus the prana available, constitute the etheric body of the undeveloped and frequently of the average man. It will be apparent, therefore, how much the undeveloped man is the victim of mass energy of a low kind, for his etheric body is responsive to, and draws its energy from a type of general environing prana, until such time as there is a definite direction and a higher control—either through oriented aspiration and mental discipline, or later as the result of soul conditioning, to use the psychological phrase.

This etheric energy, focussed in an individual etheric body, passes through two stages prior to the period of discipleship:

1. The stage wherein it assimilates the second force to which I referred—the force, latent in the dense physical form, the energy of the atomic substance, thus producing a definite fusing and blending. This causes the animal nature to conform entirely to the inner impulses,

emanating from the world of prana, where the entirely undeveloped man is concerned, or from the lower astral where the more developed or average man is concerned.

2. The moment, however, that an inner orientation towards the world of higher values takes place, then the etheric or vital force is brought into conflict with the lowest aspect of man, the dense physical body, and the battle of the lower pairs of opposites takes place.

It is interesting to note that it is during this stage that the emphasis is laid upon physical disciplines, upon such controlling factors as total abstinence, celibacy, and vegetarianism, and upon physical hygiene and physical exercises. Through these, the control of the life of matter, the lowest expression of the third aspect of divinity can be offset, and the man set free for the true battle of the pairs of opposites. This second battle is the true *kurukshetra* and is fought out in the astral nature, between the pairs of opposites which are distinctive of our solar system, just as the physical pairs of opposites are distinctive of the past solar system. From one interesting angle the battle of the opposites upon the lower spiral, in which the physical body in its two aspects is concerned, can be seen taking place in the animal kingdom. In this process, human beings act as the agents of discipline, and the domesticated animals, which are forced to conform to human control, are wrestling (even if unconsciously from our point of view) with the problem of this lower pair of opposites. Their battle is fought out through the medium of the dense physical body and the etheric forces, and in this way a higher aspiration is brought into expression. This produces in them the experience which we call "individualisation," wherein the seed of personality is sown. On the human battlefield, the kurukshetra, the higher aspect of the soul begins to dominate, producing the process of divine-human integration which we call "initiation." Ponder upon this.

When an aspirant reaches that point in his evolution wherein the control of the physical nature is an urgent necessity, he recapitulates in his own life this earlier battle with the lowest pairs of opposites, and begins then to discipline his dense physical nature.

Making a broad and sweeping generalisation, it might be said that for the human family en masse this dense physical-etheric conflict was fought out in the World War, which was the imposition of a tremendous test and discipline. Remember that our tests and disciplines are self-imposed and grow out of our limitations and our opportunities. The result of this test was the passing on to the Path of Probation of a very large number of human beings, owing to the purging and purification to which they had been subjected. This purificatory process in some measure prepared them for the prolonged conflict upon the astral plane which lies ahead of all aspirants prior to achieving initiation. It is the "Arjuna experience." This is an interesting point upon which to ponder and explains much of mystery and of difficulty in the *sequence* of human unfoldment. The individual aspirant is apt to think only in terms of himself and of his individual tests and trials. He must learn to think of the mass occurrences and their preparatory effect where humanity is concerned. The World War was a climaxing point in the process of "devitalising" the world maya. Much force was released and exhausted and much energy expended. Much was consequently clarified.

Many people are occupied today in their individual lives with exactly the same process and conflict. On a tiny scale that which was worked out in the World War is worked out in their lives. They are busy with the problem of maya and

The Nature of Glamour

hence today we find an increasing emphasis upon the physical cultures, disciplines, and physical training, such as is imposed in the world of sport, in athletic exercises and military training. In spite of all the wrong motives and the terrible and evil effects (speaking again with a wide generalisation), the training of the body and the organised physical direction of the youth of the world today in all countries, particularly the military countries in Europe, is preparing the way for millions to pass upon the Path of Purification. Is this a hard truth, my brothers? Humanity is under right direction, e'en if (during a brief interlude) they misunderstand the process and apply wrong motives to right activities.

All these points we shall later take up in greater detail when we come to our third section and begin to study the modes of ending glamour, illusion and maya. At present I am only occupied with giving you a general picture and a slight elaboration of the tabulation to be found on page 41. Study it with care and memorise it if possible, for in its right understanding lies for you much of real usefulness.

I would like to point out in connection with the problem of maya that one of the first steps to its right handling is physical coordination; hence the emphasis laid upon this today in the training of children; hence also our use of a similar process under the term "alignment" when dealing with the work of meditation and the effort to induce increased soul control. Students would do well to bear this in mind and to ponder upon the following phrases:

1. Physical co-ordination.
2. Astral orientation.
3. Mental direction.
4. Personality alignment.

These are all attempts to express the process of "right activity upon the Path of Return." This return is the objective of the human family and the culminating goal of the four kingdoms in nature. We could enlarge the concept by expressing the truth in the following manner:

Process	Correspondence	Obstacle.
1. Physical coordination	Mineral Kingdom	Maya
2. Astral orientation	Vegetable Kingdom	Glamour
3. Mental direction	Animal Kingdom	Illusion
4. Personality Alignment	Human kingdom	The Dweller on the Threshold

These processes have, therefore, their equivalents in all the kingdoms and lead up to:

1. The unfoldment of the divine consciousness.
   This starts in the mineral kingdom.
2. The expression of the soul.
   This is typified in the vegetable kingdom with its uses and beauty.
3. The manifestation of the Christ.
   This is the recognised goal of the animal kingdom which works towards individualisation.
4. The revelation of the glory of God.
   This is the objective before humanity.

4. *Glamour upon the Higher Mental Planes* . . . .
The Dweller on the Threshold.

We will now touch very briefly upon the problem of the *Dweller on the Threshold*. This Dweller is oft regarded as a disaster, as a horror to be avoided, and as a final and culminating evil. I would remind you nevertheless that the Dweller is the "one who stands before the Gate of God," who dwells in the shadow of the portal of initiation, and who faces the Angel of the Presence open-eyed, as the ancient scripture calls it. The Dweller can be defined as the sum total of the forces of the lower nature as expressed in the personality, prior to illumination, to inspiration and to initiation. The personality, at this stage, is exceedingly potent, and the Dweller embodies all the psychic and mental forces which down the ages have been unfolded in a man and nurtured with care; it can be looked upon as the potency of the threefold material form, prior to its consecration and dedication to the life of the soul and to the service of the Hierarchy, of God and humanity.

The Dweller on the Threshold is all that a man is, apart from the higher spiritual self; it is the third aspect of divinity as expressed in the human mechanism, and this third aspect must eventually be subordinated to the second aspect, the soul.

The two great contrasting Forces, the ANGEL and the DWELLER are brought together—face to face—and the final conflict takes place. Again you will note that it is a meeting and a battle between another and higher pair of opposites. The aspirant has, therefore, three pairs of opposites with which to deal as he progresses towards light and liberation.

The Pairs of Opposites

1. On the Physical Plane . . . The dense and the etheric.
    Fought out upon the Path of Purification.

2. On the Astral Plane . . . . The well-known dualities.
    Fought upon the Path of Discipleship.

3. On the Mental Plane . . . The Angel and the Dweller.
    Fought upon the Path of Initiation.

I have, I should judge, given you enough to ponder upon; I would close it, however, by pointing out to you the very practical nature of that which I have communicated and would urge you to find out in your own practical experience the nature of the battle you have each to fight. To aid you in this, I am going to help you in one very definite way.

It will be of service to you if I indicate to you—each of you—the rays which govern your threefold personality. You will then be in a position to handle yourselves with greater wisdom, to trace more easily the causes of difficulty and to study more intelligently the effect you may have upon each other and upon those you contact in daily life. I will elaborate in detail the training which should be given to each of the three bodies, taking one of the vehicles at a time and explaining the problem facing each of you in relation to that particular vehicle, and assigning a meditation which will enable you (with greater facility) to handle the personality from that specific angle.

You will note from the above that it is, therefore, my intention to give you a much more careful and intensive training. Will you profit by it? In the interim and in order that you can apprehend the truth of what I shall later tell you, will you study yourselves with care during the next six months and see if what I later suggest is not true? Use the information given in *A Treatise on the Seven Rays* as your guide in this self-analysis; I would remind you that the rays govern the three bodies in the following order:

1. Rays governing the mental body . . . . Rays 1.4.5.
2. Rays governing the astral body . . . . Rays 2.6.
3. Rays governing the physical body . . . . Rays 3.7.

Thus you will note that all the rays play their part in the mechanism of man, making all circumstances the vehicles of opportunity and all conditions the medium of development. This statement as to the governing rays is a statement of an infallible rule, except in the case of accepted disciples.

As you read and study, you would find it of value to reflect upon and then to answer the following questions:

1. What is the relation of the *intuition* to the problem of illusion?

2. In what manner can *illumination* dispel glamour, and how can it be brought about?

3. Define maya and give your understanding of *inspiration* as a factor in dispelling it.

I have purposely not elucidated this technique as I sought to draw out your own ideas. I would urge you to follow the group meditation with care. It is of deep importance to the group in the interest of integration and real spiritual cooperation. The Full Moon work will likewise increase in importance. Later will come facility in recognising and recording the nature of the glamour to be dissipated and aptitude in seeing the process of light distribution.

SECTION TWO
THE CAUSES OF GLAMOUR

1. The Racial and Individual Growth of Glamour.

We shall now employ the word "glamour" to cover all the aspects of those deceptions, illusions, misunderstandings and misinterpretations which confront the aspirant at every step of his way until he achieves unity. I would have you note that word "unity," for it holds the secret of disillusionment, as this process of release from glamour has been occultly called. It will be apparent to you (if you have studied these instructions with care) that the cause of glamour is primarily based upon the sense of duality. If such a duality did not exist, there would be no glamour, and this perception of the dual nature of all manifestation lies at the very root of the trouble or troubles with which humanity is—in time and space—faced. This perception passes through various stages and constitutes the great problem of the conscious entity. This condition is a difficulty in the realm of consciousness itself and is not really inherent in the substance or matter. The dweller in the body perceives wrongly: he interprets incorrectly that which is perceived; he proceeds to identify himself with that which is not himself; he shifts his consciousness into a realm of phenomena which engulfs him, deludes him and imprisons him until such time as he becomes restless and unhappy under the sense that something is wrong. Then he comes finally to the recognition that he is not what he seems to be and that the phenomenal world of appearances is not identical with reality as he

The Causes of Glamour

had hitherto supposed it to be. From that moment on he comes to the sense of duality, to the recognition of "otherness" and to the perception that his sense of dualism should be ended and that a process of unification and an attempt to achieve at-one-ment should be undertaken. From that moment, the troubles of the evolving man begin to be observed by him and consciously encountered, and he faces a long period of "extrication from glamour and the entering into that world wherein only unity is known." The stages from then on might be enumerated as follows:

First: The stage wherein the material world is recognised and valued. Temporarily it is made the goal of all activity and the man, refusing to recognise the difference existing between him and the material and natural world, seeks to identify himself with it and to find satisfaction in purely physical pleasures and pursuits. This stage divides itself into two parts:

a. That wherein satisfaction is sought in the almost automatic response to the physical instincts, to sex, food and warmth. These loom large in man's consciousness. The animal nature in man is made the centre of the attempt to produce some sense of unity. Because the inner and subtle man is as yet "weak in impact" (as it is esoterically called), a physical unification temporarily takes place which serves to deepen the glamour and to delay progress into freedom.

b. The stage wherein satisfaction and sense of oneness is sought in the realm of material possessions, and in the establishing of a centre of beauty and comfort in life on the physical plane. Therein the man can be at home and oblivious of a growing sense of dualism which, day by day, gets steadily stronger. This stage only takes place ages later when the aspirant is about to re-orient himself to truth and to take the first steps towards the Probationary Path. It is a correspondence towards the end of the Path of Evolution to the stage above mentioned, but the man experiencing it is a very different person to the one who now seeks synthesis in the materialisation of beauty upon the outer plane. The subtle man is now becoming dominant.

Secondly: The stage wherein the man first of all becomes aware of the duality which can be expressed by the words "the man and the forces." He becomes alive to the fact that he and all humanity are the victims of forces and energies over which they have no control and which drive men hither and thither. He becomes aware also of forces and energies within himself over which he likewise has no control and which force him to act in various ways, making him frequently the victim of his own revolts, his own acts and selfishly directed energies. Here the man discovers (unconsciously at first and later consciously), the initial duality—the physical body and the vital or etheric body. One is the mechanism of contact upon the physical plane, the other is the mechanism of contact with the inner forces, energies and worlds of being. This vital body controls and galvanises the physical body into an almost automatic activity. I referred to this duality in an earlier instruction. This stage is one of great difficulty for the man, as an individual, and for humanity as a whole. Men are still so ignorant of the "reality which shines under the envelope which envelops it"—as the *Old Commentary* calls it—that true perception is difficult and at first well-nigh impossible. Blindly and ignorantly men have to cope with this first pair of opposites. It is this that we see happening in the world at this time. The masses are awakening to the realisation that they are the victims and the exponents of forces over which they have no control and of which they have no understanding. They would like to assume control over them and are determined so to do whenever possible. This constitutes the major problem today in the economic field and in the field of daily living and of government.

World tension today consists in the fact that physical force and etheric energy are at grips. Forget not what I earlier told you that etheric force is closely related to the Monad or the highest spiritual aspect. It is life itself on the verge of externalisation. Hence the emphasis today upon the spirit of humanity, upon the spirit of a nation, and the spirit of a group. This is all the result of the battle going on between this pair of opposites in the field of human affairs and in the field of individual average human living. It is, however, this conflict—fought out to the point of synthesis and of at-one-ment—which produces the re-orientation of the race and of the individual to the truer values and to the world of reality. It is this conflict—successfully waged—which lands the man, as an individual, and the mass, as a whole, upon the Path of Purification. When there is unification of these energies upon the physical plane, you then have one-pointed activity and a determination to travel in a specific direction. There follows the resolution (note this word and its usage) of the duality into a unity.

This resolution works out in the early stages (where the average type of aspirant is concerned) into a temporary astral unity and then there emerges the one-pointed devotee. He is found in all fields—of religion, of science, of politics or in any other department of life. His etheric unity, producing re-orientation—with its results of a clear vision, a grasp of truth, and a picture of the immediate way to go—serves temporarily to glamour the man with a sense of achievement, of surety, of power and of destiny.

He goes ahead blindly, furiously and ruthlessly until suddenly he is brought sharply up against changing conditions and recognises another and far more difficult situation. The pairs of opposites upon the astral plane confront him, and he becomes Arjuna upon the field of battle. All his sense of at-one-ment, of direction, of sure and oft-times smug satisfaction disappears and he is lost in the fogs and glamours of the astral plane. This is the plight of many well-meaning disciples at this time and upon it I must for a moment dwell because this group, when it can work as a group, has for its intended task the dissolution of some of the world glamour. Some day (and let us hope that it will take place before long) this group and other such groups should work, as a group and under direction of their Master, in piercing the world glamour and letting in some light and illumination so that men may walk from henceforth more truly on the *Way* in safety.

I have, therefore, chosen for participation in this work several aspirants whose tendency is to succumb to glamour, though two of them are less prone to it than are the others. Their relative freedom from it was one of the reasons why I chose them. These two are D.L.R. and D.P.R. Let these two keep their lives free from any tendency to glamour if they are rightly to serve their brothers as desired by me. I will give indication of their tendency in that direction in their personal instructions. The other group members are quickly prone to glamour, but this is a grief to them. It can, however, be as quickly turned into an asset. How can the world glamour be dissipated except by those who recognise it for what it is and who have wrestled with it in their daily lives? How can there be success in removing world glamour through illumination, unless this illumination is brought about by those who have learned to cast the searchlight of the soul into the dark places and the glamour which sur-

The Causes of Glamour

rounds them, as individuals, and then see it disappear? Be not discouraged by this "glamorous weakness" but regard your effort to understand the problem and your ability to arrive at the solution in your own lives as part of the contribution which you can make to this most stupendous of world problems. Solve your glamour by dwelling in the light and holding the mind steady in that light, and by learning to throw this light into the fogs of glamour on the astral plane. Do not attempt to solve it, as some aspirants so frequently do, by saying, "Now I understand," whereas all that they do (and many of you do the same) is to react to a self-evident occult platitude.

Third: This stage of glamour is oft called the Arjuna Experience. Today the world Arjuna is facing the pairs of opposites, just as does the individual disciple, ready—when these pairs have been resolved into a unity—to tread the Path of Discipleship.

It might be pointed out that:

1. The masses in all lands are wrestling with the first pair of opposites, that upon the physical plane. When "resolution" has taken place, these masses will step on to the Path of Purification. This is rapidly taking place. It might be added that this is a long and slow process because the consciousness is—in this stage—not the intelligent awareness of the thinking man but the blind consciousness of the physical man, plus the forces of nature themselves.

2. The average educated citizen in all lands is facing today the Arjuna experience and the pairs of opposites upon the astral plane. Hence the intense feeling abroad in the world; hence also the search for illumination, through education, through religion, and through the many agencies of mental instruction, with the consequent

growth of knowledge, wisdom and right relationships. These people fall normally into two classes:

> a. Those who are aware of the necessity for decision and discrimination in thinking and in choice, but who are not yet truly aware of the implications or of the indications. They are called the "bewilderment phase of Arjuna's plight," and to racial, national and individual glamour, they have added a spiritual glamour which intensifies the fog.
>
> b. Those who have emerged out of this condition and are becoming aware of their problem. They see the pairs of opposites and are entering upon the "recognition stage of Arjuna's release." They see the Form of God and the indwelling Reality within that Form and are arriving at the decision to let the Warrior carry on the fight. They will then (when right decision and choice have been made) "stand up and fight," and will find themselves no longer on the Path of Purification but upon the Path of Discipleship.

With this stage you are all familiar, and aspirants such as are found in this group of students need no instruction from me as to the treading of the path out of glamour into light. The rules are well known: the glamours to which you are susceptible are equally familiar; the glamours to which humanity is prone are well recognised by you. It remains but for you to follow the ancient way of Raja Yoga and bring in the mind as a dispelling agency and thus learn to stand in the "light" between the pairs of opposites, and through that "light" achieve freedom by treading the noble middle way. Sometimes, my brothers, I feel that you know so much theoretically but have worked out relatively so lit-

The Causes of Glamour

tle. I ask myself whether I do not shoulder an unreasonable responsibility by giving you any more instructions. But I remind myself that I write for others as well as for you and that my time is short for this particular service.

The resolution of these dualities takes place when the soul, the true spiritual man, no longer identifies itself with either of the opposites, but stands free upon this middle way; the disciple then sees the "lighted *Way* ahead," along which he learns to go without being drawn into the glamorous worlds which stretch on either hand. He travels straight towards his goal.

3. The stage wherein the intelligent thinking man, whether disciple or well-meaning aspirant, or an initiate of the first and second degrees, has to learn to distinguish between the truth and the truths, between knowledge and wisdom, between reality and illusion. When this stage has been passed through it leads to the third initiation, wherein the personality (which is prone to maya, glamour and illusion) stands free. It again experiences a sense of at-one-ment. This is due to the development of the sense of the intuition which puts into the disciple's hand an infallible instrument whereby to discriminate and to discern. His perception is becoming accurate and he stands relatively free from deception and wrong identifications and interpretations.

You will have noted how the career of the man has, therefore, proceeded from a crisis of duality to one of a relative unity, only to have that sense of unification disturbed by a renewed recognition of a higher and deeper duality. This duality temporarily produces another cleavage in a man's life, and thus re-initiates a torturing process of bridging or of "occultly healing" this break in the continuity of the spiritual consciousness. I would here remind you that this sense of peace or perception of cleavage is in itself an illusion and of the nature of glamour, and is based upon the illusory sense of identification with that which is *not* the self, or soul. The entire problem can be solved if the shift of the consciousness is away from identification with the lower forms of experience into that of identification with the real and true man.

4. Stage by stage, the man has progressed from one state of illusion or glamour to another, from one point of discriminative opportunity to another until he has developed in himself three major capacities:

1. The capacity to handle force.
2. The capacity to tread the middle way between the pairs of opposites.
3. The capacity to use the intuition.

These capacities he developed by resolving the pairs of opposites on the physical, astral and lower mental planes. Now he faces his climaxing resolution, equipped with these powers. He becomes aware of those two great and apparently opposing entities (with both of whom he finds himself consciously identified)—the Angel of the Presence and the Dweller on the Threshold. Behind the Angel he dimly senses, not another duality, but a great Identity, a living Unity, which—for lack of a better word—we call the PRESENCE.

He then discovers that the way out in this case is not the method of handling force or of leaving behind both pairs of opposites, or of right recognition through the intuition, but that this Dweller and this Angel must be brought together; the lower entity must be "blotted out" in the "light," or "forced to disappear within the radiance." This is the task of the higher of the two entities, with which the disciple or the initiate, consciously and deliberately, identifies himself. With this process we will later deal. This is the problem which faces the initiate before he takes the final three initiations.

You must bear in mind that none of these three stages are, in reality, divided off from each other by clear lines of demarcation, nor do they follow each other in a clear sequence. They proceed with much overlapping and often with a partial simultaneity. It is only when the disciple faces certain initiations that he awakens to the fact of these distinctions. Therefore, it might be stated that:

1. In the first initiation the disciple demonstrates that he has resolved the dualities of the physical plane and can rightly impose etheric energy (the higher of the two) upon physical energy.

2. In the second initiation, the initiate demonstrates that he can choose between the pairs of opposites and proceed with decision upon the "middle way."

3. In the third initiation, the initiate can employ the intuition for the right perception of truth, and in that initiation he catches the first real glimpse of the Dweller on the Threshold and the Angel of the Presence.

4. In the fourth initiation, the initiate demonstrates his ability to produce complete at-one-ment between the higher and lower aspect of the soul in manifestation and sees the Dweller on the Threshold merge into the Angel of the Presence.

5. In the fifth initiation—and here words fail to express the truth—he sees the Dweller on the Threshold, the

Angel, and the Presence merged into a divine synthesis.

The question arises as to what produces this glamour and illusion. The subject is so vast (embracing as it does the whole field of planetary history) that I can do little more than indicate some of the causes. Few of them have, as yet, been susceptible of correction except in the case of individuals. This means that when individuals reach the point in evolution where they can identify themselves with their higher aspect, the soul, and can then bring in soul energy to offset, subdue and dominate the lower forces of the personality, then correction becomes possible and inevitably takes place. When, therefore, the time comes when a very large number of persons become aware of the condition of world glamour (through discovering it and dealing with it in their own lives), then we shall have a group approach to the problem. Then we shall have a definite attack upon the world glamour, and when this does take place—speaking esoterically— "an opening will be made which will admit the light of the solar orb. The fogs will slowly disappear, subdued by the solar radiance, and the pilgrims will then find the enlightened WAY which leads from the heart of the fog, straight to the door of light."

It is with the intention of discovering how far the aspirants and disciples of the world have gone in their understanding and in their handling of this problem that such an experiment as that being carried on in these groups has been undertaken and permitted.

2. The Causes Producing World Glamour.

The causes producing world glamour can be divided into three groups:

A. Planetary causes.
B. Causes initiated by humanity itself.
C. Causes induced by any individual person which are, nevertheless, founded and based in the two above groups of conditioning factors.

A. Planetary Causes. These causes are two in number and beyond your finite comprehension. I only state them and ask you to accept them as reasonable speculations and possibly accurate hypotheses:

1. Causes inherent in substance itself. The atoms of which all forms are made have been inherited from an earlier universe or solar system and are, therefore, tinged with or coloured by the results of that great creative manifestation. The effects produced in that expression of divine existence constitute predisposing factors or initiating causes in this solar system and planetary life. These conditioning and inherited factors cannot be evaded. They determine the nature of the life urge, the trend of the evolutionary unfoldment, and the innate tendencies which all forms possess, such as the capacity to grow and to unfold, to orient the type and to express in time and space the archetype or pattern, and to outline and determine the structure of the kingdoms into which science divides the natural world. These are but a few of the innate, inherent characteristics of substance itself, inherited and conditioning our present manifestation of divine life.

2. The life or manifestation of the planetary Logos, the "One in Whom we live and move and have our being," is determined by His Own Nature. To us, that great Life embodies perfection and the qualities which distinguish Him are those to which we direct our highest aspiration.

But, from the angle of Those Lives Who are ahead of Him upon the cosmic path (I speak symbolically and in terms of human experience) He is among the "imperfect Gods." These imperfections, hindering unfoldment or the perfect expression of divine energy when brought into conjunction with the inherited qualities and biases of the substances through which He must express His life, His purposes and intentions, produce the "seeds of death and of decay" which characterise our planetary evolution in all the four kingdoms in nature. They create the obstacles, obstructions and hindrances against which the soul in all created forms must struggle, gaining strength and understanding thereby and eventual liberation.

These are the two major planetary causes. They cannot finally deter the soul from emancipation but they can and do hinder and delay. It is useless for men to speculate upon these hypotheses with their present inadequate equipment and type of brain. Nothing would be achieved and you would be none the wiser.

B. Causes initiated by humanity itself. Slowly, step by step, humanity has created and intensified that glamorous condition of consciousness which we call the astral plane. All glamour is produced by the bringing together of one or more streams of energy which produce a temporary whirlpool of energies and, from the angle of man—the onlooker and participator—produce a condition of darkness, a state of bewilderment which makes clear choice and right discrimination difficult and, in the early stages, impossible. It creates an aura which is today of such a general nature and so all-enveloping that everybody is, figuratively speaking, immersed in it. This aura, in the infancy of the race,

The Causes of Glamour

only surrounded the more advanced people. To understand what I mean by this statement, I would call your attention to the fact that very unintelligent people, those who are among the lowest human types, and those who are little more than active animals, governed primarily by the instincts, are apt to deal very simply and with complete directness with the facts of existence with which they are faced and which to them are of paramount or sole importance—the facts of hunger, of birth and death, of self-protection and perpetuation. There is little true glamour in their reaction to life and living, and their simplicity, like that of a child, saves and protects them from many of the subtler ills. Their emotions are not subtle, and their minds are unawakened. But, as humanity evolved and the higher levels of the racial consciousness became more subtle and the mind factor slowly became more active, then glamour and illusion developed very rapidly.

The first indications of glamour arose when the disciples and the aspirants of the Lemurian world (whose problem was the right comprehension, correct functioning and control of the physical body) began to differentiate between themselves, as self-conscious beings, and physical and vital forces. That immediately set up a tremendous activity in the throat centre which is the higher aspect of the sacral centre (the sex centre) and thus led to the initial glamour and to the first definite recognition and consideration of the sex impulse, of sex attraction, and—for the initiate of that period—of the necessary sex transmutation. This went hand in hand with the earliest Yoga, or the cult of the physical body with the objective of its control by the soul, and the consequent merging of the conscious and the subconscious.

Around the aspirants of that time could then be seen gathering the first clouds and fogs of glamour, though illusion was nowhere present. The first recognition of the plane of the emotions, of the astral plane, was evoked in the consciousness of the groups under preparation for the first initiation which was the highest initiation possible at that time. The reason for this slowly emerging astral consciousness in the physically polarised aspirant of that time, was due to the fact that one of the secrets of initiation consists in the right understanding and use of the consciousness which is aware and capable of functioning upon a plane higher than that on which humanity as a whole is, at any given time, living. Hence, in Lemurian times, the physically centred man who was on the verge of admission to the Path was aware of:

1. The physical duality wherein his consciousness was accustomed to function normally and of the conflict between the physical body per se and the vital etheric body.

2. A dimly sensed higher consciousness which was distinguished by quality and sentiency. This was all that he could at that time contact upon the most familiar plane today, the astral plane.

3. A growing sense of self-identity which was the awakening soul or self, the Master who was to lead him out of the purely physical consciousness into the next divine stage, the astral consciousness. Forget not, through familiarity and fatigue of conflict, the divinity of each developing step.

Thus it will be apparent to you, if the above is a true statement of fact, that glamour arose from the recognition of these factors in consciousness and was the result of man's reactions to the complexities of his own constitution and to the energy of his own soul.

The Causes of Glamour

As time went on, the entire human family became aware of the new emerging dualism existing between the physical constitution and the astral plane, plus the activity of the centre within himself, which at this stage made its appearance as conscience and innate—and at that time unreasoning—realisation of an urge to higher living or a tendency to lower activity. This nebulous conscience developed eventually into what we call the Voice of Conscience. When that took place, the intricacy and the difficulty of life was greatly increased and glamour was definitely established on Earth. It was that which enfolded and over-emphasised the lower at the expense of the higher, and served to distract the attention of the aspirant away from reality. May I again re-emphasise that, at this early stage, glamour was only evoked by and recognised by the highly evolved people of that period?

Then the Lemurian race slowly passed away and the Atlantean race came into existence. During the millions of years this race flourished on Earth there were vast numbers of people with the Lemurian consciousness flourishing at the same time, just as today in this modern Aryan race, there are many, many millions of people who express the Atlantean consciousness and are polarised in their astral bodies, the victims of emotion and of consequent glamour.

In the Atlantean race, the physical duality was then solved, and the physical body and the etheric body constituted a unity, and in the healthy person still do so. The sense of duality shifted then into a growing recognition of the conflict in the realm of quality and into the field of what we today call the "pairs of opposites"—good and evil, pain and pleasure, right and wrong, sense and nonsense, and the multiplicity of opposites by which the aspirant is today faced.

Each of these racial histories sees the establishing of a temporary sense of unity in the early stages, when the previous cleavage had been healed and the initial duality had been resolved into a unity. Then there comes a growing recognition of a fresh realm of choice, based upon the emergence of the higher values, and finally a period of conflict in the consciousness of the individual and of humanity as a whole, as the attempt is made to resolve this higher duality with which the man or the race is confronted.

This resolution is brought about when a higher aspect of the consciousness is dimly visioned and men become aware of themselves as mental beings. There is then a growing demand for that mind nature to be developed and brought into play in the effort to solve the problem in this category of opposites upon the astral plane.

At the same time the sense of self-identity or the consciousness that "I am," is steadily growing, and the initiate of the day faces the effort to release himself from the thraldom of the senses upon the astral plane, from the dense glamour into which his sensory perception has thrown him, and to establish his freedom by a complete control of the astral body. This he eventually does by developing the power to pass between the pairs of opposites, unaffected by either, and thus leave them behind. He accomplishes this by using the mind as a distributor of the light which reveals the "middle way" and which dissipates the glamour with its brilliance and radiance.

This glamour has steadily deepened and intensified as more and more people have succeeded in resolving the initial physical cleavage and have become centred in the astral consciousness. Today such is the magnitude of this glamour and such the success of the evolutionary process, that humanity, as a whole, is wandering in the fogs and miasmas of the world of sentient consciousness.

The Causes of Glamour

When I use the word "sentient" I do not refer to the sensory apparatus of the physical nervous system, but to the sentient awareness of the Self which is today so immersed in glamour that the mass of men are entirely identified with the world of feeling, of quality, of sentient interplay, and of emotional reactions, with their likes and dislikes, and their dominant self-pity. Self-pity is one of the major glamours of the advanced and sensitive man. It is the advanced people who contribute the most to the world glamour. The major glamour is the reaction of the aspirant to the truth, to reality when he first becomes aware of that which lies beyond the astral plane. He interprets all that he there senses and sees in terms of glamour, of emotional understanding, of a sentient fanaticism. He forgets that truth lies beyond the world of feeling altogether, unaffected by it, and can only be sensed in its purity when feeling is transcended and transmuted. The second major glamour is self-pity.

The world today is divided into three groups, all of whom are subject to certain phases of glamour:

1. Those who are Atlantean in their consciousness and are, therefore, completely glamoured by:

    a. That which is material and to be desired.
    b. That which they *feel* in all relationships.
    c. That which they believe to be ideal, to be true or just, based on their reactions to the thinkers of the day, but which they themselves do not mentally understand.
    d. That which they demand of beauty, and of emotional comfort.
    e. That which brings to them spiritual comfort in the realm of religion and religious desire. Note the phrasing.

2. Those who are more definitely Aryan in their consciousness. This means that the mind factor is awakening and thus constituting a difficulty and that the illusions of the mental plane are now added to the glamours of the astral plane. These illusions are theoretical and intellectual in nature.

3. A group of people who are emerging out of those subject to glamour and illusion, and who are alive to the Voice of the Silence and to the demands of the soul.

The complexity of the modern psychological problem lies in the fact that our race and period sees the synthesis of all the glamours and the emergence of the illusions of the mental plane. Today we have aspirants at all stages of unfoldment, and find the masses recapitulating the different steps upon the evolutionary way, with the lowest layer of the human race definitely Lemurian in their consciousness, even though few in numbers relatively speaking.

Illusion is rapidly growing as the mental power of the race develops, for illusion is the succumbing to the powerful thoughtforms which the thinkers of the time and of the immediately preceding age have formulated, and which at the time of their creation constituted the hope of the race. They embodied then the new and emerging ideas by means of which the race was intended to progress. These forms, when old and crystallised, become a menace and a hindrance to the expanding life. The realisation of the problems of illusion lies centuries ahead when the race will have left glamour behind, when there will be few Atlantean minded people on the planet, and when there will be no people at all with the Lemurian consciousness. However, as evolution proceeds, things are greatly speeded up, and the time when humanity will be predominantly distinguished by the Aryan consciousness, is not as far ahead as

The Causes of Glamour

Race	Duality	Problem	Method	Goal
Lemurian	Physical Force versus Vital Energy	Maya	Astral Control Hatha Yoga: Aspirants Laya Yoga: Disciples	1st Initiation *Inspiration*
Atlantean	The Pairs of Opposites Qualities Sentiency	Glamour	Mental Control Bhakti Yoga: Aspirants Raja Yoga: Disciples	2nd Initiation *Illumination*
Aryan	Dweller on the Threshold Angel of the Presence	Illusion	Soul Control Raja Yoga: Aspirants Agni Yoga: Disciples	3rd Initiation *Intuition*

might be generally supposed. I speak not in terms of the Aryan race as it is generally understood today or in its Nordic implications.

C. *Causes initiated by the individual.* If you have studied all the above with the needed care, it will be apparent to you that the individual man enters upon incarnation already handicapped by existent glamour of a very ancient origin and utterly beyond his power to control at this stage. It is of great potency. I use the word "handicapped" advisedly for lack of a better term. I would like, however, to point out that the true significance of the situation exists in the fact that these conditions offer the opportunity to the man of evoking the understanding and point of view of the soul, for they provide the means whereby experience is gained. This experience will lead eventually to the soul assuming control of the mechanism, the personality, and thus giving to that soul a definite field of service. The vehicles through which the soul is seeking experience and expression are normally and naturally subject to world glamours, and to the glamours of humanity as well as illusion. When the soul, in the early stages of experience, falls into the snare of maya, of glamour and eventually of illusion, the reason is that the soul is identifying itself with those forms and therefore with the surrounding glamour, and thus failing to achieve identification with itself. As evolution proceeds, the nature of the problem becomes apparent to the soul in incarnation and a process is then instituted whereby the soul frees itself from the results of wrong identification. Every soul in incarnation which succeeds in releasing its consciousness from the world of illusion and of glamour is definitely serving the race, and helping to free humanity from this ancient and potent thraldom.

The Causes of Glamour

But it must be borne in mind that when a man is nearing the stage of consciousness when both the astral body and the mental body are active and functioning, he himself becomes a manufacturer of glamour. He struggles with forces within himself and within the world in which he lives, and the increasing potency of the inflowing soul energy (which comes in conflict with personality forces) gradually produces around him a field of glamour and an environment of illusion that brings this third category of glamour into full play.

These glamours are dependent upon the expression of the different forces which constitute a man's lower nature, of which he is becoming increasingly aware, and which pass through the stages of emergence into recognition, potency in expression, and violence in conflict until the struggling soul sits down—as did Arjuna—in the midst between the two opposing forces (personality force and soul energy) and asks himself:

1. Which is right, this or that?
2. How can I distinguish where my duty or my responsibility lies?
3. How can I find my way out of this bewildering situation?
4. How can I bring in the control of the Warrior so that the two groups of forces which I love may be resolved into a unity?
5. How can I find my way out of this impasse?
6. Why must I hurt that which I love and through which I have expressed myself for ages?
7. How can I become aware of that mental illumination which will reveal the "middle way" between the pairs of opposites?
8. How can I see God? or else the Form of God?

Many such questions arise in the mind of the aspirant. They indicate dilemma, bewilderment, a realisation of surrounding glamour, a stage of illusion and a condition of impotency. Against the disciple are fighting all the forces of his own nature, and also those of humanity as a whole and of the planetary state. He feels helpless, inert, feeble and hopeless. He cannot even see the way out. Only one clear fact remains and that is the fact of the Soul, of the immortal Identity, the Warrior behind the scenes, the Charioteer, Krishna, the Christ within.

The Bhagavad Gita can be read entirely from the standpoint of the disciple's combat with glamour and students would be well-advised so to study it.

The individual glamours of which the disciple becomes aware are consequently of five types of force. These, when brought into activity simultaneously, produce those glamours which are strictly initiated and produced by the man himself. They are:

1. The forces of his dense physical nature and of the vital body which latter, functioning through the dense physical nature, produce a condition of maya or of uncontrolled energy.

2. The forces of the astral nature, based upon desire and upon sentiency. These, at this stage, fall into two groups which we call the pairs of opposites. Their potency is accentuating at this period of individual history, for the disciple is polarised in the majority of cases in his astral body and is, therefore, subject to the glamours produced by the interplay of the opposites, plus the condition of maya, referred to above.

3. The forces of the lower mental nature, of the chitta or mind-stuff of which the mental body is composed. This is

The Causes of Glamour

coloured by past activity, as is the substance composing all the vehicles. This adds to maya and glamour, the state of illusion.

4. The personality ray then emerges and intensifies all these three aspects of force expression, producing eventually their synthetic work. Then we have the emerging of what has been called "the threefold glamorous condition," into one major glamour.

5. The soul ray or energy is all this time steadily increasing its rhythmic potency, and seeking to impose its purpose and will upon the personality. It is the united relation and the interplay between these two which—when a point of balance has been achieved—sweeps the man on to the Probationary Path, on to the Path of Discipleship, and right up to the gate of initiation. There, standing before the Gate, he recognises the final duality which awaits resolution. The Dweller on the Threshold and the Angel of the PRESENCE.

The nature of these glamours differs with different people, for the ray quality determines the type of glamour or illusion to which a man will easily succumb, and that kind of glamour which he will the most easily create. Disciples have to learn to differentiate between:

1. The glamours or glamour already existent in his environment, to which he will easily be attracted, or which he will easily attract, for they constitute the line of least resistance.

2. The glamour that he creates as he tackles life through the medium of a particular equipment, which is coloured by the experiences of past incarnations, and by the ray quality under which he has come into being.

This subject is so intricate that it will serve no useful purpose for me to go into detailed particulars. I can indicate the major glamours (and under this term I include the various maya and illusions) to which the ray types predispose the man. If you then apply these to the three vehicles of manifestation as well as to the personality and the soul, you will note how complicated is the problem. Yet remember this, my brother:

The issue is certain and determined for, in this solar system, the triumph of the soul and its final dominance and control is a foregone conclusion, no matter how great the glamour or how fierce the strife. Thus, the ascertaining (by the aspirant) of his ray influence is one of the first steps towards understanding the nature of his problem and the method of release. The psychology of the future will direct attention to the discovery of the two rays which govern the soul and personality. Having done this through a study of the physical type, emotional reactions and mental tendencies, attention will then be directed to the discovery of the rays governing the specialised vehicles. When these five rays (egoic, personality, physical, astral and mental) have been approximately ascertained, then the following factors will need consideration:

1. The nature, quality and stability of the glandular system.
2. The point attained in evolution. This will be done by a careful consideration of the centres and the glands and their relation to each other.
3. The recognition of the points of cleavage or the splits in the personality which exist. These can be:

    a. Between the etheric and the physical bodies, leading to a lack of vitality, physical weakness, obsession and many forms of difficulty.

b. In the sentient astral body, leading to a vast number of problems and psychological difficulties based upon undue sensitivity, reaction to glamour in the environment, innate tendencies to glamour in the equipment or resulting from sensitivity to the glamours of other people.

c. In the mental body, imposing mental illusions of many kinds, such as control by self-created thoughtforms, sensitivity to existing world, national, or environing thoughtforms of any school of thought, *idée fixe*, the sense of the dramatic or of importance, or a fanatical adherence to groups of ideas, inherited from the past, or mental reactions of a purely personal nature.

d. Between any of these groups of forces which we call bodies:

Between the etheric and astral bodies.

Between the astral and the mental bodies.

There is, for instance, a definite correspondence between the condition of negativity to physical plane living which is the result of a lack of integration between the physical and the etheric bodies, and that lack of interest and that failure to handle physical plane living which the thinker on abstract and scientific levels so frequently evidences. Both groups fail to make a definite and decisive manifestation upon the physical plane, both groups fail to deal with the problems of physical plane living in a clear and satisfactory manner, both are non-positive physically, but the causes producing these relatively similar conditions are totally different—though alike in their effects.

4. The comprehension of the Path of Life for an individual, through a study of his astrological indications. It is necessary in this connection to regard the sun sign into

which a man is born, as indicative of his personality trends, and as embodying the characteristics which he has inherited from the past, but to regard the rising sign as holding within it the indications of the way that a man's soul would have him go.

Many other factors will warrant careful attention. The problem of the individual is complicated by certain inherited tendencies of a family, national and racial nature. These powerfully affect the physical body in both its aspects, producing glamours of many kinds. It is also affected by certain inherited ideas which are the embodied thoughtforms of family, national and racial approaches to truth. These produce powerful illusions to which the individual man easily succumbs. There are also the inflowing forces of the sign into which the sun may be passing, such as the conditions found in the world today, due to the fact that our sun is passing into a new sign of the zodiac. Therefore powerful and new energies are playing upon humanity, producing effects in all the three bodies. They are evoking glamours in the emotional nature and illusions in the mental nature. Those easily subject to glamour become at this time conscious of an emphasised duality. The subject, as you will therefore see, is vast, and this science of the psychological influences and the results of their impact upon the human mechanism is, as yet, in its infancy. I have, however, indicated enough to arouse interest and to start investigation in this new field of psychological activity.

To return to the consideration of the many glamours which are produced by and related to certain ray types:

RAY I.

The glamour of physical strength.
The glamour of personal magnetism.

The Causes of Glamour

The glamour of self-centredness and personal potency.

The glamour of "the one at the centre."

The glamour of selfish personal ambition.

The glamour of rulership, of dictatorship and of wide control.

The glamour of the Messiah complex in the field of politics.

The glamour of selfish destiny, of the divine right of kings personally exacted.

The glamour of destruction.

The glamour of isolation, of aloneness, of aloofness.

The glamour of the superimposed will—upon others and upon groups.

RAY II.

The glamour of the love of being loved.

The glamour of popularity.

The glamour of personal wisdom.

The glamour of selfish responsibility.

The glamour of too complete an understanding, which negates right action.

The glamour of self-pity, a basic glamour of this ray.

The glamour of the Messiah complex, in the world of religion and world need.

The glamour of fear, based on undue sensitivity.

The glamour of self-sacrifice.

The glamour of selfish unselfishness.

The glamour of self-satisfaction.

The glamour of selfish service.

RAY III.

The glamour of being busy.

The glamour of cooperation with the Plan in an individual

and not a group way.

The glamour of active scheming.

The glamour of creative work—without true motive.

The glamour of good intentions, which are basically selfish.

The glamour of "the spider at the centre."

The glamour of "God in the machine."

The glamour of devious and continuous manipulation.

The glamour of self-importance, from the standpoint of knowing, of efficiency.

RAY IV.

The glamour of harmony, aiming at personal comfort and satisfaction.

The glamour of war.

The glamour of conflict, with the objective of imposing righteousness and peace.

The glamour of vague artistic perception.

The glamour of psychic perception instead of intuition.

The glamour of musical perception.

The glamour of the pairs of opposites, in the higher sense.

RAY V.

The glamour of materiality, or over-emphasis of form.

The glamour of the intellect.

The glamour of knowledge and of definition.

The glamour of assurance, based on a narrow point of view.

The glamour of the form which hides reality.

The glamour of organisation.

The glamour of the outer, which hides the inner.

The Causes of Glamour

RAY VI.

The glamour of devotion.
The glamour of adherence to forms and persons.
The glamour of idealism.
The glamour of loyalties, of creeds.
The glamour of emotional response.
The glamour of sentimentality.
The glamour of interference.
The glamour of the lower pairs of opposites.
The glamour of World Saviours and Teachers.
The glamour of the narrow vision.
The glamour of fanaticism.

RAY VII.

The glamour of magical work.
The glamour of the relation of the opposites.
The glamour of the subterranean powers.
The glamour of that which brings together.
The glamour of the physical body.
The glamour of the mysterious and the secret.
The glamour of sex magic.
The glamour of the emerging manifested forces.

I have here enumerated many glamours. But their names are legion, and I have by no means covered the possibilities or the field of glamour.

One of the groups with which I have worked had certain characteristics and difficulties, and it might be of value if I mentioned it here.

This group had a curious history in relation to other groups, because its personnel changed several times. Each time, the person who left the group had been in it from karmic right and old relation to myself or to the group members, and had, therefore, earned the opportunity to participate in this activity. Each time they failed, and each time for personality reasons. They lacked *group* realisation and were definitely occupied with themselves. They lacked the new and wider vision. So they eliminated themselves from this initial new age activity. I am explaining this, for it is valuable to disciples to grasp the fact that karmic relation cannot be ignored and that group opportunity must be offered, even though it delay functioning in group service.

Several of the group members were still struggling with glamour and it needed a longer time for them to adjust themselves to recognition of it when encountered. The major task of this group was to dissipate some of the universal glamour by a united indicated meditation. Certain of the group members also were facing or had major adjustments in their lives, and it took a little time for the needed subjective rhythm to become established. But they all worked with understanding, perseverance and enthusiasm, and it was not long before the group work was started.

You would find it of value to consider the following questions:

1. What is the method whereby ideas are developed from the moment of impressing the mind of some intuitive?

Broadly speaking, they pass through the following stages, as you have oft been told:

a. The idea . . . . . . based on intuitive perception.
b. The ideal . . . . . based on mental formulation and distribution.
c. The idol . . . . . . based on the concretising tendency of physical manifestation.

2. What glamours do you feel are particularly dominant in the world today, and why?

3. I have spoken often of the work which this group and certain other groups are intending to do in dissipating world glamour. Have you any ideas as to how this should be done, or what will be demanded of you?

3. *The Contrast between the Higher and the Lower Glamours*

In the preceding part of this section we considered (briefly and all too cursorily) some of the causes of the dense glamour which surrounds humanity. That this glamour is very ancient, powerfully organised, and is the dominant characteristic of the astral plane emerged clearly, as did the fact of the three major predisposing subsidiary causes:

1. The glamours induced by the planetary life and inherent in substance itself.
2. Those glamours which are initiated by humanity, as a whole, and intensified throughout an aeonial past.
3. Glamour engendered by the individual himself, either in the past, through participation in world glamour, or started this life.

To all of these, every human being is prone and for many lives proves himself the helpless victim of that which he later discovers to be erroneous, false and deceiving. He learns then that he need not fall supinely under the domination of the past—astral, emotional and glamorous—but that he is adequately equipped to handle it, did he but know it, and that there are methods and techniques whereby he can emerge the conqueror of illusion, the dissipator of glamour and the master of maya. This is the initial revelation, and it is when he has realised the implication of this and has set out to dominate the undesirable condition that he arrives later at a recognition of an essential duality. This is, for the time being, in no case an illusion. He discovers the relationship between himself as a personality, the true Dweller on the Threshold, and the Angel of the PRESENCE—guarding the door of initiation. This marks a critical moment in the life of the disciple for it indicates the moment wherein he can begin to tread the Path of Initiation, if he so desires and possesses the required fortitude.

In the last analysis, the partial subjugation of glamour and escape from the complete thraldom of illusion are indications to the watching Hierarchy that a man is ready for the processes of initiation. Until he is no longer completely deceived and until he is somewhat free mentally, it is not possible for him to face the waiting Angel and pass through the door. One thing I would here point out to you: after passing through the door of initiation, the disciple returns each time again to take up anew his tasks in the three worlds of activity; he there re-enacts the former processes—briefly and with understanding—after which he proceeds to master the essentials of the next initiatory lesson. I am here putting a great deal of information in a very condensed form, but that is all that is possible at this time.

For a long time, the sense of dualism pervades the disciple's being and makes his life appear to be a ceaseless conflict between the pairs of opposites. The battle of the contraries is taking place consciously in the disciple's life. He alternates between the experiences of the past and a recollection of the experience of initiation through which he has passed, with the emphasis, first of all, in the earlier experiences; later, in the final great experience which is so deeply colouring his inner life. He has prolonged moments wherein he is the baffled disciple, struggling with glamour, and brief moments wherein he is the triumphant initiate. He dis-

The Causes of Glamour

covers in himself the sources of glamour and illusion and the lure of maya until the moment arrives when again he stands before the portal and faces the major dualities in his own particular little cosmos—the Dweller and the Angel. At first he fears the Angel and dreads the light which streams from that Angel's countenance, because it throws into vivid reality the nature of the Dweller who is himself. He senses, as never before, the formidable task ahead of him and the true significance of the undertaking to which he has pledged himself. Little by little, two things emerge with startling clarity in his mind:

1. The significance of his own nature, with its essential dualism.

2. The recognition of the relationship between the pairs of opposites with which he, as a disciple, has to work.

Once he grasps the relation of the lower major duality (that of the personality and the soul) he is then prepared to pass on to the higher reality, that of the integrated Self (personality and soul) and its relation to the PRESENCE. In this statement, you have expressed in a few concise words the result of the first three initiations and the two final. Ponder on this.

It will be of real value, I believe, if I relate for your benefit the various contrasting characteristics of the intelligent man and the disciple, using the word "disciple" to cover all stages of development from that of accepted disciple to that of the Master. There is naught but the Hierarchy, which is a term denoting a steady progress from a lower state of being and of consciousness to a higher. This is in every case the state of consciousness of some Being, limited and confined and controlled by substance. You will note that I say "substance" and not "form" for it is in reality *substance* which controls spirit for a long, a very long, cycle of expression; it is not matter that controls, for the reason that gross matter is always controlled by the forces which are esoterically regarded as etheric in nature and, therefore, as substance, not form. Remember this at all times for it holds the clue to the true understanding of the lower nature.

We will study, therefore, the basic essential contrasts which the disciple must intuitively grasp and with which he must familiarise himself. We will divide what we have to say into four parts, dealing briefly, but I trust helpfully, with each:

a. The contrast between Illusion and its opposite . . . . Intuition
b. The contrast between Glamour and its opposite . . . . . . Illumination
c. The contrast between Maya and its opposite . . . . Inspiration
d. The contrast between Dweller on the Threshold
   and its opposite . . . . The Angel of the
   PRESENCE

This, you will realise, is a large subject and deals with the major problem of the disciple. I would refer you at this point to what I have already said anent these four aspects of glamour, and would ask you to refer with care to the various charts and tabulations which have been given to you from time to time.

a. The Contrast between Illusion and Intuition.

I have chosen this as the first contrast with which to deal as it should (even though it probably may not) constitute the major glamour of the members of this group. Unfortunately the emotional glamour dominates still and, for the majority of you, the second contrast, that between glamour and illumination, may prove the most useful and the most constructive.

Illusion is the power of some mental thoughtform, of some ideal, and some concept—sensed, grasped and interpreted in

The Causes of Glamour

mental form—to dominate the mental processes of the individual or of the race and consequently to produce the limitation of the individual or group expression. Such ideas and concepts can be of three kinds, as I realise you should know:

1. They can be *inherited* ideas, as in the case of those who find it so difficult to adjust themselves to the new vision of world life and of social order, as expressed in the newer ideologies. They are powerfully conditioned by their cast, their tradition and their background.

2. They can be the *more modern ideas* which are, in the last analysis, the reaction of modern thought to world conditions and situations, and to these many other aspirants are very prone and most naturally so, especially if living in the vortex of force which we call modern Europe. Such modern ideas are construed today into major currents and dominating ideologies, and to these every intelligent person must inevitably react, though they forget that that reaction is based on tradition, or upon national or international predisposition.

3. They can be *the newer dimly sensed ideas* which have in them the power to condition the future and lead the modern generation out of darkness into light. None of you as yet really sense these new ideas, though in moments of high meditation and spiritual achievement, you may vaguely and briefly react to them. That reaction may be real just in so far that it conditions, with definiteness, your service to your fellowmen. You can react correctly and can do so increasingly if you preserve your soul's integrity and are not overcome by the battle and the fever of your surroundings within your chosen field of service.

A mental illusion might perhaps be described as an idea, embodied in an ideal form, which permits no room or scope for any other form of ideal. It precludes an ability, therefore, to contact ideas. The man is tied to the world of ideals and of idealism. He cannot move away from it. This mental illusion ties and limits and imprisons the man. A good idea may consequently become an illusion with great facility and prove a disastrous conditioning factor in the life of the man who registers it.

You might well ask here if the Hierarchy itself is not conditioned by an idea and, therefore, is itself a victim of general and widespread illusion. Apart from the fact that the Directors of the Hierarchy and the Custodians of the Plan are never permitted to become such until they are free from the incentive of illusion, I would remind you that all ideas stream into the planetary consciousness along the channel of the seven rays. Thus, the Hierarchy is wide open, in any case, to the seven major groups of ideas which are the IDEA of God for any specific point in time, expressed in seven major ways—all of them equally right and serving the sevenfold need of humanity. Each of these seven formulations of God's Idea has its specific contribution to make; each of them is a true idea which has its part to play in human or planetary service; and each of them is so interrelated with the other six expressions of the same divine Idea, working out as ideals upon the mental plane, that there can be no narrowing down to one idea with its ramifications as happens among men. There is, at least, sensitivity to seven groups of ideas and their resultant ideals and—if it were no more than that—the Hierarchy is so far fluid and pliable. But it is far more than just this, for, to the members of the Hierarchy, the idea and its effects are not only interpreted in terms of human thoughtforms and human idealism, but they are also to be contacted and studied in their relation to

The Causes of Glamour

the Mind of God Himself and to the planetary kingdoms. These ideas come from and they emanate from the buddhic plane, which is seldom open to the consciousness of the average disciple and certainly is not open to the contact of the average idealist. I would here remind you that few idealists are personally in touch with the idea which has given birth to the idealism. They are only in touch with the human interpretation of the idea, as formulated by some disciple or intuitive—a very different thing.

An illusion can, therefore, be defined as the consequence of an idea (translated into ideal) being regarded as the entire presentation, as the complete story or solution and as being separated from and visioned independently of all other ideas—both religious in nature or apparently completely unrelated to religion. In this statement lies the story of separation and of man's inability to relate the various implications of a divine idea with each other. When visioned and grasped in a narrow and separative manner, there is necessarily a distortion of the truth, and the disciple or aspirant inevitably pledges himself to a partial aspect of reality or of the Plan and not to the truth as far as it can be revealed or to the Plan as the Members of the Hierarchy know it. This illusion evokes in the disciple or idealist an emotional reaction which immediately feeds desire and consequently shifts off the mental plane on to the astral; a desire is thus evoked for a partial and inadequate ideal and thus the idea cannot arrive at full expression, because its exponent sees only this partial ideal as the whole truth and cannot, therefore, grasp its social and planetary and its cosmic implications.

Where there is a real grasp of the whole idea (a rare thing indeed) there can be no illusion. The idea is so much bigger than the idealist that humility saves him from narrowness. Where there is illusion (which is usual and commonplace) and a vague interpretive reaction to an idea, we find emerging fanatics, vague idealists, sadistic enforcers of the idea as grasped, one-pointed and narrow men and women, seeking to express *their* interpretation of God's idea, and limited, cramped visionaries. Such illusionary picturing of reality and such visionary showing forth of the idea has been both the pride and the curse of the world. It is one of the factors which has brought our modern world to its sorry pass, and it is from this misuse of the divine faculty of touching the idea and transforming it into the ideal that the world is today suffering—probably inevitably. The imposition of these humanly and mentally interpreted ideas in the form of limited ideologies has had a sorry effect upon men. They need to learn to penetrate to the true idea which lies behind their ideal and to interpret it with accuracy in the light of their soul, besides employing those methods which have the warrant and the sanction of LOVE. It is, for instance, no illusion that the idea which finds expression in the statement that "all men are equal" is a fact which needs emphasis. This has been seized upon by the democratically inclined. It is indeed a statement of fact, but when no allowance is made for the equally important ideas of evolution, of racial attributes, and of national and religious characteristics, then the basic idea receives only limited application. Hence the enforced ideological systems of our modern times and of the present day, and the rapid growth of ideological illusions, which are nevertheless based on a true idea—each and all without any exception. It is again no illusion that the development of the Christ consciousness is the goal of the human family, but when it is interpreted in terms of authoritative religion and by those in whom the Christ consciousness is as yet undeveloped, it becomes simply a nice concept and often a sadistic incentive and thus enters immediately into the realm of illusion.

The Causes of Glamour

I cite these two illustrations, out of many possible ones, so that you may realise how illusions come, how they develop and how they must eventually disappear; thus you can achieve some standard of comparison whereby to grasp the relative value of the true and the false, of the immediately temporal and the basic eternality of the real.

It will, therefore, be apparent to you that the lower or concrete levels of the mental plane will have acquired or accumulated—down the ages—a vast number of ideas, which have been formulated as ideals, clothed in mental matter, nourished by the vitality of those who have recognised as much of the truth of the idea as they are capable of expressing and who have given to these ideals the emphasis of their thoughtform-making faculty and their directed attention, which necessarily implies the energising of the limited formulated ideal because—as you know—energy follows thought.

These forms of thought become objectives towards which the subjective reality, man, reaches and with which he identifies himself for long periods of time; into them, he projects himself, thus vitalising them and giving them life and persistence. They become part of him; they condition his reactions and activities; they feed his desire nature and consequently assume undue importance, creating a barrier (of varying density, according to the extent of the identification) between the man in incarnation and the reality which is his true Being.

There is no need for me here to itemise any of these prevailing thoughtforms and aspects of intellectual and mental illusion. I would not have you think for a moment that the embodied idea, which we call an ideal, is in itself an illusion. It only becomes so when it is regarded as an end in itself instead of being what it essentially is, a means to an end. An ideal, rightly grasped and used, provides a temporary aid towards the attainment of immediate and imminent reality which it is the goal of the man or the race, at any particular time, to reach. The idea before the race today is the re-establishing (upon a higher turn of the spiral) of that spiritual relationship which characterised the race in its child state, in its primitive condition. Then, under the wise guidance and the paternalistic attitude of the Hierarchy and the initiate-priests of the time, men knew themselves to be one family—a family of brothers—and achieved this through a feeling and a developed sensuous perception. Today, under the name of *Brotherhood*, the same idea is seeking *mental* form and the establishment of a renewed spiritual relationship (the idea) through training in right human relations (the ideal). This is the immediate goal of humanity.

This result will be inevitably brought about by means of the cycle of necessity through which we are now passing and the dimly sensed idea will—as a result of dire necessity—impose its rhythm upon the race and thus force the realisation of true Being upon all men. If a close study is made of the basic foundation of all the ideologies without excepting any, it will be discovered that this idea of integral relationships (often distorted in presentation and hidden through wrong methods), of spiritual objectives and of definite positive brotherly activity lies behind every outer form. I have used the current situation as an illustration of *the idea* taking form as *the ideal* and, alas, brother of mine, oft becoming *the idol* and the fanatical misunderstood and over-emphasised goal of the masses, under the guidance of some pronounced idealist. An ideal is a *temporary* expression of a basic idea; it is not intended to be permanent but simply to serve a need and to indicate a way out of the past into a more adequate future. All the present ideals, expressing themselves through the current ideologies, will serve their purpose and eventually pass away, as all else has passed in the history of the race and will give place, eventually, to *a recognised spiritual relationship, a subjective fellowship, as a defined and expressed brotherhood.* These will produce, when sufficiently developed and understood, a form of control and guidance and a species of government which it is not possible for even advanced thinkers at this time to grasp.

When ideals and mental concepts and formulated thoughtforms dominate the mind of an individual, a race or humanity in general, to the exclusion of all perspective or vision and to the shutting out of the real, then they constitute an illusion for as long as they control the mind and method of life. They prevent the free play of the intuition, with its real power to reveal the immediate future; they frequently exclude in their expression the basic principle of the solar system, Love, through the imposed control of some secondary and temporary principle; they can thus constitute a "forbidding dark cloud of rain" which serves to hide from view the "raincloud of knowable things" (to which Patanjali refers in his final book)—that cloud of wisdom which hovers over the lower mental plane and which can be tapped and used by students and aspirants through the free play of the intuition.

Let us now consider the *intuition,* which is the opposite of illusion, remembering that illusion imprisons a man upon the mental plane and surrounds him entirely with man-made thoughtforms, barring out escape into the higher realms of awareness or into that loving service which must be given in the lower worlds of conscious, manifested effort.

The major point I would seek to make here is that the intuition is the source or the bestower of revelation. Through the intuition, progressive understanding of the ways of God in the world and on behalf of humanity are revealed; through the intuition, the transcendence and the immanence of God is sequentially grasped and man can enter into that pure knowledge, that inspired reason, which will enable him to comprehend not only the processes of nature in its fivefold divine expression but also the underlying causes of these processes, proving them effects and not initiatory events; through the intuition man arrives at the experience of the kingdom of God, and discovers the nature, the type of lives and of phenomena, and the characteristics of the Sons of God as They come into manifestation. Through the intuition, some of the plans and purposes working out through the manifested created worlds are brought to his attention, and he is shown in what way he and the rest of humanity can cooperate and hasten the divine purpose; through the intuition, the laws of the spiritual life, which are the laws governing God Himself, conditioning Shamballa, and guiding the Hierarchy, are brought to his notice progressively and as he proves capable of appreciating them and working them.

Four types of people are subject to revelation through the awakening of the intuition:

1. Those on the line of the world saviours. These touch and sense the divine plan and are pledged to service, and to work for the salvation of humanity. They are found expressing different and varying degrees of realisation, stretching all the way from the man who seeks to reveal divinity in his own life and to his immediate small circle (through the medium of the changes and effects wrought in his personal life) to those great Intuitives and world Saviours, such as the Christ. The former is motivated in all probability by some one intuitive crisis which entirely remade him and gave him a new sense of values; the latter can, at will, rise into the world of intuitive perception and

The Causes of Glamour

values and there ascertain the will of God and a wide vision of the Plan. Such great Representatives of Deity have the freedom of the Holy City (Shamballa) and of the New Jerusalem (the Hierarchy). They are thus unique in their contacts and there have been relatively few of Them as yet.

2. Those who are on the line of the prophets. These touch the Plan at high intuitive moments and know what the immediate future holds. I do not refer here to the Hebrew prophets, so familiar to the West, but to all who see clearly what should be done to lead humanity out of darkness into light, beginning with the situation as it is and looking forward into a future of divine consummation. They have a clear picture in their minds of what is possible to accomplish, and the power to point it out to the people of their time. They necessarily range all the way from those who have a relatively clear vision of the cosmic picture and objectives to those who simply see the next step ahead for the race or the nation. Isaiah and Ezekiel are the only two of the Hebrew prophets who had true prophetic and cosmic vision. The others were small, but intelligent men who, from analysis and deduction, assessed the immediate future and indicated immediate possibilities. They had no direct revealing intuition. In the *New Testament,* John, the beloved disciple, was privileged to gain a cosmic picture and a true prophetic vision which he embodied in the Apocalypse, but he is the only one who so achieved and he achieved because he loved so deeply, so wisely and so inclusively. His intuition was evoked through the depth and intensity of his love—as it was in his Master, the Christ.

3. Those who are the true priests. They are priests by spiritual calling and not by choice. It is the misunderstanding of the province and duties of a priest which has led all the Churches (in the East and in the West) to their disastrous authoritarian position. The love of God, and the true spiritual incentive which recognises God immanent in all nature and peculiarly expressing that divinity in man, is lacking in the bulk of the priesthood in all the world religions. Love is not the guide, the indicator and the interpreter. Hence the dogmatism of the theologian, his ridiculous and profound assurances of correct interpretation, and his oft-times cruelty, cloaked by his claim of right principles and good intentions. But the true priest exists and is found in all religions. He is the friend and the brother of all and, because he loves deeply, wisdom is his and (if he is of a mental type and training) his intuition is awakened and revelation is his reward. Ponder on this. The true priest is rare and is not found only in the so-called "holy orders".

4. Those who are the practical mystics or occultists. These, by virtue of a disciplined life, an ardent aspiration, and a trained intellect, have succeeded in evoking the intuition and are, therefore, personally in touch with the true source of divine wisdom. This, it is their function to interpret and to formulate into temporary systems of knowledge. There are many such, working patiently today in the world, unrecognised and unsought by the unthinking. Their need today is to "assemble themselves" in this hour of the world need and so let their voice be clearly heard. These people are resolving the sense of duality into a known unity, and their preoccupation with reality and their deep love of humanity have released the intuition. When this release has taken place, no barriers are felt and true knowledge as a result of revealed wisdom is the gift which such people have, to give to their race and time.

These are the four groups who are exchanging illusion for the intuition. This is the initial resolution of the pairs of opposites, for there is no such resolution without the aid of the intellect, because the intellect—through analysis, discrimination and right reasoning—indicates what should be done.

b. The Contrast between Glamour and Illumination.

One of the aptest symbols by which one can gather some picture of the nature of glamour is to picture the astral plane on three of its levels (the second, third and fourth, counting from the top downwards) as a land shrouded in a thick fog of varying densities. The ordinary light of the ordinary man, which is similar to the headlights of a car and their self-sufficient blaze, serves only to intensify the problem and fails to penetrate into the mists and the fog. It simply throws it into relief so that its density and its deterring effects become the more apparent. The condition of fog is revealed—but that is all. So it is on the astral plane in relation to glamour; the light which is in man, self-induced and self-generated, fails ever to penetrate into or to dissipate the gloom and the foggy miasmic conditions. The only light which can dissipate the fogs of glamour and rid the life of its ill effects is that of the soul, which—like a pure dispelling beam—possesses the curious and unique quality of revelation, of immediate dissipation, and of illumination. The revelation vouchsafed is different to that of the intuition for it is the revelation of that which the glamour veils and hides, which is a revelation unique to the astral plane and conditioned by its laws. This particular utilisation of soul light takes the form of a focussed concentration of the light (emanating from the soul, via the mind) upon the state of glamour—particular or specific, or general and world-wide—so that the nature of the glamour is revealed, its quality and basis is discovered, and its power is brought to an end by a steady, prolonged period of concentration which is given to the dispelling of the condition.

In our next section we will deal in detail with the technique of this scientific use of light and, therefore, I will not elaborate the theme at this point. I will only deal with that much of it as will enable you, as a group, to begin your long awaited work upon the problem of dispelling the present world glamour—at least in some of its aspects. I am not defining glamour in this place or giving you instances of its activity as I did in the case of illusion and its contrasting correspondence, the intuition, because I covered the ground very thoroughly in the section immediately preceding, and you have only to refer to that section to read all that I am prepared to give you at this time.

I will, however, briefly define *illumination*, asking you to bear in mind that we are not here dealing with the illumination which reveals Reality, or the nature of the soul or which makes clear to your vision the kingdom of the soul, but with that form of illumination which is thrown down by the soul into the world of the astral plane. This involves the conscious use of light and its employment, first of all, as a searchlight, scanning the astral horizon and localising the glamour which is causing the trouble, and secondly, as a focussed distribution of light, turned with intention upon that area of the astral plane wherein it is proposed that some effort be made to dissipate the fog and mist which are there concentrated.

Certain basic premises are, therefore, in order and these might be stated as follows:

1. The quality and the major characteristic of the soul is light. Therefore, if that light is to be used and that quality expressed by the disciple and the worker, he must first of all achieve a recognised contact with the soul through meditation.

2. The quality of the astral plane—its major characteris-

tic—is glamour. It is the field whereon the great battle of the pairs of opposites must be fought as they are the expression of ancient desire, in the one case—glamorous, deceptive and false—and in the other, high spiritual longing for that which is real and true. It should be here remembered that astral desire, wrong and selfish emotion and astral reactions to the facts of daily life, are not natural to the soul and constitute eventually a condition which serves to veil successfully the true nature of the spiritual man.

3. A relation must then be established between the soul and the astral plane, via the astral body of the disciple. This astral body must be regarded by him as his response apparatus to the world of sensation and as the only instrument whereby his soul can contact that level of expression—temporary and non-lasting as it may be. The disciple must, therefore, establish contact with the soul and do this consciously and with the needed emphasis and so carry soul light to his own astral body, learn to focus it there in the solar plexus centre, and from that point of achievement proceed to work upon the astral plane at the arduous task of dispelling glamour.

4. When this line of contact has been made and the soul, the astral body and the astral plane have thus been intimately related, the disciple must carry the focussed light from the solar plexus (where it has been temporarily localised) to the heart centre. There he must steadily hold it and work consistently and perseveringly from that higher centre. I might here paraphrase an ancient instruction for disciples, which can be found in the Archives of the Hierarchy and which refers to this particular process. I am giving you a brief and somewhat inadequate paraphrase of this ancient symbolic wording:

"The disciple stands and, with his back to the glamorous fog, looks towards the East from whence the light must stream. Within his heart he gathers all the light available and from that point of power between the shoulder blades the light streams forth."

5. The disciple must relinquish all sense of tension or of strain and must learn to work with pure faith and love. The less he feels and the less he is preoccupied with his own feelings or sense of achievement or of non-achievement, the more probable it will be that the work will proceed with effectiveness and the glamour be slowly dispelled. In this work there is no haste. That which is very ancient cannot be immediately dispelled no matter how good the intention or how accurate may be the grasp of the needed technique.

It will be apparent to you that there are elements of danger in this work. Unless the members of the group are exceedingly watchful and unless they cultivate the habit of careful observation, they may suffer from over-stimulation of the solar plexus until such time as they have mastered the process of rapidly transferring the light of the soul, focussed in the solar plexus, and the innate light of the astral body, also found localised in that centre, into the heart centre between the shoulder blades. I would, therefore, warn each and all of you to proceed with the utmost care and I would caution you that if you suffer any solar plexus disturbance or encounter in yourselves any increased emotional instability, to be not unduly disturbed. I would ask you to regard the phenomenon of disturbance as simply a temporary difficulty, incident upon the service which you are seeking to render. If you pay this intelligent attention to the matter and no more, refusing to be distressed or to be disturbed, no bad results will be felt.

The Causes of Glamour

In connection with your anticipated group work along these lines, you will proceed with your group meditation as indicated elsewhere (*Discipleship in the New Age, Volume I,* page 61), and then—when you have arrived at Stage III in the group meditation—you will work together as follows:

1. Having linked up with all your group brothers, then consciously carry out the hints given symbolically in the ancient writing which I paraphrased for you above.

   a. Link up consciously with your soul and realise this linking as a fact.
   b. Then carry the light of the soul, through the power of the creative imagination, direct to your astral body and from thence to the solar plexus centre—which is the line of least resistance.
   c. Then transfer the light of the soul and the innate light of the astral body from the solar plexus centre to the heart centre, by a definite act of the will.

2. Then, imaginatively, stand with your back to the world of glamour and with the eye of your mind focussed on the soul, whose nature is LOVE.

3. Let a few minutes' interlude then take place wherein you stabilise yourself for the work, and definitely and consciously focus the light available, from all sources, within the heart centre. Imagine that centre between the shoulder blades as a radiant sun. I might here point out that this is, in the individual, the microcosmic correspondence to the "heart of the Sun" which is always directed by the "central spiritual Sun," localised in the head. Get this picture clearly into your consciousness, for it involves the dual, yet synthetic, activity of the head and the heart.

4. Then see a shaft of pure white light, broad and brilliant, pouring out of the heart centre between the shoulder blades, on to that localised glamour with which you, as a group, are dealing. What this localised area is, I will presently disclose.

5. When this is clearly defined in your mind and inspired by your desire and force, and when you have the entire symbolic picture clearly visualised, then see your particular shaft of light blended with the shafts of light which your group brothers are projecting. Thus a great flood of directed light coming from several trained aspirants (and are you trained, my brothers?) will pour on to that area of glamour with which you are supposed to deal.

6. Do this work for five carefully sustained minutes and then proceed as indicated in Stage IV of your meditation outline.

In defining *illumination* as the antithesis of glamour it is obvious that my remarks must necessarily be limited to certain aspects of illumination and will only concern those directed forms of work and those presentations of the problem which will concern the use of light upon the astral plane and particularly in connection with the work that you have pledged yourselves to do. There are many other definitions possible, for the light of the soul is like an immense searchlight, the beams of which can be turned in many directions and focussed on many levels. We are however only concerned here with its specialised use.

Illumination and the light of knowledge can be regarded as synonymous terms and many glamours can be dissipated and dispersed when subjected to the potency of the informative mind, for the mind is essentially the subduer of emotion through the presentation of fact. The problem is to

The Causes of Glamour

induce the individual or the race or nation which is acting under the influence of glamour to call in the mental power of assessing the situation and subject it to a calm, cold scrutiny. Glamour and emotion play into each other's hands and feeling runs so strong usually in relation to glamour that it is impossible to bring in the light of knowledge with ease and effectiveness.

Illumination and perception of truth are also synonymous terms, but it should be remembered that the truth in this case is not truth on the abstract planes but concrete and knowable truth—truth which can be formulated and expressed in concrete form and terms. Where the light of truth is called in, glamour automatically disappears, even if only for a temporary period. But, again, difficulty arises because few people care to face the actual truth, for it involves eventually the abandonment of the beloved glamour and the ability to recognise error and to admit mistakes, and this the false pride of the mind will not permit. Again, I would assure you that humility is one of the most potent factors in releasing the illuminating power of the mind, as it reflects and transmits the light of the soul. The determined facing of the factual life and the stern recognition of truth—coldly, calmly and dispassionately—will greatly facilitate the calling in of the flood of illumination which will suffice to dispel glamour.

As we are dealing with the problem of glamour and illumination, it might be of value here if I dealt with the particular glamour which I would ask your group to aid in dispelling. I refer here to the *glamour of separateness.* Work along this line will have most practical and salutary implications, for none of you (as you will discover) will be able to work effectively on this matter if you feel any sense of separativeness; this separative reaction may express itself as hatred, as an active dislike or as a voiced criticism—perhaps, in some cases, all three. There are forces which you may personally regard as separativeness or as the cause of separation. I would remind you that the favourite views and cherished beliefs of those to whom you are mentally opposed (often under the guise of a strenuous adherence to what you regard as right principles) are to those who hold them equally right; they feel that your views are erroneous and they regard them as separative in their effect and as the basis of trouble. They are, in their place, as sincere as you are and as eager for the achievement of the right attitude as you feel yourself to be. This is something often forgotten and I would remind you of it. I might also illustrate this point by pointing out to you that the hatred or the dislike (if hatred is too strong a word) that any of you may feel for the activities of the German Government, and for the line that they have taken against the Jewish people, might be turned with almost equal justification against the Jews themselves. The latter have always been separative and have regarded themselves as "the chosen of the Lord" and have never proved assimilable in any nation. The same can be said of the Germans, and from many they evoke the same reaction as they mete out to the Jew, though not the physical persecution. Neither attitude, as you well know, is justifiable from the angle of the soul; they are both *equally* wrong, and this is a point of view which the Jew and the anti-Jew must eventually understand and, through understanding, bring to an end.

I mention this because I am going to ask you to deal with that ancient and world-wide glamour—the glamour of the hatred of the Jew. In this group there are those who are, in their thought at least, violently anti-German; there are others who are definitely, though intelligently, anti-Jew. I would ask those in both these groups to recognise the problem with which they are faced. It is a problem

The Causes of Glamour

which is so very ancient and deeply rooted in the consciousness of the race that it is far bigger than the individual can possibly vision; the individual point of view is consequently so limited that constructive usefulness is noticeably impaired. After all, my brothers, the point of view of the "under dog" is not necessarily the only one or necessarily always the correct one. Both the Germans and the Jews merit our impersonal love, particularly as they are both guilty (if I may use such a term) of the same basic errors and faults. The German is powerfully race conscious; so is the Jew. The German is separative in his attitude to the world; so is the Jew. The German insists today on racial purity, a thing upon which the Jew has insisted for centuries. A small group of Germans are anti-Christian; so are an equally small number of Jews. I could continue piling up these resemblances but the above will suffice. Therefore, your dislike of one group is not more warranted than your refusal to recognise any justification for the activities and attitudes of the other. Like frequently repudiates and swings away from like, and the Germans and the Jews are curiously alike. Just as many British people and the preponderance of the British race are reincarnated Romans, so many Germans are reincarnated Jews. Hence the similarity of their points of view. It is a family quarrel and there is nothing more terrible than this.

I am going to ask you to take the Germans and the Jews into your group meditation and pour out your group love upon both these divisions of your brothers in the human family. See to it that before you begin your meditation you have freed yourselves—emotions and mind—from any latent antagonisms, from any hatreds, from any preconceived ideas of right or wrong but that you simply fall back upon the love of your souls, remembering that both Jews and Germans are souls as you are and identical in their origin, their goal and their life experience with yours.

As you pour out the stream of pure white light (as Stage III instructs you), see to it that it pours through you with purity and clarity as one stream. Then see it bisect into equal quantities or proportions—one stream of living light and love going to the Jews and the other to the German peoples. The quality of your love will count and not so much the accuracy of your analysis or the perfection of your technique.

c. The Contrast between Maya and Inspiration.

Here we come definitely into the realm of material substance. This is essentially and in a peculiar manner the realm of force. Maya is predominantly (for the individual) the aggregate of the forces which control his septenary force centres to the exclusion, I would emphasise, of the controlling energy of the soul. Therefore, you will see that the bulk of humanity, until a man stands upon the Probationary Path, are under the control of maya, for a man succumbs to maya when he is controlled by any other force or forces than those energies which come direct from the soul, conditioning and controlling the lesser forces of the personality as they eventually and inevitably must and will.

When a man is under the control of physical, astral and mental forces, he is convinced at the time that they are, for him, right forces. Herein lies the problem of maya. Such forces, however, when they control a man, determine him in a separative attitude and produce an effect which feeds and stimulates the personality and does not bring in the energy of the soul, the true Individuality. This analysis should prove illuminating to you. If men and

The Causes of Glamour

women would bring their lives under a closer scrutiny by the true inner or spiritual man and could thus determine what combination of energies conditions their life activity, they would not continue to function—as they do now—so blindly, so inadequately and so ineffectually.

It is for this reason that the study and understanding of *motives* is of such value and importance, for such a study determines intellectually (if properly investigated) what factor or factors inspires the daily life. This is a statement worth careful consideration. I would ask you: What is your major actuating motive? For, whatever it may be, it conditions and determines your predominant life tendency.

Many people, particularly the unintelligent masses, are solely inspired by desire—material, physical and temporary. Animal desire for the satisfaction of the animal appetites, material desire for possession and for the luxuries of existence, the longing for "things," for comforts and for security—economic, social and religious—control the majority. The man is under the influence of the densest form of maya, and the forces of his nature are concentrated in the sacral centre. Others are motivated by some form of aspiration or ambition—aspiration towards some material heaven (and most religions portray heaven in this manner), ambitions for power, desire for the satisfaction of the emotional or aesthetic appetites and for the possession of the more subtle realities, and the longing for emotional comfort, for mental stability and assurance that the higher desires will meet with gratification. All this is maya in its emotional form, and it is not the same thing as glamour. In the case of glamour, the forces of a man's nature are seated in the solar plexus. In the case of maya, they are seated in the sacral centre. Glamour is subtle and emotional. Maya is tangible and etheric.

Such are the forces of maya which actuate, motivate and energise the life of the ordinary man. Under their influence he is helpless for they inspire all his thinking, all his aspiration and his desire, and all his activity on the physical plane. His problem is twofold:

1. To bring all his centres under the inspiration of the soul.

2. To transfer or transmute the forces of the lower centres, which control the personality, into the energies of the centres above the diaphragm, which respond automatically to the inspiration of the soul.

It is in this thought that the potency and the symbolic value of breathing exercises consists. The motive is soul control, and though the methods employed are (in many cases) definitely undesirable yet the developing tendency of the life thought will prove inevitably determining and conditioning. The methods used may not save the unprepared physical body from certain evil and disastrous results yet, in the long run and in the last analysis, they may condition the future experience (probably in another life) in such a manner that the aspirant will find himself more able to function as a soul than might otherwise have been the case.

Before I close this particular instruction upon glamour, I would like to call the attention of the group to the occult sentences which I gave to D.L.R. prior to his leaving the group. They have a definite relation to the group work and I would like you to give them careful consideration and study. The *Old Commentary,* in speaking of the work of those whose dharma it is to dissipate world glamour, uses the following illuminating sentences:

> "They come and stand. Within the midst of whirling forms—some of beauty rare and some of horror and

The Causes of Glamour

despair—they stand. They look not here or there but, with their faces turned towards the light, they stand. Thus through their minds the pure light streams to dissipate the fogs.

"They come and rest. They cease their outer labours, pausing to do a different work. Within their hearts is rest. They run not here and there, but constitute a point of peace and rest. That which upon the surface veils and hides the real begins to disappear and from the heart at rest a beam of dissipating force projects, blends with the shining light and then the mists of man's creation disappear.

"They come and they observe. They own the eye of vision; likewise they own the right direction of the needed force. They see the glamour of the world, and seeing, they note behind it all the true, the beautiful, the real. Thus through the eye of Buddhi comes the power to drive away the veiling, swirling glamours of that glamorous world.

"They stand, they rest, and they observe. Such are their lives and such the service that they render to the souls of men."

I would commend these lines to your careful thought. They convey to you not only the field of your group service but also the desired attitude of the personal life of every member of the group.

I would also like, at this point, to touch upon a factor of real importance in this work and to repeat my earlier warning: Will you remember that the effort to free yourselves from *irritation* or from what is called in Agni Yoga "imperil" (a peculiar yet satisfying word, my brothers) is particularly essential for this group? Irritation is exceedingly prevalent these days of nervous tension and it most definitely imperils progress and retards the steps of the disciple upon the Way. It can produce dangerous group tension if present in any of you, and this induced group tension can interfere with the free play of the power and light which you are supposed to use, even when the other group members remain unconscious of the emanating source. Irritation definitely generates a poison which locates itself in the region of the stomach and of the solar plexus. Irritation is a disease, if I might use that word, of the solar plexus centre and it is definitely contagious to an almost alarming extent. So, my brothers, watch yourselves with care and remember that just in so far as you can live in the head and in the heart, you will end the disease of imperil and aid in the transference of the forces of the solar plexus into the heart centre.

d. The Contrast between the Dweller and its opposite, the Angel of the Presence.

The entire subject of the Dweller and its relation to the Angel (a symbolic way of dealing with a great relationship and possibility, and a great *fact* in manifestation) is only now possible of consideration. Only when man is an integrated personality does the problem of the Dweller truly arise, and only when the mind is alert and the intelligence organised (as is becoming the case today on a fairly large scale) is it possible for man to sense—intelligently and not just mystically—the Angel and so intuit the PRESENCE. Only then does the entire question of hindrances which the Dweller embodies, and the limitations which it provides to spiritual contact and realisation assume potent proportions. Only then can they be usefully considered and steps taken to induce right action. Only when there is adequate fusion within humanity as a whole does the

The Causes of Glamour

great human Dweller on the Threshold appear as an integrated entity, or the Dweller in a national or racial sense makes its appearance, spreading and vitalising national, racial and planetary glamour, fostering and feeding individual glamours and making the entire problem unmistakably apparent. Only then can the relation between the soul of humanity and the generated forces of its ancient and potent personality assume proportions which call for drastic activity and intelligent cooperation.

Such a time has now come, and in the two books, *Problems of Humanity* and *The Reappearance of the Christ,* and also in the Wesak and June Full Moon messages, I have dealt with this most practical and urgent situation, which is in itself the guarantee of human progress toward its destined goal as well as the assertion of its major hindrances to spiritual realisation. The sections on which we shall now be engaged are of prime importance to all who are in training for initiation. I said "in training," my brothers; I did not say that you would take initiation in this life. I know not myself whether you will or no; the issue lies in your hands and in your planned destiny—planned by your souls. Your problem is essentially that of learning to handle the Dweller on the Threshold and of ascertaining the procedures and the processes whereby the momentous *activity of fusion* can take place. Through the medium of this fusion the Dweller "disappears and is no more seen, though still he functions on the outer plane, the agent of the Angel; the light absorbs the Dweller, and into obscuration—radiant yet magnetic—this ancient form of life dissolves though keeping still its form; it rests and works but is not now itself." Such are the paradoxical statements of the *Old Commentary.*

I have earlier defined for you in as simple terms as possible the nature of the Dweller. I would like, however, to enlarge upon one or two points and give one or two new suggestions which—for the sake of clarity and for your more rapid comprehension—we will tabulate as follows:

1. The Dweller on the Threshold is essentially the personality; it is an integrated unity composed of physical forces, vital energy, astral forces and mental energies, constituting the sum total of the lower nature.

2. The Dweller takes form when a re-orientation of man's life has taken place consciously and under soul impression; the whole personality is then theoretically directed towards *liberation into service.* The problem is to make the theory and the aspiration facts in experience.

3. For a great length of time the forces of the personality do not constitute a Dweller. The man is not on the threshold of divinity; he is not consciously aware of the Angel. His forces are inchoate; he works unconsciously in his environment, the victim of circumstance and of his own nature apparently and under the lure and the urge of desire for physical plane activity and existence. When, however, the life of the man is ruled from the mental plane, plus desire or ambition, and he is controlled at least to some large extent by mental influence, then the Dweller begins to take shape as a unified force.

4. The stages wherein the Dweller on the Threshold is recognised, subjected to a discriminating discipline and finally controlled and mastered, are mainly three:

    a. The stage wherein the personality dominates and rules the life and ambitions and the goals of man's life-endeavour. The Dweller then controls.

    b. The stage of a growing cleavage in the conscious-

The Causes of Glamour

ness of the disciple. The Dweller or the personality is then urged in two directions: one, towards the pursuit of personal ambitions and desires in the three worlds; the other, in which the effort is made by the Dweller (note this statement) to take a stand upon the threshold of divinity and before the Portal of Initiation.

c. The stage wherein the Dweller consciously seeks the cooperation of the soul and, though still in itself essentially constituting a barrier to spiritual progress, is more and more influenced by the soul than by its lower nature.

5. When the final stage is reached (and many are now reaching it today) the disciple strives with more or less success to steady the Dweller (by learning to "hold the mind steady in the light" and thus controlling the lower nature). In this way the constant fluid changefulness of the Dweller is gradually overcome; its orientation towards reality and away from the Great Illusion is made effective, and the Angel and the Dweller are slowly brought into a close rapport.

6. In the earlier stages of effort and of attempted control, the Dweller is positive and the Soul is negative in their effects in the three worlds of human endeavour. Then there is a period of oscillation, leading to a life of equilibrium wherein neither aspect appears to dominate; after that the balance changes and the personality steadily becomes negative and the soul or psyche becomes dominant and positive.

7. The astrological influences can potently affect these situations and—speaking generally and within certain esoteric limits—it might be noted that:

a. Leo . . . . controls the positive Dweller.
b. Gemini . . . . . controls the processes of oscillation.
c. Sagittarius . . controls the negative Dweller.

It might be added that the three signs—Scorpio, Sagittarius, Capricorn—lead finally to the fusion of the Dweller and the Angel.

8. The soul ray controls and conditions the activity of the Angel and its type of influence upon the Dweller. It affects karma, times and seasons.

9. The personality ray controls the Dweller in all the earlier states and up to the time when the soul ray begins steadily to produce a growing effect. This personality ray is, as you know, a combination of three energies which produce the fourth or personality ray, through the medium of their interrelation over a vast period of time.

10. Therefore, the five types of energy which I indicated to you as of importance in your own lives when I gave you indications as to the nature of your five controlling rays, govern also the relation between the Dweller and the Angel, both in the individual and in humanity as a whole. These five are the rays of the physical body, the astral ray, the mind ray, the personality ray and the soul ray.

11. The rays which govern humanity and which condition humanity and the present world problem are as follows:

a. The Soul ray . . . . 2nd . . . . . . humanity must express love.
b. The personality ray . . . . 3rd . . . . . . developing intelligence for transmutation into love-wisdom.

c. Mind ray . . . . 5th . . . . . . scientific achievement.
d. Astral ray . . . . 6th . . . . . . idealistic development.
e. Physical ray . . . . 7th . . . . . . organisation. Business.

The soul ray controls for an entire life period. The personality rays given above are for the Piscean Age which is now beginning to pass out; but these have definitely and irrevocably conditioned humanity.

You will note also that the first Ray of Will or Power is missing as is the fourth Ray of Harmony through Conflict. This fourth ray is always active as it controls in a peculiar manner the fourth creative Hierarchy and might be regarded as forming the *basic* personality ray of the fourth creative Hierarchy. The one given above is a transient and fleeting personality ray of a minor incarnation.

12. In the Aquarian Age which is rapidly coming, the Dweller will present slightly different personality forces:

a. Personality ray ....5th..........basic and determining.
b. Mind ray.............4th..........the creative effect.
c. Astral ray ....6th..........conditioning incentives.
d. Physical ray..........7th..........incoming ray.

13. Each great cycle in the zodiac is in the nature of an incarnation of the human family, and each great race is a somewhat similar happening; the latter is, however, of more importance where the human understanding and consciousness is concerned. The analogy is to the few important incarnations in the life of the soul in contra-distinction to the many unimportant and rapidly succeeding incarnations. Of the important incarnations there are three which are of major import: the Lemurian, the Atlantean, and the Aryan races.

14. Each race produced its own type of Dweller on the Threshold who was faced at the close of the spiritual cycle (not the physical which goes on to crystallisation)

when maturity was achieved and a certain initiation became possible for its advanced humanity.

15. When a racial incarnation and a zodiacal cycle synchronise (which is not always the case) then there comes a significant and important focussing of the attention of the Dweller on the Angel and vice versa. This is taking place at this time at the close of the Piscean era and when the Aryan race has reached maturity and a relatively high water mark of development. Discipleship is significant of maturity, and it is with mature development that the Dweller is met. The Aryan race is ready for discipleship.

16. The development of sensitivity in the individual and in the race indicates the imminence of the recognition of the Angel from both angles of vision and the immediacy of the opportunity. This opportunity for active fusion has never been so true as now.

17. The lines of demarcation as existing between the recognised areas of influence between the Dweller and the Angel are clearer than ever before in the history of the race. Man knows the difference between right and wrong and must now choose the way that he shall go. In the Atlantean racial crisis (which was also a complete human crisis), the history of which is perpetuated for us in the *Bhagavad Gita,* Arjuna—symbol of the then disciple and the world disciple—was frankly bewildered. This is not so true now. The disciples of the world and the world disciple do see the issues today relatively quite clearly. Will expediency win or will the Dweller be sacrificed with love and understanding to the Angel? This is the major problem.

The Causes of Glamour

I will ask you, my brother, to do two things: study the above ideas in the light of the present world crisis, and in the light of your own soul-personality problem.

Advanced humanity stands, as the Dweller, on the very threshold of divinity. The Angel stands expectant—absorbed in the PRESENCE yet ready to absorb the Dweller. Humanity has advanced in consciousness to the very boundaries of the world of spiritual values and the kingdom of Light and of God. The Angel has "come to Earth" in expectation of recognition—an event of which the advent of Christ two thousand years ago was the symbol and the precursor. This is the situation where all advanced aspirants are concerned. It can be yours. It is the situation also where humanity as a whole is concerned and the approaching Hierarchy. The consciousness of humanity from the higher and spiritual standpoint functions today through the steadily growing band of world servers, world aspirants and world disciples, and their name is Legion.

Humanity today is the Dweller whilst the Hierarchy of Souls is the Angel and behind stands the PRESENCE of Divinity Itself, intuited by the Hierarchy and dimly sensed by humanity but providing in this manner that threefold synthesis which is divine manifestation in form.

All these three have powerful emanations (though the emanation of the PRESENCE via Shamballa has been wisely held in leash since the human race came into being). They all have auras, if you care so to call them, and in the three worlds at present that of the Dweller is still the most powerful, just as in the life of the aspirant, his personality is as yet the dominant predisposing factor. It is this powerful human emanation which constitutes the major glamour in the life of humanity and of the individual disciple. *It is a synthesis of glamour, fused and blended by the personality ray but precipitated by the effect of the steadily influencing soul ray.* It is the shadow or distortion of reality, now sensed for the first time on a large scale by the race of men and thrown into high relief by the light which shines from the Angel, the transmitter of energy from the PRESENCE.

And so they stand—Humanity and the Hierarchy. And so you stand, my brother, personality and soul, with freedom to go forward into the light if you so determine or to remain static and unprogressive, learning nothing and getting nowhere; you are equally free to return to identification with the Dweller, negating thus the influence of the Angel, refusing imminent opportunity and postponing—until a much later cycle—your determining choice. This is true of you and of Humanity as a whole. Will humanity's third ray materialistic personality dominate the present situation or will its soul of love prove the most powerful factor, taking hold of the personality and its little issues, leading it to discriminate rightly and to recognise the true values and thus bring in the age of soul or hierarchical control? Time alone will show.

I will give you no more today. I am anxious for these few essential statements to be mastered by all of you, prior to our taking up Section III. I am anxious too for the general group instructions, which you have lately received, to take much of your time, interest and attention. Inner group adjustments and more firmly established group relations are urgently needed and upon these I ask you to work. I would remind you here also that—as in all else in manifestation—there is a group personality and a group soul; you must learn clearly to distinguish between the two and to throw the entire weight of your influence, desire and pressure on the side of the Group Angel. In this way there might occur that stupendous recognition for which all initiation prepares the applicant—the revelation of the PRESENCE.

SECTION THREE

THE ENDING OF GLAMOUR

We come now to the consideration of the third section relating to world glamour. It is difficult to write clearly about this matter because we are in the midst of its most concentrated expression—the worst the world has ever seen because glamour, incident to centuries of greed and selfishness, of aggression and materialism, has been focussed in a triplicity of nations. It is, therefore, easily to be seen and most effective in manifestation. Three nations express the three aspects of world glamour (illusion, glamour and maya) in an amazing manner, and their powerful assault upon the consciousness of humanity is dependent not only upon the response of Germany, Japan and Italy to this ancient miasma but also upon the fact that every nation—United Nations as well as Totalitarian Nations—are tainted with this universal condition. The freedom of the world is consequently largely dependent upon those people in every nation who (within themselves) have moved forward out of one or other of these "glamorous illusions and mayavic impressions" of the human soul into a state of awareness wherein they can see the conflict in its wider terms, i.e., as that existing for them between the Dweller on the Threshold and the Angel of the PRESENCE.

These people are the aspirants, disciples and initiates of the world. They are aware of the dualism, the essential dualism, of the conflict and are not so pre-eminently conscious of the threefold nature and the differentiated condition of the situation which underlies the realised dualism. Their approach to the problem is therefore simpler and, because of this, world direction lies largely in their hands at this time.

It is right here that religion has, as a whole, gone astray. I refer to orthodox religion. It has been preoccupied with the Dweller on the Threshold and the eyes of the theologian have been held upon the material, phenomenal aspect of life through fear and its immediacy, and the fact of the Angel has been a theory and a point of wishful thinking. The balance is being adjusted by the humanitarian attitudes which are so largely coming into control, irrespective of any theological trend. These attitudes take their stand upon the belief of the innate rightness of the human spirit, in the divinity of man, and upon the indestructible nature of the soul of mankind. This inevitably brings in the concept of the PRESENCE, or of God Immanent and is the result of the needed revolt against the belief in God Transcendent. This spiritual revolution was entirely a balancing process and need cause no basic concern, for God Transcendent eternally exists but can only be seen and known and correctly approached by God Immanent—immanent in individual man, in groups and nations, in organised forms and in religion, in humanity as a whole and in the planetary Life Itself. Humanity is today (and has been for ages) battling illusion, glamour and maya. Advanced thinkers, those upon the Probationary Path, upon the Path of Discipleship, and the Path of Initiation have reached a point where materialism and spirituality, the Dweller on the Threshold and the Angel of the PRESENCE, and the basic dualism of manifestation can be seen clearly defined. Because of this clarity of demarcation, the issues underlying the present world events, the objectives of the present world-wide struggle, the modes and methods of re-establishing the spiritual contact so prevalent in Atlantean

The Ending of Glamour 163

days and so long lost, and the recognition of the techniques which can bring in the new world era and its cultural order can be clearly noted and appraised.

All generalisations admit of error. It might, however, be said that Germany has focussed in herself world glamour—the most potent and expressive of the three aspects of glamour. Japan is manifesting the force of maya—the crudest form of material force. Italy, individualistic and mentally polarised, is the expression of world illusion. The United Nations, with all their faults, limitations, weaknesses and nationalisms, are focussing the conflict between the Dweller and the Angel, and thus the three forms of glamour and the final form of the conflict between the spiritual ideal and its material opponent are appearing simultaneously. The United Nations are, however, gradually and most decisively throwing the weight of their effort and aspiration on to the side of the Angel, thus restoring the lost balance and slowly producing on a planetary scale those attributes and conditions which will eventually dispel illusion, dissipate glamour and devitalise the prevalent maya. This they are doing by the increased clear thinking of the general public of all the nations, bound together to conquer the three Axis Powers, by their growing ability to conceive ideas in terms of the whole, in terms of a desirable world order or federation, and their capacity to discriminate between the Forces of Light and the potency of evil or materialism.

The work being done by those who see the world stage as the arena for the conflict between the Dweller on the Threshold and the Angel of the PRESENCE might be itemised as:

1. The producing of those world conditions in which the Forces of Light can overcome the Forces of Evil. This they do by the weight of their armed forces, plus their clear insight.

2. The educating of humanity in the distinction between:

> a. Spirituality and materialism, pointing to the differing goals of the combatant forces.
>
> b. Sharing and greed, outlining a future world wherein the Four Freedoms will be dominant and all will have that which is needed for right living-processes.
>
> c. Light and dark, demonstrating the difference between an illumined future of liberty and opportunity, and the dark future of slavery.
>
> d. Fellowship and separation, indicating a world order where racial hatreds, caste distinctions and religious differences will form no barrier to international understanding, and the Axis order of master races, determined religious attitudes, and enslaved peoples.
>
> e. The whole and the part, pointing to the time which is approaching (under the evolutionary urge of spirit) wherein the part or the point of life assumes its responsibility for the whole, and the whole exists for the good of the part.

The dark aspect has been brought about by ages of glamour. The light is being emphasised and made clear by the world aspirants and disciples who by their attitudes, their actions, their writings and their utterances are bringing the light into dark places.

3. Preparing the way for the three spiritual energies which will sweep humanity into an era of comprehension, leading to a focussed mental clarification of men's minds throughout the world. These three imminent energies are:

The Ending of Glamour

a. *The energy of the intuition* which will gradually dispel world illusion, and produce automatically a great augmentation of the ranks of the initiates.

b. The activity of light which will dissipate, by the *energy of illumination,* the world glamour and bring many thousands on to the Path of Discipleship.

c. *The energy of inspiration* which will bring about, through the medium of its sweeping potency, the devitalisation or the removal, as by a wind, of the attractive power of maya or substance. This will release untold thousands on to the Path of Probation.

4. Releasing new life into the planet through the medium of every possible agency. The first step towards this release is the proving that the power of materialism is broken by the complete defeat of the Axis Powers and, secondly, by the ability of the United Nations to demonstrate (when this has been done) the potency of the spiritual values by their constructive undertakings to restore world order and to lay those foundations which will guarantee a better and more spiritual way of life. These constructive attitudes and undertakings must be assumed individually by every person, and by nations as collective wholes. The first is being undertaken at this time. The second remains as yet to be done.

5. Bringing home to the nations of the world the truths taught by the Buddha, the Lord of Light, and the Christ, the Lord of Love. In this connection it might be pointed out that basically:

a. The Axis nations need to grasp the teaching of the Buddha as He enunciated it in the Four Noble

Truths; they need to realise that the cause of all sorrow and woe is desire—desire for that which is material.

b. The United Nations need to learn to apply the Law of Love as enunciated in the life of Christ and to express the truth that "no man liveth unto himself" and no nation either, and that the goal of all human effort is *loving understanding*, prompted by a programme of love for the whole.

If the lives and teachings of these two great Avatars can be comprehended and wrought out anew in the lives of men today, in the world of human affairs, in the realm of human thinking and in the arena of daily living, the present world order (which is today largely disorder) can be so modified and changed that a new world and a new race of men can gradually come into being. Renunciation and the use of the sacrificial will should be the keynote for the interim period after the war, prior to the inauguration of the New Age.

Students need to remember that all manifestations and every point of crisis are symbolised by the ancient symbol of a point within the circle, the focus of power within a sphere of influence or aura. So it is today with the entire problem of ending the world glamour and illusion which fundamentally lie behind the present acute situation and world catastrophe. The possibility of such a dispelling and dissipation is definitely centred in the two Avatars, the Buddha and the Christ.

Within the world of glamour—the world of the astral plane and of the emotions—appeared a point of light. The Lord of Light, the Buddha, undertook to focus in Himself the illumination which would eventually make possible the dissipation of glamour. Within the world of illusion—the world of the mental plane—appeared the Christ, the Lord of

The Ending of Glamour 167

Love Himself, Who embodied in Himself the power of the *attractive* will of God. He undertook to dispel illusion by drawing to Himself (by the potency of love) the hearts of all men, and stated this determination in the words, "I, if I be lifted up, will draw all men unto Me." (John 12:32.) From the point they then will have reached, the world of spiritual perception, of truth and of divine ideas will stand revealed. The result will be the disappearing of illusion.

The combined work of these two great Sons of God, concentrated through the world disciples and through Their initiates must and will inevitably shatter illusion and dispel glamour—the one by the intuitive recognition of reality by minds attuned to it, and the other by the pouring in of the light of reason. The Buddha made the first planetary effort to dissipate world glamour; the Christ made the first planetary effort towards the dispelling of illusion. Their work must now be intelligently carried forward by a humanity wise enough to recognise its dharma. Men are being rapidly disillusioned and will consequently see more clearly. The world glamour is being steadily removed from the ways of men. These two developments have been brought about by the incoming new ideas, focussed through the world intuitives and released to the general public by the world thinkers. It has been also largely aided by the well-nigh unconscious, but none the less real, recognition of the true meaning of these Four Noble Truths by the masses. Disillusioned and de-glamoured (if I may use such a term), humanity awaits the coming revelation. This revelation will be brought about by the combined efforts of the Buddha and the Christ. All that we can foresee or foretell anent that revelation is that some potent and far-reaching results will be achieved by the merging of light and love, and by the reaction of "lighted substance to the attractive power of love." In this sentence I have given those who can understand a profound and useful hint as to the method and purpose of the undertaking which was staged for the June Full Moon, 1942. I have also given a clue to the true understanding of the work of these Avatars—a thing hitherto quite unrealised. It might be added that when an appreciation of the meaning of the words "transfiguration of a human being" is gained, the realisation will come that when "the body is full of light" then "in that light shall we see LIGHT." This means that when the personality has reached a point of purification, of dedication and of illumination, then the attractive power of the soul (whose nature is love and understanding) can function, and fusion of these two will take place. This is what the Christ proved and demonstrated.

When the work of the Buddha (or the embodied buddhic principle) is consummated in the aspiring disciple and in his integrated personality, then the full expression of the work of the Christ (the embodied principle of love) can also be consummated and both these potencies—light and love—will find radiant expression in the transfigured disciple. What is true, therefore, of the individual is true also of humanity as a whole, and today humanity (having reached maturity) can "enter into realisation" and consciously take part in the work of enlightenment and of spiritual, loving activity. The practical effects of this process will be the dissipation of glamour and the release of the human spirit from the thraldom of matter; it will produce, also, the dispelling of illusion and the recognition of truth as it exists in the consciousness of those who are polarised in the "awareness of the Christ."

This is necessarily no rapid process but is an ordered and regulated procedure, sure in its eventual success but relatively slow also in its establishment and sequential process. This process was initiated upon the astral plane by

The Ending of Glamour

the Buddha, and on the mental plane when Christ manifested on Earth. It indicated the approaching maturity of humanity. The process has been slowly gathering momentum as these two great Beings have gathered around Them Their disciples and initiates during the past two thousand years. It has reached a point of intensive usefulness as the channel of communication between Shamballa and the Hierarchy has been opened and enlarged, and as the contact between these two great Centres and Humanity has been more firmly established.

At the June Full Moon, 1942, the first test as to the directness of the communication between the Centre where the Will of God holds sway, the Centre where the Love of God rules, and the Centre where there is intelligent expectancy was made. The medium of the test was the united effort of the Christ, of the Buddha, and of those who responded to Their blended influence. This test had to be carried out in the midst of the terrific onslaught of the powers of evil and was extended over the two weeks beginning on the day of the Full Moon (May 30th 1942) and ending on June 15th 1942. There was a great concentration of the Spiritual Forces at that time, and the use of a special Invocation (one which humanity itself may not use), but the success or failure of the test was, in the last analysis, determined by mankind itself.

You may feel, though wrongly, that not enough people know about or understand the nature of the opportunity or what is transpiring. But the success of such a test is not dependent upon the esoteric knowledge of the few, the relatively few, to whom the facts and the information have been partially imparted. It is dependent also upon the tendency of the many who unconsciously aspire towards the spiritual realities, who seek for a new and better way of life for all, who desire the good of the whole and whose longing and desire is for a true experience of goodness, of right human relations and of spiritual enterprise among men. Their name is Legion and they are to be found in every nation.

When the Will of God, expressed in Shamballa and focussed in the Buddha, the Love of God, expressed in the Hierarchy and focussed through the Christ, and the intelligent desire of humanity, focussed through the world disciples, the world aspirants and the men of goodwill are all brought into line—either consciously or unconsciously—then a great reorientation can and will take place. This event is something that *can* happen.

The first result will be the illumination of the astral plane and the beginning of the process which will dissipate glamour; the second result will be the irradiation of the mental plane and the dispelling of all past illusions and the gradual revelation of the new truths of which all past ideals and so-called formulations of truth have only been the signposts. Ponder on that statement. The signpost indicates the way to go; it does not reveal the goal. It is indicative but not conclusive. So with all truth up to the present time.

The demand is, therefore, for knowers and for those whose minds and hearts are open; who are free from preconceived ideas fanatically held, and from ancient idealisms which must be recognised as only partial indications of great unrealised truths—truths which can be realised in great measure and for the first time IF the lessons of the present world situation and the catastrophe of the war are duly learned and the sacrificial will is called into play.

I have made this practical application and the immediate illustration of the teaching anent glamour, illusion and maya because the whole world problem has reached a crisis today and because its clarification will be the outstanding theme of

The Ending of Glamour

all progress—educational, religious and economic—until 2025 A.D.

In the section with which we are now concerned we shall consider the practical ways in which illusion, glamour and the power of maya can be brought to an end in the life of the individual, and eventually in the life of nations and finally in the world. Always we must begin with the unity of life, the Microcosm; then, having grasped process and progress in connection with the individual, the idea can then be extended to the group, the organisation, the nation, and to humanity as a whole. Thus gradually we shall approach the great Idea to which we give the name of God, the Macrocosm.

We shall in this section deal with techniques, and these might be summarised as follows:

1. The Technique of the Presence. By means of this technique, the soul assumes control of the integrated personality and of its relations, horizontal and vertical. This technique involves the unfolding of the flower of the intuition, dispelling illusion, revealing the Angel, indicating the Presence, and opening up to the disciple the world of ideas and the door of the higher initiations. Through the disciple's grasp and application of these divine ideas or seed thoughts, he becomes initiate and the third initiation becomes possible as an immediate goal. The intuition is the applied *power of transfiguration*. This technique is related to the little known yoga called Agni Yoga or the yoga of fire.

2. The Technique of Light. By means of this technique, the illumined mind assumes control over the astral or emotional body and dissipates glamour. When light pours in, glamour fades out. Illumination dominates and the vision of reality can be seen. This technique is related to Raja Yoga and its goal is the second initiation; it produces ability to tread the Path of Discipleship, and enables the man to "live a life, enlightened by divinity." Illumination is the applied *power of transformation.*

3. The Technique of Indifference. By means of this technique, maya is ended; for the control of the purified astral vehicle is consciously and technically brought into activity, producing the freeing of the energies of the etheric body from the control of matter or force-substance, and bringing men in large numbers on to the Probationary Path. Where there is "divine indifference" to the call or pull of matter, then *inspiration* becomes possible. This technique is related to Karma Yoga in its most practical form and the use of matter with complete impersonality. The goal of this technique is the first initiation, which enables man to "live a life, inspired by God." Inspiration is the applied *power of transmission*.

1. THE TECHNIQUE OF THE PRESENCE

As we enter upon our consideration of this subject, the student has three things to bear in mind: the existence of the Intuition, the fact of Illusion, and the overshadowing Presence. This Presence is revealed by the intuition through the medium of the Angel and, when revealed and recognised, brings illusion to an end.

The story of illusion is one which must not be confounded with glamour; illusion is related to the whole process of revelation. Glamour can be and often is related to the distortion of that which has been revealed, but it must be borne in mind that illusion is primarily concerned with the reaction of the mind to the unfolding revelation, as the

The Ending of Glamour

soul registers it and seeks to impress it on the highest aspect of the personal lower self. Illusion is, therefore, the failure of the mind correctly to register, to interpret or translate that which has been transmitted and it is consequently a sin (if you care for that word) of the intelligent and highly developed people, of those who stand on the Path and who are in process of becoming rightly oriented; it is also a sin of accepted disciples as they seek to expand their consciousness in response to soul contact. When they have "seen through illusion" (and I use this phrase in its esoteric sense) then they are ready for the third initiation.

Our theme is, therefore, the theme of *revelation* and I would like to make some general remarks upon the subject, because thereby the problem of world illusion can be clarified and incidentally individual illusion also.

The unfoldment of human awareness has been progressive down the ages, and has been dependent upon two major and related factors:

1. The factor of the gradual development of the human mind through the processes of evolution itself. This might be regarded as the innate capacity of that which we call the mind, the chitta, or mind stuff, to become more and more sensitive to the impact of the phenomenal world, and to the impression from the higher worlds of being. The mind is the instrument which registers the process of "becoming" but it is also—during the later stages of human unfoldment—capable of registering the nature or function of *being*. Becoming is revealed through the medium of the intellect; Being, through the medium of the intuition. In all study of illusion, the instrumental nature of the mind must be remembered and its power to register accurately, to

interpret and transmit knowledge coming from the world of phenomena and wisdom from the realm of the soul.

2. The factor of the method whereby humanity is made aware of that which is not immediately apparent. This is the method or process of what has been called "imposed revelation" or the impression conveyed to minds capable of reception of those ideas, beings, plans and purposes which exist behind the scenes, so to speak, and which are (in the last analysis) the factors which determine and condition the world process. These revelations or subjective, vital impressions are revealed by the intuition and have nothing to do with the knowledges, impressions and impacts which are related to the three worlds of human evolution, except in so far that (when grasped and apprehended) they have steadily transformed man's way of living, revealed to him his goals, and indicated his true nature. The revelations given throughout the ages and impressed on the minds of those trained to receive them deal with the great universals, are concerned with the whole, and lead to a developed appreciation of the oneness of life and with hylozoistic expression.

Two paralleling processes have produced humanity and its civilisation: One is the evolutionary process itself whereby the mind of the individual has been gradually unfolded until it becomes the dominant aspect in the personality; and at the same time a graded, wisely imparted series of revelations which have led humanity as a whole nearer to the inevitable apprehension of being; they have led him steadily away from identification with form and into those states of consciousness which are super-normal from the ordinary human angle but entirely normal from the spiritual.

The Ending of Glamour 175

Putting this concept specifically into occult terminology: *Individuality* has led to the steady perfecting of the mind with its perception, apprehension, analysis and interpretation whilst *initiation*, through the growth of the intuition, brings about (when the mental perfecting process has reached a relatively high degree of development) the apprehension of the world of spiritual values, of unified being and of intuitive understanding. This involves a consequent moving of the point of individual focus out of the world of phenomena into the world of reality. The lower use of the mind and its processes of unfoldment have produced illusion whilst the unfoldment of the higher mind and, later, its use as the transmitter of the intuition and of the higher revelation, will produce the transfiguration of the three worlds of phenomena in terms of the world of being.

Illusion is frequently misinterpreted and misapplied mental perception of truth. It has naught to do with the mental phase of glamour, though illusion can be carried down into the world of feeling and become glamour. When this happens, its potency is exceedingly great because a thoughtform has become an entity, with vital power, and the magnetic power of feeling is added to the cold form of thought. Ponder on this. But at the stage with which we are now dealing, which is that of pure illusion, a revelation has precipitated upon the mental plane and—owing to failure rightly to apprehend and interpret it or to apply it usefully—it has developed into an illusion and enters upon a career of deception, of crystallisation and of misinformation.

The theme of this technique is, therefore, concerned primarily with:

1. The process of revelation. This process has been and today is the main testimony and guarantee of the existence, behind the scenes of the phenomenal life, of a revealing Group or Agency whose task is of a triple nature:

> a. To gauge the unfoldment of the human consciousness and to meet its constant appeal and demand for further light and knowledge.
>
> b. To judge what is the next needed revelation and what form it should take, through what medium it should emerge, and where and when it should appear.
>
> c. To ascertain with what obstructions, hindrances, and preconceived ideas the new incoming revelation will have to contend.

2. The fact of the Presence. This Presence is the impelling force behind all revelation and is in reality God Immanent, striving ever for recognition and Itself impelled thereto by the fact of God Transcendent.

3. The influence of the Angel, who is the individualised seed of consciousness through whom, after due growth and response of the personal lower self, will come the revelation of the Presence. All true revelation is concerned with the unfolding glory of divinity in some field of expression, thereby testifying to the latent hidden Presence.

4. The reaction of the intuitives throughout the world to that revelation and the form in which they present it to the world thinkers. These latter are ever the first to appreciate and appropriate the new truth. The intuitives present the next phase of truth in a relatively pure form even though at the time of presentation it may be symbolically veiled.

5. The response of the thinking world to the presented truth. It is at this point that illusion appears and misinterpretation and misrepresentation take place. These untrue interpretations of revealed truth, when they have lasted long enough and have acquired momentum, add to the general illusion and become part of it and thus feed and are fed by the world illusion. This is the built-up illusory form of thought, developed down the ages, which controls so much of the mass belief. When the revelation reaches this stage, the mass of men become involved; they recognise the illusion as the truth; they regard this illusion as reality; they fail to grasp the significance of the veiled, symbolically presented revelation but confuse it with the illusory presentation, and thus the intuitively perceived revelation becomes a distorted, twisted doctrine.

Theological interpretations and dogmas fall into this category and there ensues a re-enactment of the ancient drama of the blind leading the blind, to which Christ referred as He faced the theologians of His time.

The above statements are true of all revelation as it comes forth from the emanating centre of light, whether they concern so-called religious truth or scientific discoveries or the great standard of spiritual values whereby advanced humanity of both hemispheres seek to live and which, from time to time, move on a step in significance and in importance.

a. Intuition dispels Individual Illusion

Today we have reached a crisis in the field of human apprehension and can now enter into a new era wherein illusion can be dispelled and thinkers can begin to register accurately and without misapprehension that which the intuitives convey to them. This statement does not as yet apply to the general public. It will be a long time before they will respond without illusion, because illusion is based upon the thought-form-building activity of the lower mind. The masses are just beginning to use that lower mind and illusion is, therefore, for them a necessary stage of testing and training and one through which they must pass or they will lose much valuable experience, leaving undeveloped their powers of discrimination. This is a point which all teachers of occultism should have in mind. It is essential consequently that the masses are taught the significance of illusion and be trained to see and choose the kernel of pure truth in any presentation of truth with which they may be confronted. It is essential likewise that the world intuitives learn to use and control and understand the faculty of spiritual perception, of divine isolation and appropriate response which characterises the intuition. This they can do through the practice of the Technique of the Presence, but not as it is usually taught and presented.

Perhaps I shall make my meaning clearer if I state that this technique falls into certain scientific lines or modes of work, for which much of the training given in schools of true meditation and in the Raja Yoga systems have prepared the aspirant. These stages begin where the usual formulas leave off, and presuppose facility in approach to the Angel or the soul, and an ability to raise the consciousness to a point of soul fusion. I will list the processes or stages as follows:

1. The evocation of the stage of tension. This is basic and essential. It is a tension brought about by complete control of the personal self so that it is "fitted for contact with the real."

2. The achieving of a state of fusion with the soul or with the Angel which guards the approach to the Path of the Higher Evolution.

The Ending of Glamour 179

3. The holding of the mind steady in the light of the soul, which remains the attitude of the lower self for the entire remaining period of work, held at the point of tension by the soul and not by an effort of the personality. The soul undertakes this holding when the personal self has done its utmost to achieve the desired tension.

These are the three preliminary steps for which the practice of alignment should have prepared the student of the higher mysteries. These steps must precede all effort to develop the intuition, and this may take several months (or even years) of careful preparation. Fire is the symbol of the mind and these are the first three stages of the Agni Yoga discipline or of the yoga of fire for which Raja Yoga has prepared the student.

Next come six more stages in the Technique, and these must be thoroughly understood and form the basis of prolonged brooding and intelligent reflection, carried on whilst the daily avocations and duties are being performed and not carried out at certain set times. The trained intuitive or disciple lives ever the dual life of mundane activity and of intense and simultaneous spiritual reflection. This will be the outstanding characteristic of the Western disciple in contradistinction to the Eastern disciple who escapes from life into the silent places and away from the pressures of daily living and constant contact with others. The task of the Western disciple is much harder, but that which he will prove to himself and to the world as a whole will be still higher. This is to be expected if the evolutionary process means anything. The Western races must move forward into spiritual supremacy, without obliterating the Eastern contribution, and the functioning of the Law of Rebirth holds the clue to this and demonstrates this necessity. The tide of life moves from East to West as moves the sun, and those who in past centuries struck the note of Eastern mysticism must strike and are now striking the note of Western occultism. Therefore, the following stages must follow upon the three earlier. We will continue with the numbering as given, for what I here suggest is a formula for a more advanced meditation attitude. I said not form.

> 4. Definite and sustained effort to sense the Presence throughout the Universe in all forms and in all presentations of truth. This could be expressed in the words: "the effort to isolate the germ or seed of divinity which has brought all forms into being." I would point out that this is not the attainment of a loving attitude and a sentimental approach to all people and circumstances. That is the mystical way and though not intended to be negated in the disciple's life, is not used at this time in the process of effective approach. It is the effort primarily to see *in the light which the Angel radiates* the point of light behind all phenomenal appearances. This is, therefore, the transference of the mystical vision to the higher levels of awareness. It is not the vision of the soul but the vision or the spiritual sensing of that which the light of the soul can aid in revealing. The flickering soul light in the personal self has enabled the disciple to see the vision of the soul and in that light to reach union with the soul, even if only temporarily. Now the greater light of the soul becomes focussed like a radiant sun and it reveals in its turn a still more stupendous vision—that of the Presence, of which the Angel is the guarantee and promise. As the light of the Moon is the guarantee that the light of the Sun exists, so the light of the Sun is the guarantee, did you but know it, of a still greater light.

The Ending of Glamour

5. Then, having sensed the Presence—not theoretically but in vibrating response to its Existence—there next comes the stage of the ascertaining of the Purpose. Hope of identification with the purpose lies too far ahead even for the average initiate, under the status of Master. With that unattainable stage (for us) we are not concerned. But we are concerned with the effort to achieve an understanding of that which through the medium of form is seeking to embody the high purpose at any particular point in the evolutionary cycle. This is possible and has been achieved down the ages by those who have rightly approached and duly reflected upon the Way of the Higher Evolution. This Way is revealed to the disciple, e'en though it may not concern the intuitive message which he may bring back from his high adventure.

6. He then carries some world problem, some design which his mind has evolved or his heart desired for the helping of humanity into what is esoterically called "the triple light of the intuition." This light is formed by the blending of the light of the personal self, focussed in the mind, the light of the soul, focussed in the Angel, and the universal light which the Presence emits; this, when done with facility through concentration and long practice, will produce two results:

a. There will suddenly dawn upon the disciple's waiting mind (which still remains the agent of reception) the answer to his problem, the clue to what is needed to bring relief to humanity, the information desired which, when applied, will unlock some door in the realm of science, psychology or religion. This door, when opened, will bring relief or release to many. As before I have told you, the intuition is never concerned with individual problems or enquiries, as so many self-centred aspirants think. It is purely impersonal and only applicable to humanity in a synthetic sense.

b. The "intruding agent of light" (as the *Old Commentary* calls these adventuring intuitives) is recognised as one to whom can be entrusted some revelation, some new impartation of truth, some significant expansion from a seed of truth already given to the race. He then sees a vision, hears a voice, registers a message, or—highest form of all—he becomes a channel of power and light to the world, a conscious Embodiment of divinity, or a Custodian of a divine principle. These forms constitute true revelation, imparted or embodied; they are still rare but will increasingly be developed in humanity.

7. The next few stages are called, in preparation for the revelation:

   a. The relinquishing of the Higher Way.
   b. The return to the Angel, or a refocussing in the soul.
   c. A pause or interlude for constructive thinking, under the influence of the Angel.
   d. The turning of the mind to the formulation of those forms of thought which must embody the revelation.
   e. Then again a pause which is called "the pause preceding presentation."

8. The presentation of the revelation or of the imparted truth and its precipitation into the world of illusion comes next. In that world of illusion, it undergoes the "fiery ordeal" wherein "some of the fire within that which is revealed wings its way back to the source from whence it came; some of it serves to destroy the revealer, and some

The Ending of Glamour 183

to burn those who recognise the revelation." This is a phase of Agni Yoga which, as you can see, is only for those who can penetrate beyond the Angel into the place "where fire dwelleth," and where God, the Presence, functions as a consuming fire and waits for the hour of total revelation. This is a symbolic rendering of a great truth. In the case of the individual initiate, the third initiation, the Transfiguration, marks the consummation of the process. Only glory then is seen: only the voice of the Presence is heard and union with the past, the present and the future is reached.

9. The succumbing of the revelation to the prevailing illusion, its descent into the world of glamour, and its subsequent disappearance as a revelation and its emergence as a doctrine. But, in the meantime, humanity has been helped and led forward; the intuitives continue to work and the inflow of that which is to be revealed never ceases.

This basic technique underlies both primary and secondary revelations. In the case of the first, the time cycle is long; in the second, the time cycle is short. A very good instance of this process is demonstrated by one of the secondary points of revelation in connection with the teaching which emanated from the Hierarchy (the Custodian of secondary revelations, as Shamballa is of primary) fifty years ago and which took the form of *The Secret Doctrine*. H.P.B. was the "penetrating, sensing, appropriating intuitive." The revelation she conveyed followed the accustomed routine of all secondary revelation from the Source to the outer plane. There the minds of men, veiled by illusion and clouded by glamour, formulated it into an inelastic doctrine, recognising no further revelation and holding steadily—many of the theosophical groups—that *The Secret Doctrine* was a final revelation and that naught must be recognised but that book and naught deemed correct but their interpretations of that book. If they are correct, then evolutionary revelation is ended and the plight of humanity is hard indeed.

Even the neophyte upon the way of the intuition can begin to develop in himself the power to recognise that which the lower mind cannot give him. Some thought of revealing potency, to be used for the helping of the many, may drop into his mind; some new light upon an old, old truth may penetrate, releasing the truth from the trammels of orthodoxy, thus illumining his consciousness. This he must use for all and not for himself alone. Little by little, he learns the way into the world of the intuition; day by day, and year by year, he becomes more sensitive to divine Ideas and more apt in appropriating them wisely for the use of his fellowmen.

The hope of the world and the dispelling of illusion lies in the development of intuitives and their conscious training. There are many natural intuitives whose work is a blend of the higher psychism with flashes of true intuition. There must be the training of the exact intuitive. Paralleling their intuitive response and their effort to precipitate their intuition into the world of human thought, there must also be the steady development of the human mind so that it can grasp and apprehend what is projected, and in this too lies the hope of the race.

b. Group Intuition dispels World Illusion

Today the world is full of illusions, many of them veiled under the form of idealisms; it is full of wishful thinking and planning, and even though much of this is rightly oriented and expresses the fixed determination of the intelligentsia to create better living conditions for the entire population of the

The Ending of Glamour

world, the question arises: Is there in the sum total of this wishful thinking enough of the essential dynamic livingness which will carry it down into physical demonstration and factual expression and thus truly meet human need? I would point out that the two greatest revealing Agents Who have ever come to Earth within the range of modern history made the following simple revelations to humanity:

> 1. The cause of all human suffering is desire and personal selfishness. Give up desire and you will be free.
> 2. There is a way of liberation and it leads to illumination.
> 3. It profits a man nothing to gain the whole world and lose his soul.
> 4. Every human being is a Son of God.
> 5. There is a way of liberation and it is the way of love and sacrifice.

The lives of these Revealers were symbolic representations of that which They taught, and the rest of Their teaching but an extension of Their central themes. Their contribution was an integral part of the general revelation of the ages which has led men from the primitive state of human existence to the complex state of modern civilisation. This general revelation can be called the Revelation of the Path which leads out of form to the Centre of all life; the purity of this revelation has been preserved down the ages by a small handful of disciples, initiates and true esotericists who have always been present upon the Earth—defending the simplicity of that teaching, seeking for those who could respond to and recognise the germ or seed of truth, and training men to take Their place and to tread the way of intuitive perception. One of the major tasks of the Hierarchy is to seek for and find those who are sensitive to revelation and whose minds are trained so that they can formulate the emerging truths in such a way that they reach the ears of the world thinkers, relatively unchanged. All revelation, however, when put into words and word forms, loses something of its divine clarity.

Much of the revelation of the past has come along the lines of the religious impulse and, as the illusion has deepened and grown in time, the original simplicity (as it was conveyed by its Revealers) has been lost. All basic revelations are presented in the simplest forms. Accretion after accretion crept in; the minds of men made the teaching complex through their mental dissertations until the great theological systems were built up which we call, for instance, the Christian Church and the Buddhist system. Their Founders would have much difficulty in recognising the two or three fundamental and divine facts or truths which They sought to reveal and emphasise, so great is the mantle of illusion which has been thrown over the simple pronouncements of the Christ and of the Buddha. The vast cathedrals and the pompous ceremonies of the orthodox are far removed from the humble way of the life of the Christ, the Master of all the Masters and the Teacher alike of angels and of men, and from the simplicity of His present way of life as He watches and waits for the return of His people to the simple way of spiritual realisation.

So great has been the illusion that in the West today men talk of the "temporal power of the Catholic Church"; the Protestant Churches are split up into warring factions; the Christian Science Church is known for its ability to amass money and to teach its adherents to do so and to achieve temporary good health; the Greek Orthodox Church was corrupt throughout, and only the simple faith of the uncultured and the poor has preserved any semblance of the truth in its original simple form. They have no ability

The Ending of Glamour

for high sounding theological discussions, but they do believe that God is love—just simply that—that there is a way which leads to peace and light, and that if they deny their own material desires they are pleasing God. I am, I know, widely generalising, brother of mine, for I do know also that there are wise and good Christians and churchmen within the theological systems; these, however, spend not their time in theological discussions but in loving their fellowmen, and this they do because they love Christ and all for which He stands. They are not interested in building great churches of stone and marble and in gathering together the money needed for their support; they are interested to gather out those who form the true Church upon the inner spiritual plane and in helping them to walk in the light.

The illusion of power, the illusion of superiority, taints them not. After the world crisis is over, Churchmen everywhere will not rest until they can discover how to penetrate through the illusion of doctrine and dogma which engulfs them, and find their way back to Christ and His simple message which has in it the power to save the world, if recognised and practised.

Much of the true revelation since the time of Christ has come to the world along the line of science. The presentation, for instance, of material substance (scientifically proven) as essentially only a form of energy was as great a revelation as any given by the Christ or the Buddha. It completely revolutionised men's thinking and was—little as you may think it—a major blow struck at the Great Illusion. It related energy to force, form to life, and man to God and held the secret of transformation, transmutation and transfiguration. The revelations of science when basic and fundamental are as divine as those of religion, but both have been prostituted to meet human demand. The era is close at hand when science will bend every effort to heal humanity's sores and build a better and happier world.

The revelations of science, though focussed often through one man or woman, are more specifically the result of group endeavour and of trained group activity than are the revelations of religion, so called. Revelation, therefore, comes in two ways:

1. Through the effort, aspiration and achievement of one man who is so close to the Hierarchy and so imbued with conscious divinity that he can receive the message direct from the central divine Source. He has joined the ranks of the Great Intuitives and works freely in the world of divine Ideas. He knows His mission clearly; He chooses His sphere of activity with deliberation and isolates the truth or truths which He deems appropriate to the need of the time. He comes forth as a Messenger of the Most High, leads a dramatic and arresting life of service and symbolises in His life-events certain basic truths which have already been revealed but which He pictorially re-enacts. He epitomises in Himself the revelations of the past, and to them adds His Own contribution of the new revelation which it is His specific function to present to the world.

2. Through the effort of a group of seekers, such as the scientific investigators in every country, who *together* are searching for light on the problems of manifestation or for some means to alleviate human suffering, a revelation comes. The effort of such a group often lifts upon the wings of its unrealised aspiration some one man who can then penetrate into the world of divine Ideas and there find the longed for cure or key and thus he intuitively discovers a long sought secret. The discovery, when of

the first rank, is as much a revelation as the truths presented by the World Teachers. Who shall say that the statement that God is Love is of more value than the statement that All is Energy?

The route which the revelation then follows is the same in both cases, and illusion overtakes both forms of revelation but—and here is a point upon which I would ask you to reflect—there is a little less illusion gathered around the revelations of science than has gathered around the revelations of what humanity calls the more definitely spiritual truths. One reason lies in the fact that the last great spiritual revelation, given by the Christ, was given two thousand years ago, and the development of man's mind and his responsiveness to truth has grown greatly since that time. Again, the revelations of science are largely the result of group tension, eventually focussed in one intuitive recipient, and the revelation is thereby protected.

Today, as humanity awaits the revelation which will embody the thoughts and dreams and constructive goal of the New Age, the demand comes for the first time from a large group of intuitively inclined people. I said not intuitives, brother of old. This group is now so large and its focus is now so real and its demand so loud that it is succeeding in focussing the massed intent of the people. Therefore, whatever revelation may emerge in the immediate future will be better "protected by the spirit of understanding" than any previous one. This is the significance of the words of the *New Testament*, "every eye shall see Him"; humanity as a whole will recognise the revealing *One*. In past ages the Messenger from on High was only recognised by and known to a mere handful of men, and it took decades and sometimes centuries for His message to penetrate into the hearts of humanity.

The stress of the times also and the development of the sense of proportion, plus an enforced return to simplicity of living and requirements may save the coming revelation from too swift and quick submergence in the fire of the *Great Illusion*.

It will be apparent to you from the above that the mode of handling world affairs, states of consciousness and conditions in the three worlds is one in which the disciple and initiate work from above downwards. The method is in reality a repetition of the involutionary arc in which—like the Creator, from a vantage point of exterior direction—energy, force and forces are directed into the world of phenomena and produce definite effects upon the substance of the three planes. This is a point which should be most carefully remembered; and it is for this reason that the Technique of the Presence must always be employed, prior to all other techniques. It establishes contact with the directing spiritual Agent and enables the disciple to assume the attitude of the detached Observer and an agent of the Plan. When this technique is correctly followed, it brings the intuition into play and the world of meaning (lying behind the world of phenomena) stands revealed, thereby dispelling illusion. Truth, as it is, is seen and known. Forms in the outer world of phenomena (outer from the angle of the soul and therefore encompassing the three worlds of our familiar daily living) are seen to be but symbols of an inward and spiritual Reality.

2. THE TECHNIQUE OF LIGHT

We come now to the consideration of the next development and service to be rendered through the medium of another technique.

This theme is so vast and there is so much literature to be found in all the world Scriptures, commentaries and theological

The Ending of Glamour

dissertations on the subject of Light that the simple truth and a few basic principles are lost to sight in a welter of words.

In my various books I have given much anent this subject and in the book, *The Light of the Soul*, which I wrote in collaboration with A.A.B., an effort was made to indicate the nature of the light of the soul. The key to this technique is to be found in the words: In that Light shall we see LIGHT. A simple paraphrase of these apparently abstract and symbolic words could be given as follows: When the disciple has found that lighted centre within himself and can walk in its radiating light, he is then in a position (or in a state of consciousness, if you prefer) wherein he becomes aware of the light within all forms and atoms. The inner world of reality stands visible to him as light-substance (a different thing to the Reality, revealed by the intuition). He can then become an efficient cooperator with the Plan because the world of psychic meaning becomes real to him and he knows what should be done to dispel glamour. It might be stated that this process of bringing light into dark places falls naturally into three stages:

1. The stage wherein the beginner and the aspirant endeavour to eradicate glamour out of their own life by the use of the light of the mind. *The light of knowledge* is a major dispelling agent in the earlier phases of the task and effectively eliminates the various glamours which veil the truth from the aspirant.

2. The stage wherein the aspirant and disciple work with the light of the soul. This is *the light of wisdom* which is the interpreted result of long experience, and this streams forth, blending with the light of knowledge.

3. The stage wherein the disciple and the initiate work with *the light of the intuition*. It is through the blended

medium of the light of knowledge (personality light) and the light of wisdom (soul light) that the Light is seen, known and appropriated. This light puts out the lesser lights through the pure radiance of its power.

You have therefore the light of knowledge, the light of wisdom and the light of the intuition, and these are three definite stages or aspects of the One Light. They correspond to the physical Sun, the heart of the Sun, and the Central Spiritual Sun. In this last sentence you have the clue and the key to the relation of man to the Logos.

These stages and their corresponding techniques are apt to be misunderstood if the student fails to remember that between them lie no real lines of demarcation but only a constant overlapping, a cyclic development and a process of fusion which is most confusing to beginners. Just as the result of innate reaction to environment produces the apparatus needed to contact that environment, so the unfoldment of the powers which these techniques serve produces modes of contact with soul and spiritual environments. Each of these techniques is related to a new environment; each of them eventually develops power in the initiate or disciple which can be used in the service of humanity and in higher spheres of divine activity; each is related to the other techniques, and each releases the disciple into a conscious relationship with a new environment, new states of awareness and new fields of service. For instance:

1. *The Technique of the Presence,* when successfully followed, enables the intuition to flow in and to supersede the activity of the rationalising mind and to dispel illusion, substituting for that illusion divine ideas, formulated into concepts which we call ideals. The Masters, it should be remembered, only use the mind for two activities:

The Ending of Glamour

a. To reach the minds of Their disciples and attract aspirants through the medium of an instrument similar to the disciple's mind.

b. To create thoughtforms on concrete levels which can embody these divine ideas. The directing Agent, the Angel of the Presence, produces the power to create in this manner, and this we call the result of the intuition—idea or truth, its perception and its reproduction.

2. The Technique of Light is more closely related to the mind and signifies the method whereby the illumination which flows from the soul (whose nature is light) can irradiate not only ideals but life, circumstances and events, revealing the cause and the meaning of the experience. When the power of the disciple to illumine is grasped, he has taken the first step towards dispelling glamour; and just as the technique of the Presence becomes effective upon the mental plane, so this technique produces powers which can become effective on the astral plane and eventually bring about the dissipation and the disappearance of that plane.

3. The Technique of Indifference renders ineffective or neutralises the hold of substance over the life or spirit, functioning in the three worlds, for soul is the evidence of life.

In connection, therefore, with this second technique, I would like to take some words out of the Bible, substituting the word "light" for the word "faith." I give you this definition: *Light is the substance of things hoped for, the evidence of things not seen.* This is perhaps one of the most occult definitions of the light of the world that has yet been given and its true meaning is intended to be revealed in the next two generations. The word "faith" is a good instance of the method of rendering "blind" some of the ancient truths so that their significance may not be prematurely revealed. Light and substance are synonymous terms. Soul and light are equally so, and in this equality of idea—light, substance, soul—you have the key to fusion and to the at-one-ment which Christ expressed so fully for us in His life on Earth.

When, therefore, students and aspirants have made progress in soul contact, they have taken one of the first important steps towards the comprehension of light and its uses. They must however be careful not to confuse the light which they can bring to bear on life, circumstance, events, and on environment with the intuition. The light with which we are concerned expresses itself in the three worlds and reveals form and forms, their reaction and effects, their glamour and attractive appeal, and their power to delude and imprison consciousness. The light concerned is soul light, illuminating the mind and bringing about revelation of the world of forms in which that life is immersed.

The intuition is concerned with nothing whatsoever in the three worlds of human experience but only with the perceptions of the Spiritual Triad and with the world of ideas. *The intuition is to the world of meaning what the mind is to the three worlds of experience.* It produces understanding just as the light of soul produces knowledge, through the medium of that experience. Knowledge is not a purely mental reaction but is something which is found on all levels and is instinctual in some form in all kingdoms. This is axiomatic. The five senses bring physical plane knowledge; psychic sensitivity brings a knowledge of the astral plane; the mind brings intellectual perception, but all three are aspects of the light of knowledge (coming from the soul) as it informs its vehicles of expression in the vast threefold environment in which it chooses to imprison itself for purposes of development.

On a higher turn of the spiral, the intuition is the expression of the threefold Spiritual Triad, placing it in relation to the higher levels of divine expression; it is a result of the life of the Monad—an energy which carries revelation of divine purpose. It is in the world of this divine revelation that the disciple learns eventually to work and in which the initiate consciously functions. Of this higher experience, the active life of the three worlds is a distorted expression but constitutes also the training ground in which capacity to live *the initiate life of intuitional perception* and to serve the Plan is slowly developed. These distinctions (in time and space, because all distinctions are part of the great illusion, though necessary and inevitable when the mind controls) must be carefully considered. Disciples will reach a point in their development where they will know whether they are reacting to the light of the soul or to the intuitional perception of the Triad. They will then come to the point where they will realise that intuitive perception—as they call it—is only the reaction of the illumined personality to the identification tendency of the Triad. But these concepts are beyond the grasp of the average man because fusion and identification are by no means the same.

The rules for the Technique of Light have been adequately laid down in the Raja Yoga system of Patanjali, of which the five stages of Concentration, Meditation, Contemplation, Illumination, and Inspiration are illustrative; these, in their turn, must be parallelled by a following of the Five Rules and the Five Commandments. I would ask you to study these. They, in their turn, produce the many results in psychic sensitivity, of which hierarchical contact, illumination, service and discipline are descriptive and, finally, the stage of "isolated unity," which is the paradoxical term used by Patanjali to describe the inner life of the initiate.

Most of what I have said above is well known to all aspirants whether they study the Raja Yoga teaching of India or the life of practical mysticism as laid down by such mystics as Meister Eckhart and the more mentally polarised modern esotericist. These latter went beyond the mystical vision by arriving at fusion. I need not enlarge on this. It is the higher stage of at-one-ment to which all true mystics bear witness.

What does concern us here is how this light is recognised, appropriated and used in order to dispel glamour and render a deeply esoteric service to the world. It might be said that the inner light is like a searchlight, swinging out into the world of glamour and of human struggle from what one Master has called "the pedestal of the soul and the spiritual tower or beacon." These terms convey the idea of altitude and of distance which are so characteristic of the mystical approach. Power to use this light as a dissipating agent only comes when these symbols are dropped and the server begins to regard *himself* as the light and as the irradiating centre. Herein lies the reason for some of the technicalities of the occult science. The esotericist knows that in every atom of his body is to be found a point of light. He knows that the nature of the soul is light. For aeons, he walks by means of the light engendered within his vehicles, by the light within the atomic substance of his body and is, therefore, guided by the light of matter. Later, he discovers the light of the soul. Later still, he learns to fuse and blend soul light and material light. Then he shines forth as a Light bearer, the purified light of matter and the light of the soul being blended and focussed. The use of this focussed light as it dispels individual glamour teaches the disciples the early stages of the technique which will dispel

The Ending of Glamour

group glamour and eventually world glamour, and this is the next point with which we will deal.

The theme with which we are dealing—the light of the soul as it dissipates glamour in the three worlds—is the most practical and useful and needed subject for study to be found today: it concerns the astral plane, and the service to be rendered is vital and timely. The ridding of the world of the individual and the world of humanity as a whole of the all-enveloping glamour which holds humanity in thrall is an essential requirement for the race. The new era which will open up before mankind at the close of the war will be distinguished by its mental polarisation and consequent freedom from glamour; then illusion will for a time control until the intuition is more fully developed. This illusion will produce vastly different results to those which follow when men live and work in the midst of glamour. The second characteristic of the new era will be the scientific approach to the entire problem of glamour which will then be recognised for what it is and will be scientifically dissipated by the use of the illumined minds of groups, working in unison for just that purpose.

The proposition, therefore, which I am laying before you (who are the aspirants and the disciples of the world) is the possibility of a definite world service. Groups will eventually be formed of those who are working at the dissipation of glamour in their individual lives and who are doing so not so much in order to achieve their own liberation but with the special objective of ridding the astral plane of its significant glamours. They will work unitedly on some major phase of world glamour by the power of their individual illumined minds; unitedly they will turn "the searchlight of the mind, reflecting the light of the sun but at the same time radiating its own inner light upon the mists and fogs of Earth, for in these mists and fogs all men stumble.

Within the lighted sphere of the focussed radiant light, reality will issue forth triumphant."

It is interesting to note that the most ancient prayer in the world refers to the three aspects of glamour, and it is for these that the three techniques must be used to make release and progress possible. As you know, this prayer runs as follows (Brihadaranyaki Upanishad I, 3, 28):

"Lead us, O Lord, from darkness to light; from the unreal to the real; from death to immortality."

"Lead us from darkness to light" refers to the mind as it becomes eventually illumined by the light of the intuition; this illumination is brought about by the means of the Technique of the Presence from Whom the light shines. This is the mediating factor producing the Transfiguration of the personality, and a centre of radiant light upon the mental plane. This statement is true whether one is speaking of an individual or of that focal point of light which is formed by the mental unity and the clear thinking of advanced humanity. These, through the power of their unified minds, will succeed in ridding the world of some aspects of the Great Illusion.

"Lead us from the unreal to the Real" has specific relation to the astral plane and its all-encompassing glamours. These glamours embody the unreal and present them to the prisoners of the astral plane, leading them to mistake them for the Reality. This imprisonment by glamour can be ended by the activity of the Technique of Light, utilised by those who work—in group formation—for the dissipation of glamour and for the emergence in the consciousness of men of a clear conception and recognition of the nature of Reality.

This particular work of dissipation is our immediate theme. It is of vital importance that those who recognise the

The Ending of Glamour

open door to the future through which all men must pass should begin to carry forward this work. Only thus can humanity be helped to leave behind the errors, the glamours and the failures of the past. It is this technique which brings freedom from glamour and which can transform human living, and so bring in the new civilisation and culture. This dissipation can be carried forward by disciples in all parts of the planet, aided by the world aspirants; it will, however, be primarily the work of those whose ray focus makes astral living the line of least resistance and who have learnt or are learning to dominate it by the power of thought and mental light. These are the sixth ray people in the first instance, aided by aspirants and disciples upon the second and fourth rays.

In time and space, this task will be first of all instituted and controlled in group formation only by aspirants whose soul or personality rays are the sixth or by those whose astral bodies are conditioned by the sixth ray. When they have grasped the nature of the work to be done and "fanatically adopted the technique of light in the service of the race," their work will be completed by second ray disciples, working from the Ashrams of those Masters Who take disciples. The work done by these two groups will be finally revealed (and at a much later date) by those aspirants and disciples who will swing into astral activity when the fourth ray again begins to manifest. Therefore, the work of dissipating glamour is carried forward by those who come out into manifestation along the lines of energy which embody the second, fourth and sixth rays. I emphasise this as disciples frequently undertake tasks for which they are not particularly fitted and whose rays do not aid them in accomplishment and sometimes prevent that accomplishment.

The whole subject is related to consciousness, to the second aspect, and concerns the forms through which mankind becomes progressively aware. Glamour is caused by the recognition of that which man has himself created and, as has occultly been said, "Man only becomes aware of reality when he has destroyed that which he has himself created." These forms fall into two major groups:

1. Those forms which are of very ancient origin and which are the result of human activity, human thinking and of human error. They embrace all the forms which *the desire nature* of man has created down the ages and are the nebulous substance of glamour—nebulous from the physical angle but dense from the angle of the astral plane. They are that which provides the incentive behind all striving and activity upon the outer plane as man attempts to satisfy desire. From these forms the individual aspirant has ever to rid himself, emerging after so doing through that gate which we call the second initiation into a wider consciousness.

2. Those forms which are being constantly created and ceaselessly produced in response to *the aspirational nature* of humanity and which provide the enticements which lead the man along towards high personal achievement in the first instance and spiritual achievement later. They have in them the indications of the new and the possible. These likewise (strange as it may seem) constitute a glamour, for they are temporary and illusory and must not be permitted to hide the Real. That Reality will precipitate itself at the right moment once the higher light pours in. They are indicative of the Real and are often mistaken for the Real; they are in conflict with the old thoughts and desires of the past and must eventually give place to the factual presence

The Ending of Glamour

of the Real. They provide (in times of crisis) the great testing for all aspirants and disciples, evoking the subtlest kind of discrimination; but once that testing has been triumphantly passed, then can the task of dissipating both these types of glamour be given to the disciple and aspirant, with the emphasis upon the immediate need or any particular and current world glamour.

It will be apparent to you, therefore, that groups working consciously at the service of dissipating glamour will have the following characteristics:

1. They will be composed of sixth ray aspirants and disciples, aided by second ray spiritual workers.

2. They will be formed of those who:

> a. Are learning or have learnt to dissipate their own individual glamours and can bring understanding to the task.
>
> b. Are focussed upon the mental plane and have, therefore, some measure of mental illumination. They are mastering the Technique of Light.
>
> c. Are aware of the nature of the glamours which they are attempting to dissipate and can use the illumined mind as a searchlight.

3. They will count among their numbers those who (occultly speaking) have the following powers in process of rapid development:

> a. The power not only to recognise glamour for what it is, but to discriminate between the various and many types of glamour.
>
> b. The power to appropriate the light, absorbing it into themselves and then consciously and scientifically project it into the world of glamour. The

Masters, the higher initiates and the world disciples do this alone, if need be, and require not the protection of the group or the aid of the light of the group members.

c. The power to use the light not only through absorption and projection but also by a conscious use of the will, carrying energy upon the beam of projected light. To this they add a persistent and steady focus. This beam, thus projected, has a twofold use: It works expulsively and dynamically, much as a strong wind blows away or dissipates a dense fog or as the rays of the sun dry up and absorb the mist. It acts also as a beam along which that which is new and a part of the divine intention can enter. The new ideas and the desired ideals can come in "on the beam," just as the beam directs and brings in the airplanes to a desired landing place.

a. The Dissipation of Individual Glamour

Let us first of all consider the mode by which the individual aspirant can succeed in dissipating the glamours which have for ages conditioned his life in the three worlds. He has been dominated by desire for four-fifths of his incarnated experience. He has begun to transmute his desire into aspiration and to seek—with all the devotion, emotion and longing of which he is capable—for realisation. It is then that he becomes aware of the appalling nature of the glamours in which he automatically and normally walks. Glamour arose when man recognised and registered desire as an incentive, thus demonstrating his humanity and his distinction from the animal, because it is the mind which reveals the existence of desire. The instinctual effort to satisfy desire—innate and inherent in the lower nature—gave

The Ending of Glamour 203

place to *planned* efforts to meet desire, involving the directive use of the mind. Thus the line of demarcation between the animal and the human has become increasingly apparent and the first and basic expression of pure selfishness appeared aeons ago. Later, as evolution proceeded and desire shifted from one planned satisfaction to another, it began to take on a less physical aspect and men sought pleasure in emotional experience and in its dramatisation: this led to the establishment of the drama as its first artistic expression; by means of this, down the ages, man has supplemented individual emotional and dramatic living with a vicarious submergence in it, thus exteriorising himself and supplementing his personal dramas, desires, and objectives with those which were developed by means of the creative imagination, thus laying the foundation for the recognition—intelligent and real—of the part in relation to the whole. Thus from earliest Atlantean times the foundation was laid for the unfoldment of the sense of mystical duality through the various stages of an anthropomorphic recognition of deity to the recognition of the real in man himself, until finally we arrive at the proposition which faces the disciple. Then the Dweller on the Threshold confronts the Angel of the Presence and the last and major conflict is fought out.

This dualistic consciousness culminates at the time of the third initiation in the final fight between the pairs of opposites and the triumphant victory of the Angel—the embodiment of the Forces of Good in the individual, in the group and in humanity. Then dualism and the desire for that which is material and not oneself (as identified with the Whole) dies out. Unity and the "life more abundantly" is achieved.

The process followed by the disciple who is consciously working at the dissipation of glamour in his life can be divided into four stages to which the following definitions can be given:

1. The stage of recognition of the glamour or glamours which hide the Real. These glamours are dependent in any particular life crisis upon the ray of the personality.

2. The stage of focussing the disciple's consciousness upon the mental plane and the gathering of the light to that point of focus so that the illumination is clear, the work to be done is plainly seen, and the searchlight of the mind is directed upon the glamour which it is intended should be dissipated.

3. The stage of direction. This involves the steady pouring of the light (under intelligent direction) into the dark places of the astral plane, remembering that the light will enable the disciple to do two things:

   a. Dissipate the glamour—a satisfying experience.
   b. See the Real—a terrifying experience, brother of mine.

4. The stage of identification with the Real as it is contacted after the dissipation of the glamour. In the added light which is now available, there will be a further recognition of still subtler glamours which in their turn must be dissipated.

This process of recognition, focussing, dissipation and consequent revelation goes on continually from the time a disciple treads the Path of Accepted Discipleship until the third initiation.

The clue to all success in this process is, therefore, connected with meditation and the holding of the mind steady in the light. Only through steadiness can the beam of light be formed, intensified, focussed and projected and then—at the right moment—withdrawn. I cannot here enter upon an elucidation of the process of meditation, based on the right understanding of the nature of concentration. I have written much upon the subject and the Raja Yoga discipline is well known. Mental concentration and control is now the ordinary theme of all instructions given by educators and enlightened parents. It is difficult for the average person today to realise that there was a time when such phrases as "Use your mind" or "If you will only think" or "A little mental control on your part would be useful" were totally unknown because the mind was so little developed. It was then only recognised as a functioning factor by those with initiate consciousness. The Path of Evolution is in fact the path of recognitions, leading to revelation. The whole process of evolution is initiatory in character, leading from one expansion of consciousness to another until the worlds of the formless and of form stand revealed in the light which the initiate generates and in which he walks. These lights are varied and variously revealing; there is:

1. The light of matter itself, found in every atom of substance.
2. The light of the vital or etheric vehicle—a light which is the reflection of the One Light because it unifies the three types of light within the three worlds.
3. The light of the instinct.
4. The light of the intellect or the light of knowledge.
5. The light of the soul.
6. The light of the intuition.

From light to light we pass, from revelation to revelation until we pass out of the realm of light into the realm of life which is, as yet to us, pure darkness.

It will be obvious to you that this increasing light brings with it a constantly developing series of revelations which, like all else in the world of human experience, unfolds before the eyes first of all the world of forms, then the world of ideals, then the nature of the soul, of ideas and of divinity. I am choosing but a few of the words which embody the revelation and are symbolic of its character. But all these revelations constitute one great unified revelation which is slowly unfolding before the eyes of humanity. The light of the personal lower self reveals to man the world of form, of matter, of instinct, of desire and of mind; the light of the soul reveals the nature of the relation of these forms of life to the world of the formless and of the conflict between the real and the unreal. The light of the intuition unfolds before the vision of the *soul within the personality*, the nature of God and the unity of the Whole. The restlessness of material desire, seeking its satisfaction in the three worlds, eventually gives place to aspiration towards soul contact and soul life. This in its turn is recognised as a step towards those great fundamental experiences to which we give the names of the five major initiations. These reveal to man the hitherto unrealised fact of his non-separateness and of the relation of his individual will to the divine will.

We are now going to study the mode whereby these phases of work upon the astral plane are carried forward: first, the individual learns to use the light of the mind, generated by the soul as it becomes closely related to the personality and impulsed by the intuition. By means of this light the disciple learns to dissipate his personal and private glamours. I mention this because I would have you appreciate the extent of the task a man undertakes when he consciously sets about ridding himself of glamour preparatory to extended service. He is in conflict then with the whole glamour of the entire plane and is apt to be overwhelmed by a realisation of what he is facing. This is one of the causes of the deep depression and those profound inferiority complexes which render some people completely futile or lead eventually to suicide. Their own personal glamours tie them in to national or planetary glamour and thus condition their life expression and their thinking. I would ask you to remember this as you deal with people and find them set in their ideas and unable to see the truth as you see it. They are as they are because their individual glamour is fed by the greater glamours, and this is as yet too much for them.

It is not my intention to deal specifically with particular glamours but to give you a formula which—with slight changes and additions—can serve the individual and the group in the task of eradicating glamour. I would begin by saying that the first need is for the man to realise that his reactions, ideas, desires and life experience, as far as his emotional nature is concerned, are conditioned by some one glamour or glamours, that he is the victim of several glamours, engendered over many lives, deeply rooted in his past history, and to which he instinctually reacts. The time, however, comes when the probationary disciple becomes aware of these instinctual glamours and recognises them on appearance, even when reacting to them; he seeks to free himself, working at first spasmodically, trying to use the mind to rationalise himself out of them and alternating between temporary success, when he can with deliberation act as if free from glamour, and long periods of defeat when he is overwhelmed, can see no light anywhere and acts like a blind, bewildered person. This indicates that he is drawn as by a magnet (the force of accumulated ancient glamour with its karmic effects) into the midst of the very glamour he would seek to avoid. Later comes the stage (a result of this alternating process) when the pull of the soul begins to offset the pull of these glamours: he aspires to free expression and to liberation from astral plane control. The balancing process then takes place.

It is during this stage that meditation is instituted so that the man becomes aware of soul light as it blends with the inherent light of the mental body, and this blended light steadily intensifies as he persists in the meditation work. A point then comes where the aspirant discovers that this inner light can be used, and he begins tentatively and with uneven success to turn that light upon the problems of his particular glamour. It is also at this point that we now carry forward the Technique of Light, employing it so that the vague unscientific technique of the past comes to an end. The indicated technique is of use only to the man who knows something of the light of the mind, of the light in the head, and of the light of the soul. The light in the head is produced by the definitely planned bringing together of soul light and personality light, focussed in the mental body and producing an effect in the brain. This focussing process falls into three stages:

1. The attempt to focus the light of the mind and of matter in the mental vehicle.

This signifies a bringing together of the light of matter and substance (dense material and etheric light) and the light of the mind itself. There is no peculiar or specific light in or of the astral body itself, for it is only an aggregate of forms, created by individual man, by nations and by races, and these in their entirety constitute the astral plane and possess no inherent light as do other forms. They are not created as a form of expression for some dynamic life by the planetary Logos, and this is the real meaning of what I have earlier told you that the astral plane in reality does not exist. It is the phantasmoric creation of human desire down

The Ending of Glamour

the ages and its false light is a reflection of either the light of matter or of the mind. This process of focussing is undertaken through alignment and by the effort to bring to a point of illumination the positive light of the mind and the negative light of the brain and is carried forward through mental control, developed in meditation. When these two opposite poles are in relation then (by an act of the personality will) these two aspects of the lesser light can form a pin point of light—like a small torch light—revealing some phase of the glamour to which the aspirant most easily responds. This first focussed light is not of such a nature that it can do more than reveal. It has no dissipating power, nor can it render existing glamour ineffective. It can only make a man aware in his waking or brain consciousness that glamour holds him. This is related to the stage of concentration in the meditation process.

2. The second stage of the focussing process is produced through the effort to meditate. In the previous stage, the blending of the two material lights was entirely a form process and the aspirant is actuated entirely by his personality forces and expediency. An illustration of this and of its effectiveness can be seen in the man who, from purely selfish motives and through an intense concentration, focusses his mind and brings about the gratification of his desires and the achievement of his goals. He kills out all emotional reactions and goes a long way towards dissipating glamour. He develops the ability to draw on the light of matter itself (physical matter and mental substance) and thus he generates a false light from which soul light is rigorously excluded. It is this power which eventually produces a black magician. He has developed the capacity to draw

upon the light energy of matter itself and to focus it so powerfully and effectively that it becomes a great destructive force. It is this which has given Hitler and the six evil men associated with him their power to destroy upon the material plane. But, in the case of the aspirant, the power to meditate upon spiritual reality and to contact the soul offsets the dangers inherent in focussing on and using solely the light of matter; to the lesser light of matter is added the light of the soul and then these two blended lights, or aspects of the One Light, are focussed upon the mental plane through the power of the creative imagination. This enables man eventually to dissipate glamour and liberates him from the astral plane.

3. The third stage is that in which the light of matter, the light of the mind and the light of the soul (as a channel for the intuition) are consciously blended, fused and focussed. The man then turns this blended light, under soul direction, upon the world of glamour and upon the particular glamour with which he is at any one time pre-occupied. The false light of the astral plane disappears in this triple blended light just like a fire can be nearly put out if subjected to the full rays of the sun; or a burning glass, focussing the rays of the sun, can start a destructive blaze. It is the use of a powerful light which can obliterate a lesser light and dissipate a fog.

All this has to be understandingly and consciously carried forward as a preliminary to the technique proper. His work will be experimental at first, and scientifically applied eventually. It will be based upon a recognition of truth—a truth which is faced and accepted. This work is not a form of rationalisation, though that precedes the definitely scientific

The Ending of Glamour

work I am outlining; it is not the cultivation of fresh interests of a mental and spiritual kind which gradually supersede desire and drive out glamour. That is all preparatory in character and leads to an unfoldment which prepares the aspirant to work scientifically; it is not a process of "killing out desire" as some schools of thought teach, but is a process of gradually eradicating desire by stern discipline and hard trained work and this, incidentally, involves the dissipation of glamour. Such have been the slow techniques of the past. Today the process is to be changed because enough people are now the product of understanding and can work wisely and also scientifically.

The process I am developing for you is one of rapid and effective dissipation and is based upon the acceptance of the hypothesis of light, upon the recognition of the fact that the astral plane has no true existence, upon a trained use of the creative imagination and upon the unquestioning following of instructions, individually and as a group.

It is my intention to give you two formulas—one for the use of the individual and the other which groups can use as they contribute their united effort to the dissipation of glamour, either of group glamour or in relation to some aspect of the prevalent world glamour. Two things will be apparent to you:

First: that those participating in the eradication of glamour must be able to distinguish between glamour and the reality. These often closely resemble each other on a superficial examination. They must be in a position to recognise that an emotional or astral condition constitutes a veil over the truth and is a distortion of the presentation or the appearance of the individual's or the group's expression of divinity. They must, therefore, be capable of vision, clear thinking, and prompt recognition as to what is preventing the materialising of that vision and the accurate reception of the truth. They must also be able to distinguish between a major and a minor glamour. A minor glamour, a passing evanescent thoughtform of an easily recognisable nature does not warrant the use of either of the formulas. Such a minor glamour would be a sense of self-pity in an individual or the glorification of some notable individual by an individual, a group or a nation. Time and commonsense suffice to take care of such a situation. A major glamour in the world (prior to the war) was the emphasis put upon possessions and the belief that happiness was dependent upon things and upon material good and comfort.

Second: that the three stages of focussing, referred to above, constitute a preparatory process. These three stages must be somewhat developed before effective use of the formulas can be possible, and those intending to work at the task of ridding the world of glamour must subject themselves constantly to these phases in the art of polarisation, if I might so call it. They must have an understanding of the apparatus of thought, of the creation of thoughtforms, and of the nature of the thinker. They must be emotionally polarised, yet, in group work relatively free from astral control. This astral liberation must to a certain extent control the choice of those who are to work at major dissipations. In the case of the individual who is seeking to break up glamour in his individual life, he should be mentally polarised by decision and effort even if the emotional nature is for him in any one life the line of least resistance. Those working in group formation will have achieved a measure of mental focus but for the purposes of the work to be done they will focus themselves consciously and deliberately upon the emotional plane through

The Ending of Glamour

their control of their natures. Workers must therefore have practised meditation, have reflected much upon the nature of thought and its uses, and must be aware of the light within.

When these three stages are established as related activities, habits and automatic reactions, and when the intention is fixed and the ability to focus has become an almost instinctual reaction, then sound and effective work can be done; to this work must be added persistence and patience. It is not necessary, I might add, to have achieved perfection in the process before starting this work and service. Disciples and aspirants must cultivate the consciousness of cooperation and realisation that in service such as is proposed, they are definitely participating in a hierarchical activity and are, therefore, in a position to render help even if they could not—alone and unaided—achieve the desired results. They can hasten the process by their combined help. The power of united effort upon the physical plane is being realised today on a large scale, and the war effort in all countries has greatly hastened this realisation. The power of unified emotion (often expressing itself in what is called mob psychology) is everywhere recognised and feared as well as exploited. The power of unified thought is little grasped as yet, and the power inherent in the light of many minds, rendering them effective instruments in world affairs, penetrating and dissipating glamour and proving creative upon the physical plane, will prove to be a part of the new modes of work which will be employed in the new age. For this, the Hierarchy has planned and worked and it is now prepared to test the effectiveness of that work by organising a group or groups which will work upon the problem of glamour.

You can see, consequently, that what I am outlining is relatively new. The faint impression of the coming technique as far as the individual is concerned has been registered. Men and women everywhere are attempting to rid themselves of glamour by the power of clear thinking, stern discipline and commonsense, and by a recording consciously of their relation to the whole—which prompts them to eliminate out of their lives all that could hinder others or increase world deception through glamour. To this will be added (perhaps as an aspect of the new world religion now on its way towards externalising) the realisation that groups can successfully clear away the glamours which darken humanity's way to its goal, through the power of combined and projected thought.

In order to make the first step towards united group activity along this line of service, I present a formula or group ritual which—if employed by those whose lives are relatively free from glamour, who are realists and who are recognised by the group as thus relatively free, and who are animated by good intent—will do much to bring to an end certain aspects of the world glamour. Their effort, combined with that of similar groups, will so weaken the power of these ancient glamours that the "Day of Clarification" will eventually come.

First, however, let me briefly offer for the use of the individual aspirant a formula whereby he may aid in freeing himself from his particular glamour or glamours. I will tabulate the process, and the aspirant would do well to follow it as given, having in his mind no sense of time, and being willing to do this work regularly for months, and if necessary for years, until he has freed himself and the light breaks in on the astral plane through the medium of his astral body. I would suggest that no aspirant attempt to tackle the problem of glamour as a whole or seek to dissipate all the glamours to which he is susceptible. He is dealing with very ancient evil and with firmly established

The Ending of Glamour

habits of glamour. They are closely connected with aspects of his daily living, with his sex life or with his ambitions, with his relations to other people, with his pet ideals and ideas, his dreams and visions. He should choose the glamour that is the most apparent and the most hindering at any given time (and there is always one) and for its dissipation he should work conscientiously, if he would lay the foundations for effective service in the dissipation of world glamour.

FORMULA FOR THE DISSIPATION OF GLAMOUR
(For the Individual)

I. Preparatory Stages.

1. Recognition of the glamour to be dissipated. This involves:
    a. A willingness to cooperate with the soul in physical, astral and mental ways in order to aid in the more technical work. Ponder on the implications in this sentence.
    b. A recognition of the ways in which this glamour affects the daily life and all relationships.
2. The three stages of focussing outlined (pp. 208-210) must be undertaken.
    a. *The stage of focussing the light of the mind and the light of matter in the mental vehicle.* This is done by a process of lifting up and of blending and fusion, and to do this the activity of the creative imagination is employed.
    b. *The stage of meditation* which in time brings about the fusion of the light of matter, the light of the mind and the light of the soul upon the mental plane.

c. *The stage in which these three lights are realised to be one unified light*—a searchlight, ready to be turned in the needed direction.

3. The recognition of two aspects of preparedness:

   a. Alignment of the personality, so that the three aspects of the lower nature are seen as constituting one functioning personality.
   b. An act of integration in which the personality and the soul are seen also as a unit. This is done through the dedication of the personality to the soul and its acceptance by the soul.

   These two lines of thinking produce a field of magnetic thought and realisation in which all the work is done.

4. A pause in which the whole man braces himself for the work to be done. From a profound pre-occupation with the stage of soul contact and initial preparation he now focusses his attentive mind upon the glamour to be eradicated. This does not involve a consciousness of the glamour and its why and wherefore. It means a *turning of the attention of the integrated soul-personality to the astral plane and the particular glamour; the attention is not turned to the astral body of the aspirant,* seeking to do the work. This is a statement of major importance because in destroying the peculiar type of glamour with which he is concerned, the aspirant or disciple begins to destroy his share in it—that in him which gives him contact with the glamour—and at the same time he is preparing himself for group service along the same line. This will not prove an easy task.

The Ending of Glamour

II. The Technique or Formula.

5. By an act of the creative imagination the worker endeavours to see and hear the soul—the source of light and power in the three worlds—breathing out the O M into the mind of the attentive waiting personality. There the light and power of the soul is retained and held by the positive personality, for a negative attitude is not desirable.

6. The retained light and power, combined with the dual light of the personality (focussed as we know on the mental plane) is seen generating an intense light which can be visualised as a searchlight of great brilliance and strength. It must be seen as a sphere of vivid brilliant light but not yet radiating out or projecting outwards.

7. When this act of visualisation is deemed to be satisfactorily accomplished, a pause then ensues wherein the aspirant focusses all the will he has behind the light thus created by the fusion of the three lights. This refers to the stage spoken of by Patanjali as that of the "mind held steady in the light." This use of the will—soul-personality will—is dynamic but at this stage quiescent and not magnetic or radiatory.

8. Next follows a process wherein the glamour to be dissipated and the searchlight of the mind are brought into relationship by the power of thought. The glamour and its quality and the searchlight and its power are recognised to be as they are, and the effect or effects to be brought about by that relationship are carefully thought out. This must not be done in such a way that the mind process,

light and power will strengthen the already powerful glamour. It must be done in such a way that at the close of the process the glamour will be appreciably weakened and eventually dissipated. This is an important realisation.

9. Having, as far as possible, achieved the needed concentration, realisation and relationship, the aspirant then (by an act of the will and of the creative imagination) turns on the searchlight and sees a vivid beam of light stream forth and pierce the glamour. He must visualise a broad brilliant beam, pouring forth from the illumined mind on to the astral plane. He must believe that this is so.

10. Then comes an important and difficult phase of the work in which the worker *names the glamour* and sees it in process of dissipation. He aids the process by saying with tension and inaudibly:

> The power of the light prevents the appearance of the glamour (Naming it).
> The power of the light negates the quality of the glamour from affecting me.
> The power of the light destroys the life behind the glamour.

The saying of these three sentences constitutes an affirmation of power and of purpose and must be enunciated at a point of tension, with the mind held in steadiness and with a positive orientation.

11. Again the Sacred Word is sounded with intent to produce what in occult parlance is called an "Act of Penetration"; the light is then seen accomplishing three things:

The Ending of Glamour

   a. Making a definite impact upon the glamour.
   b. Penetrating the glamour and being absorbed by it.
   c. Dissipating it slowly; as time elapses the glamour will never again be so powerful and will eventually disappear altogether.

12. This is followed by a process of withdrawing wherein the aspirant consciously and deliberately withdraws the beam of light and re-orients himself upon the mental plane.

I would point out that glamour is never immediately dissipated. It is of too ancient an origin. But a persistent use of this formula will weaken the glamour and slowly and inevitably it will vanish and the man will walk free from that particular hindrance. This may seem like a very long formula but I have purposely detailed it in as full a manner as possible so that the aspirant may clearly apprehend what he is intended to do. After due practice and a faithful following of the required conditions, the aspirant will follow it well-nigh automatically and all that he will then need will be the formula reduced to the following brief outline:

Brief Outline of the Formula

1. The four Preparatory Stages:
   a. Recognition of the glamour to be dissipated.
   b. The stage of focussing the light of the personality, a dual light.
   c. The stage of meditation and the recognition of the greater light.
   d. The unification of the dual light of matter and the light of the soul, creating thus the searchlight of the mind.

2. A process of alignment and of recognised integration.
3. A deliberate turning of the searchlight of the mind to the astral plane.

The Formula

4. Soul activity and the retention of the light.
5. The generating and visualising of the searchlight.
6. The evocation of the will behind the searchlight of the mind.
7. The generated unified light is turned upon the glamour by the power of thought.
8. The naming of the glamour and the triple affirmation.
9. The Act of Penetration.
10. The Process of Withdrawing.

You will see, brother of mine, that what I am in fact doing is teaching the coming generation how to destroy those forms of thought which hold the race in bondage and which in the case of glamour are the forms which desire, emotion, sensitivity to environment, developing aspiration and old ideals have taken and which prevent the light of the soul from illuminating the waking consciousness. The energies taking form upon the astral plane are not pure emotion and feeling, clothed in pure astral matter, for there is no such thing. They are the instinctual desires, evoked by the evolving substance of the physical plane and this, in its entirety and through the activity of the human family, is being redeemed and drawn upwards until some day we shall see the transfiguration of that substance and the "Glorification of the Virgin Mary"—the Mother Aspect in relation to divinity. They are also the descending thoughtforms which the developing human being is always creating and drawing

The Ending of Glamour

downwards into manifestation, clothing them with the substance of desire. When the descending forms of thought (a reflection in the three worlds of that vast "cloud of knowable things" in process of perception, as Patanjali calls it, and which hovers upon the buddhic plane, awaiting precipitation) and the ascending mass of instinctual demands from the lower aspect of the human unit and from humanity as a whole, meet at a point of tension then you have the appearance of what is known as the astral plane—a man-created sphere of activity. The subhuman kingdoms of nature know no astral plane; the superhuman kingdoms have surmounted it and discovered the secret of its delusion and no longer recognise it except as a temporary field of experience wherein man lives. In that sphere he learns the fact that reality is "none of these but only the One and the Other in relation with each other." This is one of the occult phrases which the disciple has to learn to understand and which is descriptive of manifestation.

b. The Dissipation of Group Glamour and of World Glamour

Group work in dissipating world glamour must be handled (as will be obvious to you) by those who are working at the dissipation of glamour in their own lives and have learnt to use the formula just given. The majority of those so working are sixth ray aspirants—those who have sixth ray personalities or whose soul ray is the sixth, plus those on all rays who have powerful sixth ray astral vehicles. These make the most effective workers in the group but are subject to one major difficulty. In spite of aspiration and good intention, they are seldom aware of the glamours which control them. It is exceedingly hard to induce the sixth ray aspirant to admit that he is held by a glamour, particularly when it is glamour of spiritual connotation and of a very high order. In their case, the glamour is enhanced by the energy of devotion which stiffens it and brings in a quality which makes it most difficult to penetrate. Their complete assurance proves a serious obstacle to clear-sighted work because that has all to go before the work of dissipation can be carried forward successfully. First ray people can overcome glamour with relative ease once they become aware of it as a personality limitation. Third ray people are as susceptible to it as are those of the sixth ray and their devious, twisting, planning minds and the rapidity with which they can deceive themselves (and seek often to deceive others) greatly hinders their work of clearing away glamour. Their pronounced tendency to be the victims of glamour is evidenced by the inability of the third ray aspirant and disciple to convey his meaning clearly by speech. He has guarded himself for many lives by devious formulations of thought and of ideas and can seldom convey his meaning clearly. This is why sixth ray people and third ray people almost inevitably prove themselves unable to teach. Both these groups must, therefore, learn to use this formula and they would greatly hasten the process of dissipation if they would force themselves to speak or write their thoughts clearly, if they would never be ambiguous or deal in half thoughts, innuendo or suggestion. They should clearly enunciate the ideas with which they may be dealing.

The seventh ray person is faced with the difficulty of being able to create exceedingly clear-cut thoughtforms and the glamours, therefore, which control him are precise and definite and, to him, all compelling. They rapidly crystallise, however, and die their own death. Second ray aspirants are usually fully aware of any glamour which may be seeking to hold them because they have an innate faculty of

The Ending of Glamour 223

clear perception. Their problem is to kill out in themselves their rapid response to the magnetic pull of the astral plane and its many and widespread glamours. They are not so frequently responsive to *a* glamour as to all glamours in a relatively temporary manner but one which is nevertheless exceedingly delaying to their progress. Because of their clearsightedness, they add to this sensitivity to glamour an ability to suffer about it and to register their responsiveness as a sin and failure and thus delay their liberation from it by a negative attitude of inferiority and distress. They will profit enormously from a constant use of the formula until the time comes when they are aware of the glamour or glamours but are not touched by them. Fifth ray people suffer the least from glamour but are primarily the victims of illusion, and for them the Technique of the Presence is all-important because it brings in a factor which the true fifth ray person is apt to negate and refuse to admit, the fact of the Higher Self. He feels self-sufficient. They respond so easily and with such satisfaction to the power of thought; pride in their mental competence is their besetting sin and they are, therefore, set in their purposes and preoccupied with the world of the concrete and the intellectual. The moment that the Angel of the Presence is a reality to them, their response to illusion weakens and disappears. Their major problem is not so much the negation of the astral body, for they are apt to despise its hold, but they have a major difficulty in recognising that which the mind is intended to reveal—the divine spiritual Self. Their lower concrete mind interposes itself between them and the vision.

Fourth ray people are peculiarly prone to fall into glamour and thus to produce a condition which is one of extreme difficulty. I might define their problem by saying that they tend to bring their illusions down to the astral plane and there clothe them with glamour and have consequently a double problem upon their hands; they are faced with a unification of glamour and illusion. They are, however, the group of souls which will eventually reveal the true nature of the intuition and this will be the result of their illusory glamorous fight in the world of appearances.

We come now to the consideration of the formula to be used by those who seek to serve humanity by deliberately breaking up and dispersing the glamours which hold the race in thrall and who know the need to do this in group formation. Certain individual characteristics are essential for the personnel of such groups. First of all there must be an ability to work "without attachment" to results and to use the formula for a given length of time (for instance, once a week for two years or more) without looking for results; they need to realise that they can never know whether they are successful or not, because the glamours they are attempting to dissipate are so widespread and general that effects cannot be grasped by their individual minds. They are too close to the picture; their perspective has necessarily to be that of the immediate foreground. Secondly, they must have an intelligent appreciation of what constitutes a world glamour so that they can occultly "name it" and, by so doing, contact it. They must, thirdly, be accustomed to the work of dispersing glamour in their own lives; the necessity to do this and their success in so doing are factors which indicate their suitability for the task.

They must, finally, love their fellowmen. This they must not do as the sixth ray person loves them, with an isolating devotion, but as the second ray person loves—with an all round appreciation of humanity, an understanding heart, plus a critical mind, which loves steadily in spite of error seen, with a clear sighted perception of the assets and the debits of an individual or a race. The ability

The Ending of Glamour

to do this is one of the factors which enables the sixth ray aspirant to transfer off the minor sixth ray and find his place upon the major second ray, as must all sixth and fourth ray initiates.

One of the requirements in this group work is a most careful choice of those who are to participate in the work. They must be chosen because they *can* work together. They must either know each other exceedingly well and be free from personality frictions or they must be relatively unknown to each other as personalities but are drawn to each other as soul-collaborators in this particular work. They must, as far as in them lies, endeavour to work with regularity so that a rhythm can be set up which will lead to a steady rhythmic impact of the light upon the glamour. They must also adhere faithfully to the formula given. This is one of the initial formulas and is most powerful because it is one of the very first to be used in group dissipation of glamour. This whole procedure is entirely new as far as man is concerned, and the work to be done will necessarily prove hard as it involves an interesting situation. The groups who will do this work of piercing the glamours which dim the vision of humanity and of dissipating them will be the first non-initiate groups to work this way upon the physical plane and to work consciously and with fixed intent. Hitherto the work has been carried forward by members of the Hierarchy, and then only with the idea of holding back the glamours until such time as humanity was ready to destroy that which it had created. Glamours have also been pierced before now by massed effort carried forward for a long time and usually without any very real conscious understanding. An illustration of this would be the work done by the Church in a diffused and vague way in piercing the glamour of material desire and material good by substituting the idea of a heavenly substitute. The work that is now planned is dynamic and clear cut, consciously carried forward and specific in its impact. It is a definite method of handling and projecting the energy of light with the objective of destroying the impediments of an emotional-mental nature upon the Path of Return to God.

It is desirable and aids an easier and more concentrated form of work if the group can meet together for the use of the formula. If, however, this proves not possible, then the personnel of the group can arrange to work apart but with the idea of the work being group work firmly realised and with a steady recognition of the members who form the group body. This is necessary both for the "pooling of the light" and also for protection from the glamour to be attacked. This "pooling of the light" is a major requirement and must ever be borne in mind. Whenever possible, the rule should be that the work is done at some definite planned group meeting, even if this entails quite drastic sacrifice on the part of some of the members.

I advise that some glamour which all the group members recognise as a major hindrance to the progress of humanity be one of the first handled by the group. I would also advise that in the early stages of their work, they deal with a glamour affecting aspirants and that they do not attempt to tackle the more widely spread and deeply centred glamours of the race as a whole. Let them develop facility in handling some of the lesser and more easily visualised glamours. Then as time goes on and facility in the work is gained, the group can pass to the more difficult tasks and handle the glamours further removed from their own orbit of difficulties. It is surely needless for me to point out that the group members be but those who are endeavouring to keep their own lives free from glamour. I would also add that if a group member is in the thick of glamour himself and is occupied with wrestling with it, he should abstain from the group work until he has freed himself with the aid of the individual formula.

Those who can face themselves with an open eye and who see the truth as it is, who can face the same facts in connection with humanity, and can stand serene and unafraid in the face of the worst kind of discoveries about themselves and the world of men, are those who will employ this technique with the most success. I would also remind you that the group will need to protect itself from the glamour or glamours which it is attempting to dissipate. Their individual tendency to glamour is the factor which gives them the right to serve in this way but it also lays them open to danger, and for this a protective formula will be necessary.

The formula will, therefore, be divided into three parts:

1. The Preparatory Stages.
2. The Use of the Protective Formula.
3. Group Formula for the Dissipation of Glamour.

The work done by the individual in dealing with his personal problems of glamour will greatly facilitate the preparatory work of the group.

You will note that in outlining to you this work, I make no reference to the type of room, to the position of the group members, to posture assumed, to the use of incense, or to any of the paraphernalia which so many occult groups deem of importance. The set physical rituals are today (from the angle of the Hierarchy) entirely obsolete and of no importance where disciples and advanced aspirants are concerned. They are of value to the little evolved in whom the sense of drama has to be developed and who need external aids, and they do provide a setting which serves to help beginners to keep the theme of their work and their objective in view. The only ritual which is still regarded as of value to the human family as a whole—particularly to the advanced person—is the Masonic Ritual. The reason for this is that it is a pictorial representation of the process of Creation, of the relation between God and man, of the Path of Return and also of those great Initiations through the means of which the liberated initiate passes into the Council Chamber of the Most High. But with the exception of this, the small petty rituals of position and of physical relations in respect to attitude and seating arrangements are regarded as unnecessary and as usurping frequently the attention which should be given to the work in hand.

Those using these formulas are presumed to have acquired some measure of inner polarisation and to be able to withdraw themselves to their spiritual centre in any place and at any time. This is the centre of quiet thought from whence the work is carried on.

All that is needed as a preface to this group work is ten minutes of complete silence in which the group members attempt to set up that magnetic field of positive receptive activity (note here the paradoxes of the occult sciences) which will make the rest of the work possible.

The leader of the group (chosen in rotation so that all the members of the group occupy that position) starts the work by calling the names of the group members and as each name is called, the other group members look directly into the eyes of the one named, who rises and for a minute faces them. Thus a rapport and a relationship is established because the directive magnetic force of each soul is always reached from "eye to eye." This is the occult significance of the words "Can you look me in the eye?" or "They eyed each other" and similar phrases. Then, having established this interlocking relationship, the group sits in silence for ten minutes. This is done in order to withdraw the conscious-

The Ending of Glamour

ness from all world and personal affairs and centre it upon the work to be done. At the end of that time, the leader names the glamour with which the group is to be occupied. There will be no dissension anent the glamour at the time of the group meeting because the group members—outside the meetings and for a month prior to undertaking the task of dissipating the glamour will have made a study of it, its implications, its historicity and effects—psychological, individual, group and national, and also its widespread influence over humanity as a whole. The experience of the group in this type of work will determine the nature of the glamour to be dealt with. As I earlier pointed out, the inexperienced group of workers will begin by dealing with one of the glamours which hinder aspirants and will pass on from these to handle the more powerful and more widely dispersed glamours which trouble humanity as a whole. This preface to the work is frequently called the *Act of Naming,* because both the group members and also the glamour are named.

The next stage is similar to the preparatory stages in the formula for the dissipation of glamour for the individual. You have therefore the following:

THE PREPARATORY STAGES

1. The Act of Naming.
2. The Protective Formula.

    The Protective Formula is very simple. The members of the group will say in unison:

    > "As a soul I work in light and darkness cannot touch me.
    > I take my stand within the light.
    > I work and from that point I never move."

As they say this, each person in the group makes the sign of the Cross by touching the centre of the forehead, the centre of the chest, and each of the two eyes, thus forming the long limbed Cross of the Christ or of divine humanity. The Cross is not, as you well know, simply a Christian symbol. It is the great symbol of light and of consciousness and signifies the vertical light and the horizontal light, the power of attraction and the power of radiation, soul life and service. The Cross as now made in the Catholic Churches, touching the forehead, the heart and the two shoulders is the sign of matter. It signifies in reality the third Aspect. The Cross which the group will make is the Cross of Christ and of the Christ consciousness. Gradually the Cross of Christ (the Cross of the Risen Christ) will supersede the Cross of matter and of the Mother aspect. Its likeness to the swastika is obvious and will be one of the reasons for its disappearance.

3. The Preparatory Stages:
   a. Focussing the dual personality light of matter and of mind.
   b. Meditation on soul contact and the recognition of soul light.
   c. The blending and fusion of the two lesser lights and of soul light. This is carried forward as a group, each member making his contribution and consciously attempting to visualise the process of blending the triple light which each contributes, into one sphere of light.
4. Then the group says in unison, at a signal from the leader:

> "The light is one and in that light shall we see light.
> This is the light that turns the darkness into day."
>
> O M.　　　　O M.　　　　O M.

The processes of individual and group alignment and integration can now be regarded as completed and when it is really correctly accomplished, each meeting thereafter should see a more rapid integration and fusion and a greater brilliance of the sphere of light thus created. The sounding of O M indicates both the fusion and the sphere of action because O M is first of all sounded forth by the group soul (the realised unity of the souls of all the group members) and then as the soul upon the mental plane, and finally as the soul ready to function as lightbearer and distributor of light upon the astral plane. These are all symbolic ways of registering the inner reality and are an attempt to externalise force, for that is what all symbols and symbolic ways of acting are capable of doing; they thus serve to keep the workers at a point of tension. This is an important recognition and should keep the workers from attributing undue power to the form aspect of the simple ritual and aid them in focussing their attention in the world of meaning and of subjective spiritual activity. These three stages are called:

1. The Act of Naming.
2. The Act of Protection.
3. The Act of Focussing the Light.

It will be apparent to you that much depends upon the ability of the group members to visualise clearly as well as to think clearly. Practice naturally tends to perfect both processes. At the close of these three stages, the group members are united as souls insulated against the attractive power of the glamour, and united as souls with mind and brain held steady and positive in the light. Their blended light is looked upon by them as a great searchlight whose beams are to be directed through an act of the will downward from the mental plane on to the glamour existing on the astral plane and which has been brought into relation with the group by the very act of naming it. I am going into detail on this matter because the work is a new venture and I am anxious for you to start it with a clear understanding as to how the task is to be carried out. At the close of this instruction you will find the two long and two short formulas so that they can be seen and grasped apart from their explanatory context. This initial work should take fifteen minutes at first and later not more than five (excluding the ten minutes of silent preparation which precedes the formal work) for the group members will get used to working together and will eventually attain the objectives of the preparatory work with great rapidity.

The Technique or Formula

5. Then together and in vocal unison the group says:

> "Radiance we are and power. We stand forever with our hands stretched out, linking the heavens and the earth, the inner world of meaning and the subtle world of glamour.
>
> "We reach into the Light and bring it down to meet the need. We reach into the silent Place and bring from thence the gift of understanding. Thus with the light we work and turn the darkness into day."

As they say this, the group visualises the turning of the great searchlight which they have jointly created by their unified light on to the glamour to be dissipated, holding

The Ending of Glamour

the light steady and realising mentally the work of dissipation it is intended to do. This is called the *Act of Direction*.

6. Then follows a pause for a few minutes in which the group attempts to throw behind the searchlight their united directed and dynamic will or intent; this carries along the projected beam of light the destructive quality of the spiritual will—destructive to all that hinders the manifestation of divinity. This is done by attaining a united point of tension, and the dedication of the individual and group will to the will of God. This is called the *Act of Will* and is carried on by each member of the group silently and with a deep realisation that all are thus accepted and that it is the group will which is being silently focussed. Then together they say:

> "With power upon its beam, the light is focussed on the goal."

7. Then comes the *Act of Projection* and the saying of the words of power which—again naming the particular glamour which is the subject of attention and thus bringing it consciously into relation with the focussed light—begins the task of dissipation.

> "The power of our united light prevents the appearance of the glamour of ... (naming it). The power of our united light negates the quality of the glamour from affecting men. The power of our united light destroys the life behind the glamour."

These words are very nearly the same as those in the individual formula and gain strength from the experience of the aspirant and from his familiarity with their use. This constitutes an *Act of Affirmation* which is the second part of the Act of Projection.

8. Then comes an important aspect of the work in which the group members visualise the gradual dissipation and dispersal of the glamour by the penetration of the light into its darkness. They endeavour to see it disintegrating and the reality emerging, doing this by an effort of the creative imagination. Each will do this in his own way and according to his understanding and capacity. This is the *Act of Penetration.*

9. Now follows five minutes of silence and intensity of purpose while the group waits for the work instituted to go forward. Then follows the group withdrawal of its consciousness from the astral plane and the world of glamour. The group members refocus their attention first of all on the mental plane and then on the soul, relinquishing all thought of the glamour, knowing that the work has been successfully carried forward. They re-organise themselves as a group in relation to the kingdom of souls and to each other. Occultly speaking, the "searchlight of the soul is shut off." This is the *Act of Withdrawal.*

10. The O M is then sounded in group formation; and then, in order to emphasise that the group work is ended, each member of the group sounds the O M alone, saying:

> "So let it be, and help me in my own life to end all glamour and untruth."

It will take aspirants some time to gain facility in this work, but it is surely obvious that in learning what is an entirely new technique of service each step must be mastered and practised for quite a long time. Every new branch of learning takes some time to become familiar and this one is no exception. But the effort is well worth while both from the individual angle and as an act of service to humanity.

That all the groups may learn to function in the light and that glamour may disappear from all your lives so that you may walk freely in that light and use that light for others is the wish of my heart for you.

Formula for the Dissipation of Glamour
(For the Individual)

Preparatory Stages.

1. Recognition of the glamour to be dissipated. This involves:

    a. A willingness to cooperate with the soul.

    b Understanding the nature of the particular glamour.

2. The three stages of focussing:

    a. Focussing the dual light of matter and mind in the mental body.

    b. Focussing, through meditation, this dual light and the light of the soul.

    c. Focussing these three lights and so creating the searchlight for the dissipation of glamour.

3. Preparedness through alignment and integration. This is the production of a field of magnetic thought substance.

4. The turning of the attention and of the searchlight of the mind on to the astral plane.

The Formula.

5. The soul breathes out the O M into the waiting personality and the light and power thus generated are retained for use.
6. An intense light is slowly and consciously generated.
7. The spiritual will is invoked whilst the mind is held steady in the light.
8. The glamour to be dissipated and the searchlight of the mind are brought into relationship.
9. The searchlight is then turned on by an act of the will and a strong beam of light is projected into the glamour.
10. The glamour is named and the aspirant says with tension inaudibly:

    "The power of the light prevents the appearance of the glamour (naming it). The power of the light negates the quality of the glamour from affecting me. The power of the light destroys the life behind the glamour."

11. The O M is sounded by the aspirant, producing an Act of Penetration. This produces impact, penetration and dissipation.
12. The aspirant, having done his work, withdraws himself consciously on to the mental plane and the beam of light fades out.

Brief Form of the Individual Formula.

1. The four preparatory stages:

    a. Recognition of the glamour to be dissipated.

The Ending of Glamour

    b. Focussing the dual light of the personality.
    c. Meditation and recognition of soul light.
    d. Unification of the three lights.

2. The process of alignment and of recognised integration.
3. The turning of the searchlight of the mind to the astral plane.

The Formula.

4. Soul activity and the retention of the triple light.
5. The generating and visualising of the searchlight.
6. The evocation of the WILL behind the searchlight of the mind.
7. The searchlight of the mind is turned upon the glamour, directed by thought.
8. The naming of the glamour and the triple affirmation.
9. The Act of Penetration.
10.   The process of Withdrawing.

FORMULA FOR THE DISSIPATION OF WORLD GLAMOUR

(Technique for a Group)

The Preparatory Stages.

1. The naming of the group members, followed by ten minutes silence.
2. The Protective Formula: The group members say in unison:

> "As a soul I work in light and darkness cannot touch me.
> I take my stand within the light.
> I work and from that point I never move."

As these words are uttered, each group member makes the sign of the Cross of Divinity.

3. The three preparatory stages:

    a. Focussing the dual light of matter and mind.
    b. Meditation on soul contact and recognition of soul light.
    c. The fusion of the two lesser lights with soul light.

4. On a signal from the leader, the group says together:

    > "The light is one and in that light shall we see light. This is the light that turns the darkness into day."

    O M.   O M.   O M.

The Formula.

5. Then together the group says:

    > "Radiance are we and power. We stand forever with our hands stretched out, linking the heavens and the earth, the inner world of meaning and the subtle world of glamour.
    >
    > We reach into the light and bring it down to meet the need. We reach into the silent Place and bring from thence the gift of understanding. Thus with the light we work and turn the darkness into day."

As these words are said, the group members visualise the great searchlight they have created turning its light upon the astral plane.

6. A pause follows and then comes the invocation of the spiritual will. When this has been done the group says:

> "With power upon its beam, the light is focussed on the goal."

7. The glamour to be dissipated is named and the light is thrown upon it. The Words of Power are uttered :

> "The power of our united light prevents the appearance of the glamour of... (naming it).
>
> The power of our united light negates the quality of the glamour from affecting man.
>
> The power of our united light destroys the life behind the glamour."

8. Visualisation of the light, penetrating into the glamour and producing its weakening and dissipation.

9. Five minutes of silence and intensity of purpose whilst the work is seen proceeding. Then the group members refocus themselves upon the mental plane, turning their attention away from the astral plane. The searchlight of the soul is shut off.

10. The sounding of the O M individually and aloud by each member.

Brief Form of the Group Formula.

1. The Act of Naming.
2. The Act of Protection.
3. The Act of Focussing the Lights.
4. The Act of Direction.

5. The Act of Invoking the Will.
6. The Act of Projection and Affirmation.
7. The Act of Penetration.
8. The Act of Withdrawal.

Our consideration of glamour is nearing its close. We have carried a consecutive theme steadily and have traced the threefold aspect of the world illusion as it appears upon the mental plane, and there conditions the intelligentsia of the world; as it appears upon the astral plane where it constitutes the glamour to which the masses of men succumb; we shall now consider the world of maya in which we, physically, live and move and have our being.

I wonder if those who read my words appreciate the importance of this entire subject or if they are aware of the wide field of service which it opens up, making practical—as it does—all human living, and indicating likewise the steps whereby Reality can be known and all veiling forms disappear. Behind these words of illusion, glamour and maya, lies TRUTH. This truth is the clear consciousness of Being, of Existence and of essential, initial Reality. That is the reason that Christ stood mute before Pilate who symbolised the human intellect; He knew that no reply could convey meaning to that veiled, inhibited mind.

Illusion is the mode whereby limited understanding and material knowledge interpret truth, veiling and hiding it behind a cloud of thoughtforms. Those thoughtforms become then more real than the truth they veil, and consequently control man's approach to Reality. Through illusion, he becomes aware of the apparatus of thought, of its activity, expressed in thoughtform building, and of that which he succeeds in constructing and which he views as the creation of his intellect. He has, however, created a barrier between himself and that which is and, until he has exhausted the resources of his intellect or has deliberately refused to utilise it, his divine intuition cannot function. It is the *intuition* which reveals true Being and which induces a state of spiritual perception. Then the technique of the PRESENCE becomes an established habit.

Glamour, in its turn, veils and hides the truth behind the fogs and mists of feeling and emotional reaction; it is of unique and terrible potency, owing to the strength of human nature to identify itself with the astral nature and to the vital nature of conscious and sentient response itself. As you know and have been taught, glamour can only be dissipated by the inflow of clear, directed light; this is true of the life of the individual or of humanity as a whole. *Illumination* reveals first of all the existence of glamour; it provides the distressing contrasts with which all true aspirants wrestle and then gradually it floods the life to such an extent that eventually glamour completely vanishes. Men see things then as they are—a facade hiding the good, the beautiful and true. The opposites are then resolved and consciousness is superseded by a condition of realisation—a realisation of Being for which we have no adequate term. The technique of LIGHT becomes a permanent condition.

3. THE TECHNIQUE OF INDIFFERENCE

We come now to a brief study of the third aspect of illusion, to which we give the name *Maya*, and to the technique which can overcome it. We will deal next with the Technique of Indifference which is concerned with the distribution of soul force upon the physical plane, via the etheric plane, leading to inspiration. This is related to the Science of the Breath.

What then is maya? This, my brother, is not easy to define because it is related to the form-building activity of the planetary Logos Himself. However, a consideration of the analogy existing between the microcosm and the Macrocosm may help somewhat. The soul creates a threefold expression in the three worlds of human living. This is an occult truism. The outer form, the dual physical body (dense and vital or etheric) is produced, created, motivated, energised and conditioned by certain energies and forces, emanating from those levels whereon the soul has—rightly or wrongly—*engineered a reaction of identification.* Note this phrase, my brother. These make the man what he is; they give him his temperament, profession and quality upon the physical plane; they make him negative or positive to various types of impacting energy; they give him his character and make him what he appears to be to others; they produce his colouring, his capacities and his personality. With all of these the average man identifies himself; he believes himself to be the form, the medium through which he attempts to express his desires and his ideas. This complete identification with the transient creation and with the outer appearance is maya. It must be remembered that individual maya is a fractional part of the world of energies and forces which constitute the life expression of the planetary Logos, which condition our outer planetary life, and make our planet what it appears to be to the other planets.

The difference between man, the microcosm, and the planetary Logos, the Lord of the World, the Macrocosm, lies in the fact that the Lord of the World is not identified with the maya which He has created, and which has its purpose in eventually bringing about the release of the "prisoners of the planet." To that Maya, HE is supremely indifferent and it is this divine indifference which has led to the great theological illusion of an anthropomorphic Deity and to the belief (in the East) that our planet is but the back-

The Ending of Glamour 243

ground or the plaything of the Gods. It is this cosmic indifference which has led to the human glamour concerning the "inscrutable will of God" and to the affirmation that God is far away and not immanent in every creature and in every atom of which creatures are made. These are some aspects of the glamours and illusions which must be dispelled and dissipated and, in the process, discovery will be made that the form is only maya and can be disregarded, that forces can be organised and directed by energy and that the world of thought, the field of sentient consciousness and the playground of the energies are something apart from the Thinker, from the One who feels and from the Actor and Player of the many parts which the Soul undertakes to play.

The disciple learns eventually to know himself to be, above everything else (whilst in incarnation), the director of forces: these he directs from the altitude of the divine Observer and through the attainment of detachment. These are things which I have oft told you before. These truths are, for you, only the platitudes of occultism and yet, if you could but grasp the full significance of detachment and stand serene as the observing Director, there would be no more waste motion, no more mistaken moves and no more false interpretations, no wandering down the bypaths of daily living, no seeing others through distorted and prejudiced vision and—above all—no more misuse of force.

Again and again, down the ages, the Masters have told Their disciples (as I have told you) that the occultist works in the world of forces. All human beings live and move and express themselves in and through that same world of ever-moving, ever-impacting, outgoing and incoming energies. *The occultist, however, works there*; he becomes a conscious directing agent; he creates upon the physical plane that which he desires, and that which he desires is the pattern of things and the design laid down upon the trestle board of the spiritual consciousness by the great divine Architect. Yet he identifies himself not with the pattern or with the forces which he employs. He moves in the world of maya, free from all illusion, unhindered by glamour and uncontrolled by the mayavic forces. He is rapidly arriving, as far as his own little world is concerned, at the same "divine indifference" which characterises Sanat Kumara, the Lord of the World; therefore increasingly he becomes aware of the Plan as it exists in the Universal Mind and the Purpose which motivates the Will of God.

It is this divine indifference which is responsible for the fact that in attempting to describe "Pure Being" or God, and in the effort to arrive at some understanding of the nature of divinity, the formula of negation has been evolved. God is not this; God is not that; God is no-thing; God is neither time nor space; God is not feeling or thought; God is not form or substance. God simply *IS*. God *IS*—apart from all expression and manifestation as the Manipulator of energy, the Creator of the tangible and the intangible worlds, the Pervader of life, or the Indweller in all forms. God is the ONE WHO can withdraw and, in withdrawing, *dispel, dissipate* and *devitalise* all that has been created—using those words in their fullest significance.

It will be obvious to you, therefore, that in these three activities of that Reality which is not identified with appearance, the will of God, the Destroyer aspect of Deity, is beneficently present. The act of abstraction produces the dispelling of the illusory world of thought; the withdrawal of the divine attention dissipates the sentient universe and brings glamour to an end; the cessation of divine direction brings death to the physical world. All these activities are evidences of the will or of the first aspect—the will-to-good which can and will function in perfection only when goodwill is

The Ending of Glamour

finally and fully developed on Earth, through the agency of humanity.

The will and the breath, my brother, are occultly synonymous terms. In this statement you have the clue to the ending of maya.

The above remarks are preliminary to our study of the Technique of Indifference. It is necessary to point out analogies and to link together the various aspects of related teaching if true perception is to be developed. Let us divide our consideration of this subject as follows:

1. Activity upon the etheric plane, i.e., the world of forces.
    a. Their distribution.
    b. Their manipulation.

2. The Science of the Breath.
    a. The relation of the will and the breath.
    b. Inspiration.

3. The Technique of Indifference.
    a. Through concentration.
    b. Through detachment.

We enter now the field of practical occultism. This is not the field of aspiration or the sphere of a planned moving forward towards that which is higher and desirable. It is, in some ways, a reverse activity. From the point reached upon the ladder of evolution, the disciple "stands in spiritual Being" (as far as in him lies), and consciously, deliberately works with the energies in the three worlds. He directs them into the etheric body from whatever level he chooses to work—mental, emotional, or from the vital plane itself. He does this in conformity with some visioned idea, some cherished ideal, some sensed divine pattern, some spiritual hope, some consecrated ambition or some dedicated desire.

The etheric body of the individual is, as you know, a part of the etheric body of humanity and this, in its turn, is an aspect of the etheric body of the planet, which is likewise an intrinsic part of the etheric body of the solar system. Incidentally, in this far-reaching factual relationship, you have the basis of all astrological influences. Man moves, therefore, in a whirlpool of forces of all types and qualities. He is composed of energies in every part of his manifested and unmanifested expression; he is, therefore, related to all other energies. His task is one of supreme difficulty and needs the great length of the evolutionary cycle. With the mass of world energies and systemic forces we cannot here deal, but we will confine ourselves to the consideration of the individual problem, advising the student to endeavour to extend his understanding of the microcosmic situation to the macrocosmic.

a. Force distribution and manipulation upon the etheric plane.

We will now assume that the aspirant is aware of the need for him to establish a new and higher rhythm in his physical plane life, to organise his time in obedience to the injunction of his higher self, and to produce, consciously and scientifically, those effects which—in his highest moments—are presented to him as desirable. He has now a certain amount of knowledge as to the equipment available for his task and has mastered some facts anent the etheric vehicle. The pairs of opposites are clearly seen by him, even if he is as yet influenced by one or other of them; he is aware of a basic disagreement between his vision of goodness and his expression of that goodness. He has learnt that he is a triple reflection of a higher Trinity and that this Trinity is—for him—the Reality. He understands that

The Ending of Glamour 247

mind, emotions and physical being are intended eventually to manifest that Reality. In the last analysis, he knows that if that intermediate aspect of himself, the etheric body, can be controlled and rightly directed, then vision and expression will and must finally coincide. He is also aware that the dense physical body (the outer tangible appearance) is only an automaton, obedient to whatever forces and energies are the controlling factors in the subjective, conditioning the man. Is that physical body to be controlled by emotional force, pouring through the sacral centre and producing desire for the satisfaction of the physical appetites, or through the solar plexus leading to emotional satisfaction of some kind? Is it to be responsive to the mind and work largely under the impulse of projected thought? Is it perhaps to be directed by an energy greater than any of these but hitherto apparently impotent, the energy of the soul as an expression of pure Being? Is it to be swept into action under the impulse of sentient reactions, ideas and thoughts, emanating from other human beings or is it to be motivated and spurred into activity under the direction of the spiritual Hierarchy? Such are some of the questions to which answers must be found. The stage of aspiring, dreaming and of wishful thinking must now be superseded by direct action and by the carefully planned use of the available forces, swept into activity by the breath, under the direction of the inner eye and controlled by the spiritual man. Which energies can and must be thus used? What forces must be brought under direction? In what manner can they be controlled? Should they be ignored and so rendered futile by that ignoring, or are they forces which are needed in the great creative work?

It will be apparent to you that the first step the spiritual investigator has to take is to ascertain—truly and in the light of his soul—where exactly is his focus of identification. By that I mean: Is his major use of energy to be found upon the mental plane? Is he predominantly emotional and utilising force from the astral plane the greater part of the time? Can he contact the soul and bring in soul energy in such a manner that it negates or offsets his personality force? Can he thus live like a soul upon the physical plane, via the etheric body? If he earnestly studies this problem, he will in time discover which forces are dominant in the etheric body and will become aware *consciously* of the times and experience which call for the expenditure of soul energy. This, my brother, will take time and will be the result of prolonged observation and a close analysis of acts and sentient reactions, of words and thoughts. We are here concerned, as you can see, with an intensely practical problem which is at the same time an intrinsic part of our study and which will be evocative of basic changes in the life of the disciple.

He will add to this observation and analysis of the strength of the force or the forces engaged, the conditions which will swing them into action, the frequency of their appearance, indicating to him novelty or habit, and likewise the nature of their expression. In this way, he will arrive at a new understanding of the conditioning factors which work through his vital body and make him—upon the physical plane—what he essentially is. This will prove to him of deep spiritual and significant help.

This period of observation is, however, confined to mental and intelligent observation. It forms the background of the work to be done, giving assurance and knowledge but leaving the situation as it was. His next step is to become aware of the quality of the forces applied; in ascertaining this, he will find it necessary to discover not only his soul ray and his personality ray but to know also the rays of his mental apparatus, and his emotional nature. This will lead

The Ending of Glamour

necessarily to another period of investigation and careful observation, if he is not already aware of them. When I tell you that to this information he must add a close consideration of the potencies of the forces and energies reaching him astrologically, you will see what a stern task he has set himself. Not only has he to isolate his five ray energies, but he has to allow for the energy of his sun sign as it conditions his personality, and of his rising sign as it seeks to stimulate that personality into soul responsiveness, thus working out soul purpose through personality cooperation.

There are, therefore, seven factors which condition the quality of the forces which seek expression through the etheric body:

1. The ray of the soul.
2. The ray of the personality.
3. The ray of the mind.
4. The ray of the emotional nature.
5. The ray of the physical vehicle.
6. The energy of the sun sign.
7. The influence of the rising sign.

Once, however, these are ascertained and there is some assurance as to their factual truth, the entire problem begins to clarify and the disciple can work with knowledge and understanding. He becomes a scientific worker in the field of hidden forces. He knows then what he is doing, with what energies he must work, and he begins to *feel* these energies as they find their way into the etheric vehicle.

Now comes the stage wherein he is in a position to find out the reality and the work of the seven centres which provide inlet and outlet for the moving forces and energies with which he is immediately concerned in this particular incarnation. He enters upon a prolonged period of observation, of experiment and experience and institutes a trial and error, a success and failure, campaign which will call for all the strength, courage and endurance of which he is capable.

Broadly speaking, the energy of the soul works through the highest head centre and is brought into activity through meditation and applied aptitude in contact. The energy of the integrated personality is focussed through the ajna centre, between the eyes; and when the disciple can identify himself with that, and is also aware of the nature and the vibration of his soul energy, then he can begin to work with the power of direction, using the eyes as directing agencies. There are, as you have gathered in your studies, three eyes of vision and direction at the disposal of the disciple.

1. *The inner eye,* the single eye of the spiritual man. This is the true eye of vision and involves the idea of duality (of the see-er and that which is seen). It is the divine eye. It is that through which the soul looks forth into the world of men and through which direction of the personality takes place.

2. *The right eye,* the eye of buddhi, the eye which is in direct responsive relation to the inner eye. Through this eye the highest activity of the personality can be directed upon the *physical plane.* You have therefore in this connection a triangle of spiritual forces which can be swept into unique activity by the advanced disciple and initiate.

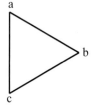

a. the spiritual eye.
b. the ajna centre.
c. the right eye.

It is through this triplicity, for instance, that the trained initiate works when dealing with a group of people or with an individual.

3. *The left eye,* the eye of manas, the distributor of mental energy under correct control—correct as far as personality purposes are concerned. This eye is also a part of a triangle of forces, available for the use of the aspirant and the probationary disciple.

a. the ajna centre.
b. left eye
c. right eye.

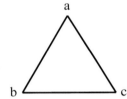

The inner or divine eye is quiescent and relatively inactive, being only the organ of observation where the soul is concerned and it is not yet—in the majority of cases—a distributor of directing soul energy. The disciplined reoriented aspirant, however, integrated and focussed in his purified personality, is using both buddhic and manasic force; he is beginning to be intuitional and predominantly mental. It is when these two triangles are under control and are beginning to function properly that the seven centres in the etheric body are brought under clear direction, become the recipients of the established rhythm of the developed human being, and present consequently an instrument to the soul through which appropriate energies can flow and the full organisation and purpose of a functioning son of God can be manifested on Earth.

Next comes what we have called the stage of direction. The soul or the integrated personality is in command or—on a higher turn of the spiral—the Monad is in command and the personality is simply then the agent of spirit. Through the two triangles or through both of them working synchronously, the centres up the spine (five in all) are brought under rhythmic control. Energy is directed into them or through them; they are steadily brought into a beauty of organisation which has been described as a "life aflame with God"; it is a life of spiritual application and service wherein the higher triangle is the most potent.

The following three statements sum up the story of the eventual release of the disciple from the Great Illusion:

> First: As the soul, working through the higher triangle, becomes the directing agent, illusion is dispelled. The mind becomes illumined.

> Second: As the personality (under the growing influence of the soul) works through the second triangle, glamour is dissipated. The control of the astral nature is broken.

> Third: As the disciple, working as the soul and as an integrated personality, assumes direction of his life expression, maya or the world of etheric energies becomes devitalised, and only those forces and energies are employed which serve the need of the disciple or the initiate as he fulfils divine intent.

You will note that this is all embodied and brought about in the sevenfold work described above. This can be summarised as follows:

1. The disciple discovers the focus of his identification.

2. He ascertains the nature of the forces he is in the habit of using and which perpetually seem to swing him into action.

The Ending of Glamour

3. He becomes aware of the strength and frequency of this force expression.

   All this is carried forward as the mental observer.

4. He becomes conscious of the quality of the forces employed, their ray relation or their astrological significance.

   This is a sentient, feeling activity and is not so basically mental as the previous three stages.

5. He identifies the centres in the etheric body and becomes aware of their individual existence as force agents.

6. The two "triangles of vision and direction" in the head reach a stage of organisation and become

   a. Active and functioning mechanisms.

   b. Related and functioning, as one expressive instrument. This is an objective and subjective activity.

7. The galvanising of the physical body into activity through the medium of the directing agencies in the head and through the centres up the spine.

The question now arises as to how this is to be brought about. This brings us to our second point.

b. The use of the Science of the Breath.

There has been a great deal of nonsense talked and taught about the science of the breath. Many groups give a great deal of dangerous instruction anent breathing—dangerous because it is based on book knowledge and its exponents have never practised it extensively themselves, and dangerous because many groups simply exploit the unready, usually for commercial gain. Fortunately for the mass of aspirants, the information and the instruction given are both feeble, inaccurate and frequently innocuous, though there are many cases of significantly bad reaction; fortunately, also, the purpose of the average aspirant is so weak that he is incapable of persistent, daily, unchanging compliance with the requirements and fails to render that application which would be the guarantee of a dubious success; hence, in these cases, no danger exists. Many occult groups exploit the subject in order to build up mystery and to hold out inducements to the unwary, or give their adherents something to do and thus gain kudos for themselves as learned and well trained occultists. Anyone can teach breathing exercises. It is largely a matter of periodic in-breathing and exhalation, timed and spaced according to the wish of the teacher. Where there is persistence in effort, results will be achieved and these will usually be undesirable because the average teacher emphasises the technique of the breath and not the ideas which—upon the energy which that breath engenders—should take form in the life of the disciple.

The entire science of the breath is built around the use of the Sacred Word, the O M. The use of the Word is intended to be confined to those aspirants who are earnestly pledged to tread the Way, but it has been passed on and its use enjoined by many unscrupulous teachers, particularly those swamis who come from India, pose as Holy Men and get the silly women of the occident into their clutches. The Word is then used with no spiritual intent but simply as a sound which, carried on the breath, produces psychic results which indicate to the gullible their deep spirituality. The trouble is that breathing is inevitably related to the O M, but the effects are dependent upon motive and inner fixed intention. The oriental, unless he has attained the fourth or fifth initiation, has no true understanding of the

The Ending of Glamour 255

occidental or of his mechanism and equipment which, as the result of a civilisation and a mode of living, differs widely from that of the oriental. In the East, the problem of the teacher or Guru is to take negatively polarised people and make them positive. In the West, the races are as a whole positive in attitude and need no such training as is rightly given to the oriental. What exactly do I mean when I make this statement? I mean that in the East, the will factor (the quality of the first aspect) is absent. The oriental, particularly the inhabitant of India, lacks will, dynamic incentive and the ability to exert that inner pressure upon himself which will produce definite results. That is why that particular civilisation is so unadaptable to modern civilisation, and that is why the people of India make so little progress along the lines of regulated municipal and national life, and why they are so behind the times as far as modern civilised living is concerned. Generalising, the occidental is positive and needs the directive force of the soul and can produce it with very little teaching. In the Aryan race, a fusion is today taking place between the will aspect, the mind and the brain. This is not so in the Orient. It will be so later.

The only factor which makes the breath effective is the thought, the intent and the purpose which lie behind it. In this statement, you have the clue to dynamic useful breathing exercises. Unless there is a clear appreciation of purpose, unless the disciple knows just what he is doing as he practises esoteric breathing, and unless the significance of the words "energy follows thought" is understood, breathing exercises are sheer waste of time and can be dangerous. From this it can be gathered that only when there is an alliance between breathing and thinking will results be possible.

Behind this lies a third and even more important factor—the WILL. Therefore, the only person who can safely and usefully practise breathing exercises is the man whose will is active—his spiritual will and, therefore, the will of the Spiritual Triad. Any disciple who is in process of building the antahkarana can begin to use, with care, directed breathing exercises. But, in the last analysis, it is only the initiates of the third degree and who are coming under monadic influence who can properly and successfully employ this form of life direction and reach effective results. This is fundamentally true. However, a beginning has to be made and to this effort all true disciples are invited.

If all the implications in the above paragraph are considered, it will be apparent that the disciple has to establish—as a preliminary step—a direct relation between his brain, his mind and the will aspect of the Spiritual Triad; in other words, the negative receptor of thought (the brain), the agent of the will (the mind), and the Triad itself, have to be brought into contact with each other, via the antahkarana. When such a relation exists or is beginning to be established, then breathing exercises can safely and profitably be attempted. You see, my brother, only the directed will, using the organised rhythmic breath as its agent, can control the centres and produce an ordered purpose in life. Therefore, it is the dominating idea or line of mental activity with which the disciple must be concerned as he performs a breathing exercise. This idea must embody some purpose, some planned activity and some recognised goal before the breath which will engineer or implement it is generated, assembled, sent forth and thus becomes the carrier of power. This has to be done upon the wings of conscious intention, if I may here speak symbolically. I would urge you to read these last sentences with frequency because they concern the Science of the Breath and hold the clue to needed work. This science is primarily and fundamentally concerned with ideas as formulated into clear thoughtforms and

The Ending of Glamour

thus condition the life of the disciple upon etheric levels. From there, they eventually condition his physical plane life.

I have no intention here of giving any breathing exercises which disciples or aspirants could use—or, more probably, misuse. Their first responsibility is to become aware of the impulses within themselves which could galvanise the centres into activity and so produce conditions and events upon the physical plane. When these are clear and firmly established in the mind consciousness of the disciple, nothing can then stop their emergence in due time into the light of day. But they must follow an ordered process of gestation and of timed appearance.

When there is true idealism, right thought, plus an understanding of the vehicle of expression and the world of forces into which the idea has to be launched, then the student can safely follow certain scheduled breathing exercises and the second phase or the result of sound rhythmic breathing will appear. *This is Inspiration.*

Breathing exercises, my brother, have a purely physiological effect when not impelled or motivated by directed thought and when they are not the result of the aspirant attaining and adhering to a point of tension. Steadily, whilst the process of inhalation and exhalation is being carried forward, a clear line of active thinking must be preserved so that the breath (as it is sent out) is qualified and conditioned by some idea. It is here that the average aspirant fails so often. He is usually so intensely pre-occupied with the process of directing breathing and so expectant of some phenomenal results, that the living purpose of the breath is forgotten; this is to energise and add quality to the life of the centres through the medium of some projected and presented thought, expressing some sensed and determined idea. Where this background of idealistic thought is lacking, then the results of the breath will be practically nil or— where there are results of any kind under these circumstances—they will be in no way concerned with thought but will be psychic in nature. They can then produce lasting psychic trouble, for the emanating source of the activity is astral and the projected energy goes to centres below the diaphragm, thus feeding the lower nature, enriching and strengthening its astral content and thereby enhancing and deepening glamour. The results can also be physiological, producing the stimulation of the etheric body leading to the strengthening of the physical nature; this often leads to serious results, for the breath is carried to centres which should be in "process of elevation" as it is esoterically called; this increases their physical potency, feeds the physical appetites and makes the task of the aspirant much harder as he seeks to sublimate the lower nature and anchor or focus the life of the centres above the diaphragm or in the head.

Glamour and maya are then increased and for the life in which these exercises are misapplied, the aspirant remains in a static and unprofitable condition. As he breathes in or inhales, he draws the breath from within his own aura, his auric ring-pass-not; he feeds the lower nature and sets up a vicious circle within himself which strengthens day by day until he is completely enmeshed by the glamour and maya which he is constantly establishing and re-establishing. The lower centres are steadily vitalised and become extremely active and the point of tension from which the aspirant then works is found in the personality and is not focussed in relation to the soul; the consciousness of the uniqueness of special breathing and the expectancy of phenomenal results bar out all thought, except lower reactions of a kama-manasic nature; emotion is fostered and the power of the astral body is tremendously increased; very frequently also the physiological results are potent and noticeable, such as a great chest development and the muscular strengthening of the diaphragm. Something of this can be seen in the case of operatic singers. Singing, as now taught, is an expression of some of the lower aspects of the breath, and the breathing in the case of the above vocalists produces much breast development, intensifying emotionalism, producing instability in the life expression (which is often referred to as temperament) and keeps the singing aspect entirely astral in nature.

There is a higher and better mode of song, actuated by a difference in the point of tension and involving a breathing process which draws the needed energy upon the breath from sources higher and far more extensive than those normally used; this will produce the inspiration which will involve the whole man and not simply his emotional reaction to the theme of his song and his audience. This will bring into being a new mode and type of singing and of breathing, based on a form of mental breathing which will carry energy and consequent inspiration from sources without the personality aura. The time for this is not yet. My words will be little understood today, but the singing in the next century will be by those who will know how to tap the reservoirs of inspiration by means of a new method and technique in breathing. These techniques and exercises will be taught, to start with, in the new and coming schools of esotericism.

Inspiration is a process of qualifying, vitalising and stimulating the reaction of the personality—via the centres—to that point of tension where soul control becomes present and apparent. It is the mode whereby energy from the soul can flood the personality life, can sweep through the centres, expelling that which hinders, ridding the aspirant of all remaining glamours and maya, and perfecting an instrument whereby the music of the soul and, later, the musical quality of the Hierarchy can be heard. Forget not that sound permeates all forms; the planet itself has its own note or sound; each minute atom also has its sound; each form can be evoked into music and each human being has his peculiar chord and all chords contribute to the great symphony which the Hierarchy and Humanity are playing, and playing now. Every spiritual group has its own tune (if I may employ so inappropriate a word) and the groups which are in process of collaborating with the Hierarchy make music ceaselessly. This rhythm of sound and this myriad of chords and notes blend with the music of the Hierarchy itself and this is a steadily enriching symphony; as the centuries slip away, all these sounds slowly unite and are resolved into each other until some day the planetary symphony which Sanat Kumara is composing will be completed and our Earth will then make a notable contribution to the great chords of the solar system—and this is a part, intrinsic and real, of the music of the spheres. Then, as the Bible says, the Sons of God, the planetary Logoi, will sing together. This, my brother, will be the result of right breathing, of controlled and organised rhythm, of true pure thought and of the correct relation between all parts of the chorus.

Think out this theme as a meditation exercise and gain inspiration thereby.

c. The Technique of Indifference

I have, in my other books, given much information anent the etheric body and the centres—major and minor—which are to be found within its radius. There is a tendency among students to identify the centres with the physical body in their thinking and not so clearly with the etheric body. This concerns location in the majority of cases and is a mistake. Aspirants would do well to avoid any concentration at all upon

The Ending of Glamour

the physical body and learn gradually to shift their focus of attention into the etheric body. Necessarily the physical body is active and potent but increasingly it should be regarded as an automaton, influenced and directed by:

> 1. The vital body and the forces of maya; or by inspiration, emanating from points of spiritual tension.
>
> 2. The astral vehicle and the forces of glamour; or sentient, conscious love, emanating from the soul.
>
> 3. The mind and the forces of illusion; or by illumination, coming from higher sources than the life in the three worlds.
>
> 4. The soul, as the vehicle of monadic impression, until such time as the antahkarana is built—that bridge in mental matter which will eventually link the Monad and the personality.

One of the problems which disciples have to solve is the source of the incentive, impulses, impressions or inspiration which—via the etheric body—sweep the physical vehicle into activity upon the physical plane, thus giving a demonstration of the quality, purpose and point of tension of the incarnating man, and manifesting the nature of the man as he is at any particular point upon the ladder of evolution. According to the tensions and impulses indicated, will be the activity of the centres. You can see, therefore, how much that I teach reverses the usual occult procedures. I teach no mode of awakening the centres because right impulse, steady reaction to higher impulses and the practical recognition of the sources of inspiration will automatically and safely swing the centres into needed and appropriate activity. This is the sound method of development. It is slower, but leads to no premature development and produces a rounded out unfoldment; it enables the aspirant to become truly the Observer and to know with surety what he is doing; it brings the centres, one by one, to a point of spiritual responsiveness and then establishes the ordered and cyclic rhythm of a controlled lower nature. That breathing exercises may eventually find a place in the training of the disciple is true and possible, but they will be self-initiated as a result of rhythmic living and a constant right use of the Sacred Word, the O M. When, for instance, a disciple in meditation sounds the O M seven times, it is the equivalent of a breathing exercise; when he can send the energy thus generated on the wings of conscious planned thought to one or other of the centres, he is bringing about changes and readjustments within the mechanism which handles force, and when this can be carried out with ease and with the mind held at a point of "thought-full tension," then the disciple is well on the way to shifting his entire focus of attention away from the world of illusion, glamour and maya and into the realm of the soul, in the world of the "clear cold light" and into the kingdom of God.

When he also adds to this an understanding and the practice of the Technique of Indifference, he stands free and liberated and is essentially at all times the Observer and User of the apparatus of manifestation.

What is this technique? What is indifference? I wonder, brother of mine, if you understand the significance of this word "indifference"? It means in reality the achieving of a neutral attitude towards that which is regarded as the Not-self; it involves a repudiation of similarity; it marks the recognition of a basic distinction; it signifies refusal to be identified with anything save the spiritual reality as far as that is sensed and known at any given point in time and space. It is, therefore, a much stronger and vital thing than what is usually meant when the word is used. It is active repudiation without any concentration upon that which is re-

The Ending of Glamour

pudiated. That is a statement of moment and warrants your careful consideration. It is concerned with the point of tension from which the observing disciple or aspirant is working. The point of tension becomes the emanating source of some type of energy, and this pours down into and through the etheric body without being in any way affected by maya or by the concentration of diverse forces of which the etheric body is ever composed. Indifference, technically understood, signifies direct descent from there to here, without deviation or distortion. The manifesting entity, the disciple, stands steady and firm at this point of tension and his first step is, therefore, to ascertain where that is, on what plane it is found, and what is the strength of the tension upon which he has to depend. The next step is to discover if that which he seeks to convey to the physical body, and thus produce effects upon the outer world of experiment and experience, is distorted by illusion of any kind, arrested in its expression by glamour, or liable to be sidetracked by uncontrolled forces and by the maya which these produce. This he ascertains not by identifying himself, stage by stage of descent, with the hindrances and possible obstructions but by intensifying his point of tension, by the constant recollection of the truth that he is the Self and not the not-self and by a process of projection; this projection is defined as sending of energy, qualified and recognised, from the point of tension direct and undeviatingly to the vital body from whence it can find its way to the seven centres of control.

It is at this point that he applies the technique of indifference for, if he does not, that which he is seeking to express may be held up and arrested by etheric force or by the veils of maya. He works consequently from a point of intense concentration; he refuses any "attachment" to any form or plane as he projects the energy into and through the three worlds. When he discovers any arresting or sidetracking of progress through active illusion, or glamour, he "detaches" himself consciously from such contacts and braces himself for the final stage of indifference or repudiation of all forces except those which he—consciously and with purpose—is seeking to use upon the physical plane.

In the last analysis, my brother, the point of tension for the average disciple will be found on mental levels, involving the illumined mind and a growing soul contact:

> a. He will be able then to "see" clearly in the light of the soul, and with a developed sense of values; he can consequently dispel illusion.
> b. He will be able to project light, consciously, on to the astral plane and can thus dissipate glamour.
> c. He will be able to pour light energy through the etheric body and anchor the light or energy in the appropriate centres because there will be complete indifference or non-identification with maya.

Where the initiate is concerned, the process is carried on at first from a point of tension within the soul and later from a point of tension in the Spiritual Triad. In all cases, however, once within the ring-pass-not of the three worlds, the directing energy produces results as outlined in this book and brings about:

1. The dispelling of illusion.
2. The dissipation of glamour.
3. The overcoming of maya.

It sounds fairly simple and easy of accomplishment as the aspirant reads these fairly simple elucidations of a difficult process but that in itself is delusion. Age-long identification with the form side of life is not easily overcome and the task ahead of the disciple is a long and arduous one but one which promises eventual success, provided there is clear thinking, earnest purpose and planned scientific work.

SECTION FOUR

THE TECHNIQUE OF FUSION

In this, our final point, we are concerned with the control—constant and unremitting—of the soul over the personality. We are therefore concerned with the stage of initiation which brings to an end the path of development for humanity and inaugurates a cycle of existence of which we know, and can know, nothing except that the liberated Master then begins to function in a dual manner: as a member of the Hierarchy, cooperating with the Plan and occupied with the salvaging of humanity and, secondly, as a disciple of Sanat Kumara. The task of Sanat Kumara in relation to the Masters is to prepare Them to tread the Way of the Higher Evolution. When this becomes possible, the shift of the spiritual "attention" (I use this inadequate word for lack of a better one) is away from the soul and the Angel of the Presence to the mysterious Presence itself; this has hitherto only been sensed and dimly visioned. The Master—freed from the three and five worlds of human and so-called superhuman evolution—has now the full gifts of omnipresence and omniscience. He is aware of the underlying unity, brought about by the factual nature of the One Life and Being Who pervades all manifestation; He has also mastered all possible techniques and modes and methods of activity, of control and of fusion. But having developed those capacities, He now becomes faintly aware of that which conditions the One Being, and senses energies and contacts which are extra-planetary and of which He has hitherto been totally unaware. Knowledge comes to Him after the fifth initiation.

The Technique of Fusion

Before Him lies the attainment of a still higher range of perceptions and, in order to garner the reward of those possible contacts, He has to master techniques and methods of development which will make Him omnipotent and, therefore, expressive of the highest of the three divine aspects. This development will put into His grasp potencies and experiences which can only be manipulated and understood through the scientific activity of the WILL and this must be implemented from a point of tension, focussed in whatever is meant by the word "Monad." Do you know what that means, my brother? I am sure that you do not. Only the Masters of the Wisdom have any appreciation of these final unfoldments and then only in the sense of the Will-full aspiration—a phase of aspiration which is characterised by the conscious will, just as the aspiration of the disciple is characterised by sublimated desire. These things are, however, beyond the comprehension of the average disciple; their sole value is to depict the unending opportunity which presents itself at every stage and point of crisis upon the everlasting Way.

We are concerned at this time with the great point of crisis which faces the disciple when he attempts to resolve the final pair of opposites, prior to certain major initiations; this is the confronting the personality by the Angel of the PRESENCE. There is no need for me to define the two aspects of the disciple's nature, for that is what they essentially are. You have been told and have known that the Dweller upon the Threshold is the fully developed personality—the sum total of all the past and the composite presentation upon the physical plane of all unresolved problems, all undeclared desires, all latent characteristics and qualities, all phases of thought and of self-will, all lower potencies and ancient habits of any of the three bodies (both bad and good). These, in their totality, are brought to the surface of consciousness, there to be dealt with in such a way that their control is broken. The disciple is then free to take the final initiations. This process is not consummated in one particular facing of the two antagonistic forces. It is a threefold process, covering each of the three periods before the first three initiations or (from the angle of the Hierarchy) before the two initiations of the threshold and the first major initiation, the Transfiguration.

For many lives, the disciple has been dwelling upon the threshold. He himself is the Dweller. Behind the slowly opening door he senses life, energy, spiritual embodiment, and the *fact* of the Angel. Between him and that door is a burning-ground; this he faces, and this he knows he has to cross if he seeks to pass through the door. The question for him to answer is whether his will to achieve is strong enough for him to submit his personal lower self to the fires of the final purification. The personal self is now very highly developed; it is a useful instrument which the soul can use; it is a highly trained agent for service; it is essentially a piece of adequate and useful equipment. It has, however, its points of weakness which are liable at any time to present points of crisis; it has likewise its points of strength which can be transmuted with relative ease into points of tension; on the whole, it is a dependable instrument and one which can render good service. Can it and should it be sacrificed so that (esoterically speaking) its life is lost and in its place consecration and devotion are substituted? This is a hard problem for all disciples to solve, to understand and to make effectively practical. Only by crossing the burning ground three successive times are all impediments to the free use of the will destroyed. The relation between the Angel and the Dweller must be released, by means of the will, to full expression. I here refer to the spiritual will and to its three aspects which must be brought into play before the divine will can begin to control. The disciple brings the two aspects of his nature together in full consciousness and with clear intention through a planned act of the will, and this *act* produces a point of tension in the "centre of the burning-ground wherein the two can meet," as the ancient Archives put it.

I would call your attention to the fact that it is at a "midway point" that the great submission of the lower to the higher takes place. It does not happen when the disciple hovers uncertainly upon the periphery of the burning-ground or when he stands before the door with the burning ground experience behind him. The essential point of crisis, producing the needed point of tension, is the result of the "invocative decision" of the personality which, in time, produces an "evocative response" from the Angel. The two factors involved (and forget not, my brother, that all this takes place within the field of consciousness of the disciple) move together and towards each other. In the centre of the burning ground they meet, and then the lesser light (a true light in its own right) of the personality is absorbed into the greater light of the Angel or soul. The Angel, therefore, "occultly obliterates" the Dweller who becomes lost to sight in the radiant aura of the Angel. This has been symbolically portrayed for us in the picture book of the heavens when, according to Catholic Festivals, the Assumption of the Virgin takes place and the constellation Virgo is lost to sight in the radiance of the sun. There you have the three factors:

1. The Virgin . . . . . material form . . . . personality . . . . . . Dweller
2. The Sun . . . . spiritual nature . . . soul . . . . Angel
3. The Earth . . . . . . aspiring man . . . . . the disciple . . . . . .

The personality remains; it still exists but it is seen no more as of old. The light of the Angel envelops it; the burning ground has done its work and the personality is now nothing more or less than the purified shell or form through which the light, the radiance, the quality and the characteristics of the Angel can shine. It is a fusion of lights, with the stronger and the more powerful obliterating the lesser.

How has this been brought about? I refer not here to the preparation of the Dweller on the Threshold for this great event or to the aeon of disciplining, of preparation, of experiment and of experience from life to life which has made this consummating event possible and successful. The two aspects in man can only meet in full power and with intention and finality when illusion can no longer control the mind, when glamour has lost all power to veil and when the forces of maya can no longer hinder. Discrimination, dispassion and indifference have produced the dispelling through focussed light, the dissipating potency of distributed light and the directing power of light energy. Only five recognitions now control the disciple:

1. The fact of his discipleship.
2. The perception of the Angel, waiting and dynamic.
3. The invocative appeal of the Dweller on the Threshold.
4. The necessity to use the will in a new and different manner.
5. The need to cross the burning ground.

The issues are now entirely clear. It is a question of timing and of decision. I would remind you that in all these processes, it is the disciple who, in full consciousness, *acts*. He initiates all the processes himself. It is not the Angel or the Dweller but the spiritual man himself who has to employ the will and take definite forward moving action. Once the disciple has taken the necessary steps and moved irrevocably forward, the response of the Angel is sure, automatic and all-enveloping. Complete obliteration of

The Technique of Fusion

the personal self in three successive stages is the immediate and normal result. It was to this that John the Baptist referred when he said "He shall increase but I must decrease." When he spoke these words, he spoke as a disciple, prior to the second initiation of the threshold. This occult waxing and waning is portrayed for us in the phases of the moon and, for the planet as a whole, in the sign Gemini, where the light of one of the twins is slowly dimming and the light of the other is gaining in intensity.

When this "occult obliteration" has taken place, what then is the destiny of the disciple? It is complete control by the soul and this, in practice, connotes group realisation, group work, group service and eventually group initiation. With these developments, it is not my intent to deal, for I have covered much of these matters in my other books. Here I have been dealing in this short elucidation with the effects that substances and the substantial forces, found in the three worlds, produce in the disciple and as they affect the aspirant. I have not considered the problem of glamour, illusion and maya from the angle of average man. The latter is necessarily immersed in them, and under their constant impact he passes his life. By their means he learns. He is not at the point where he seeks deliverance from them as does the man upon the Path. I have, therefore, considered the problem from the angle of the disciples and aspirants.

From them the WAY opens up, and for them comes the conscious recognition of the light. The need for the service of men and women, free from illusion and glamour, has never been so dramatically present as it is today and it is for these potential servers of a desperate necessity that I have written.

That the Angel of the PRESENCE may make His nearness felt and inspire you to pass courageously through the fires of the burning ground is my earnest prayer; that the *fact* of the PRESENCE may be sensed by you and lead you to greater activity—once the burning ground is passed—is my deepest wish for you; and that the light may shine upon your way and bring a certain and assured consummation of all the travail and struggle which has characterised your way of life is my heart's desire for you. To more active and steady enterprise I call you.

THE TIBETAN

See also the Techniques of Fusion and Integration in *A Treatise on the Seven Rays, Vol. II, Esoteric Psychology,* pp. 345-401.

THE ARCANE SCHOOL

Training for new age discipleship

is provided by the *Arcane School.*

The principles of the Ageless Wisdom

are presented through esoteric meditation,

study and service as a *way of life.*

Contact the publishers for information.

www.lucistrust.org/arcaneschool

INDEX

A

Act of—
  abstraction, 244
  affirmation, 233-234, 240
  direction, 233, 239
  focussing the Lights, 231, 239
  integration, 216
  naming, 229, 231, 232, 239
  penetration, 218, 220, 234, 236, 237, 240
  projection, 233, 234, 240
  protection, 231, 239
  will, 232, 233, 236, 240
  withdrawal, 234, 240
Affirmation of power and purpose, 218
Ajna—
  awakening, 7
  focus of energy, 250
  in triangles of forces, 250, 251
Alignment—
  in dispelling glamour, 43, 209, 216, 220, 231
  need for, 89
  of will and love of God and desire of humanity, results, 170
  practice, 179
  process, 237
  soul, 54
  use, 209, 235
  value, 89
Angel of the Presence—
  absorbed in Presence, 159
  agency in revelation, 172
  attention, focus on Dweller, 158
  confronting personality, 267
  contrast with Dweller, 128, 152-160
  facing by Dweller, 90, 91, 102-103
  fusion with Dweller, 156, 159
  influence, 176
  keynote to solution of problem, 159
  occult obliteration of Dweller, 269
  on mental plane, 91
  penetration beyond, 183
  recognition of, 158
  relation to Dweller, 39-40, 156-157
  return to, stage, 182
  sensing, 152
  transmitter of energy, 160
  victory, 203
  See also Presence.
Angel, Solar—
  right to rule, 46
  See also Soul.
Animals, domesticated, battle of opposites, 87
Antahkarana, use, 256, 261
Aquarian Age—
  Dweller, personality forces, 157
  prophecy regarding, 22
  techniques, x
  See also New Age.
Architect, Divine, 244
Archives of Hierarchy, quotation, 141-142
Arjuna experience, 88, 98, 99, 100, 158
Aryan Race, 32, 40, 157, 158, 255
Aspirants, needs, 15, 85
Aspiration of Master and disciple, 267
Astral—
  body—
    fades out, 66
    function, 141
    nature of 66, 208-209
    planetary, appearance, 69-70
  life of race, disappearance, 73, 112
  nature, control broken, 252
  plane—
    disappearance, 193, 210
    illumination, 43, 170, 214
    liberation from, 210
    nature of, 31-32, 140-141, 208-210
    origin, 221
    pairs of opposites, 91, 99
    purified, control, 172
    Technique of Presence effective, 193
  results of breathing exercises, 258
Astrological—
  considerations, 119-120
  influences, 155-156, 246, 249
Atlantean—
  racial crisis, 158
  spiritual contact, 162-163
Atlantis—
  glamour, 32, 40
  illusion, 40
  mystical duality, 203
Atom, point of light, 196
At-one-ment—
  achievement, desire for, 95
  key, 194
Attachment to form or plane, refusal, 263-264
Aura—
  purification, 27
  study, 34-35
Auras of group members, 28

Avatars. *See* Buddha; Christ.
Awareness—
    human, unfoldment, factors, 173-174
    of reality, 200
Axis powers, 163, 164, 169

B

Beam of projected light, 202, 236
Bhagavad Gita—
    Atlantean racial crisis, 158
    symbolism of combat with glamour, 116
Blavatsky, H. P., work, 183
Blind, rendering, 194
Body—
    etheric. *See* Etheric.
    outer dual, production, 242
    physical. *See* Physical.
Brain—
    consciousness, 42, 43, 67, 209
    effect of union of soul light and personality life, 208
    functions, 43, 256
    relation to mind and spiritual will, 256
    structure, esoteric, 1
Breath—
    effectiveness, factors, 254, 255, 256
    organised rhythmic, use, 256
    Science of, 241
    synonymous with will, 245
Breathing—
    dangerous, 253-254, 255, 258
    exercises, 150, 254, 255-256, 257-258
Brotherhood, goal, 134-135
Buddha, Lord—
    and Christ, combined work, 165-169
    blow at world glamour, 40, 166, 167
    light on world problem, 23
    Noble Eightfold Path, 59
    teaching, 165-166
Buddhi, eye of, 250
Buddhic—
    faculty, 8
    force, use, 251
    plane, 9, 43, 131, 221
    principle, expression, 81
Buddhist system built up, 186
Builders, lesson, 6
Burning ground—
    center, meeting, 269
    crossing, 268

C

Catholic Church, cross, 230

Cell light, 5
Children, training, 89
Christ—
    advent, symbol and precursor, 159
    and Buddha, combined efforts, 167, 169
    and Buddha, work, 165-169, 186
    before Pilate, 240
    consciousness, 132
    dispelling illusion, 167, 187, 189
    expression, 194
    task, 23
    teaching, application, 166, 168
Church—
    Catholic, 186
    Christian, 186
    Christian Science, 186
    Greek Orthodox, 186-187
Churches—
    condition, 137-138
    Protestant, 186
Civilisation—
    new, bringing in, 199
    production, two processes, 174
Cloud of knowable things, 221
Compassion, true, 3
Concentration—
    intense, point, work from, 263
    nature of, understanding, importance, 205
Consciousness—
    basis of glamour, 94
    dualistic, culmination, 203
    human, impact by groups, 18
Contemplation, effect on illusion, 67-68
Creation—
    on physical plane, 243-244
    See also Imagination, creative.
Crisis, point, 267, 269
Cross of the Christ, or of divinity, 230, 238
Culture, new, 199

D

Darkness, pure, 205
Decentralisation of life from personality to soul, 61
Deception, types, differentiation, 85
Depression, deep, cause, 207
Desire—
    elimination, 66, 211
    not between brain consciousness and soul, 67
Destiny planned by souls, 153
Destroyer aspect, 244

Destroyers, lesson, 6
Detachment—
    attainment, 243
    necessity for, 17, 19, 264
    personality, 4
    value, 243
Devotee, one-pointed, 97-98
Dharma, definition, 1
Diaphragm, centres above, 150
Director, observing, serene, 243
Disciple—
    and intelligent man, contrast, 127-128
    ascertainment of nature of forces, 252
    capacities, three, development, 102
    contact with soul, establishment, 141
    directing agencies, 250, 252
    direction of life expression, 252
    director of forces, 243
    focus of identification, discovery, 252
    freed from influence of force, 84
    knowledge of forces, attainment, 252-253
    obligation, 1
    occidental, traits, 179, 255
    point of tension, 264
    power to illumine, 193
    problem, 33
    process of dissipating glamour, stages, 203-206
    quality equipment, 42
    recognitions, five, 270
    release from Great Illusion, 252
    self-examination, 246-250
    stand in spiritual being, 245
    training objective, 33
    western, 179, 255
    work, 190, 245, 250, 252
Disciples—
    work, factor of Ray, 199, 248-249
    world, 159, 202
Disciplines—
    physical, 87, 89
    self, 5, 88
Discrimination between forces and energy, 42
Disillusionment—
    secret, 94
    See also Illusion.
Distinctions needed by aspirant, 58-59
Divine indifference. *See* Indifference.
Doctrine—
    distorted twisted, 177
    emergence, 183

Dualistic consciousness, 203
Dualities, resolution, 101
Duality—
    mystical, sense of, unfoldment, 203
    sense of, basis of cause of glamour, 94
    sense of, recognition, 95
Dweller in body—
    extrication and entrance into unity, 95-103
    mistakes, 94
Dweller on Threshold—
    and Angel, brought together, 90-91, 102-103, 203, 267-268
    attention focussed on Angel, 158
    conflict, focussing, 163
    contrast with Angel, 152-160
    control broken, stages, 268
    definition, false, 21
    definitions, 22, 26-27, 90-91, 154, 160, 267
    emergence, 39
    fusion with Angel, 156
    individual, form, 34
    limitations resulting, 152
    occult obliteration, 269, 271
    of humanity, national or racial, 152-153
    on mental plane, 91
    personality forces in Aquarian Age, 157
    planetary, blow to, 23
    problems, 152, 154
    racial types, 157-158
    recognised and mastered, 154-155
    relation to Angel, factor of Rays, 156-157
    synthesis, 159

E

Earth, contribution to chords of solar system, 260
Eckhart, Meister, 196
Emotional—
    stability, 33
    types, susceptible to glamour, 31
Energies—
    human, 246
    in three worlds, work with, 245
    of dual body, sources, 242, 249
    three spiritual, imminent, 164-165
    uncontrolled and undirected, 85
    world of, 243
Energy—
    currents, distorted, 29
    direction, 252

discrimination from forces, 42
follows thought, 255
form, material substance, 187
mental distribution, 251
of—
    inspiration, world-wide, 164-165
    integrated personality, 250
    intuition, world-wide, 164-165
    light, handling and projecting, method, 226
    soul, vehicle, 250
use, major, 248
use or misuse, 42

Esoteric—
    sense, 1, 4
    training, need, 64

Esotericism, true, definition, 10

Esotericist, modern, 196

Etheric—
    bodies, pattern-forms, 2
    bodies, relationship, 246
    body—
        composition, 263
        energy reception, 245, 264
        forces, 249, 251, 253, 256, 260-262
        functions, 261
        of undeveloped and average man, 86
    plane, function, 241

Evocative response from Angel, 269

Evolution—
    character, 205-206
    point in, factor in distortion of idea, 56-57

Expression, arrest by etheric force or maya, 263

Eye—
    inner spiritual, 250, 251
    left, 251
    right, 250
    to eye, 228

Eyes—
    three, 250-251
    use as directing agencies, 250

Ezekial, vision, 137

F

Facts, facing, 145

Fanatic—
    holding of ideas, 170
    production, 29-30, 119, 132, 134

Fear, source of glamour, 46

Fire, symbolism, 179

Focus—
    in meditation, 209-210
    of—
        identification, 247-248
        light, 143, 144, 208-209, 210, 235
        mind, 209, 235

Focussed light, 141-142, 196, 198

Focussing—
    dual light, 230, 235, 237, 238
    process, stages, 208-210, 215
    three lights, 235

Force—
    agents, centres, 252, 253
    buddhic, use, 251
    circulation and mutation, 42-43
    distribution on etheric plane, 246-253
    manasic, use, 251
    misuse, 243
    physical-plane influence, freedom from, 84
    use or misuse, 42

Forces—
    director, 243
    distinction from energy, 42
    knowledge of, attainment, 252-253
    of dual body, 242
    of life, work with, 42
    organised and directed, 243
    seeking expression through etheric body, 249
    seven centres, 249-250
    spiritual, triangle, 250-251
    world of, 243

Forces of Light, 163

Form, human—
    identification with, 242
    nature of, 243

Forms—
    all, permeation by sound, 260
    divine, germ, 3
    from which to rid oneself, 200-201
    light of, 3
    reality in, 82
    symbolism, 190
    through which man becomes aware, 200-201

Formulas for dissipation of glamour—
    by group, 227-240
    for individual, 214-221, 235-237
    for world glamour, 227-235
    protective, 227, 229-230
    requirements for participants, 211-215

Four Freedoms, 164

Four Noble Truths, 23, 40, 165-166, 167

Freedom—

INDEX 279

from maya, illusion, and glamour, 244
of world, 161
Full Moon, June, 1942, undertaking, 168, 169
Fusion—
  active, opportunity for, 158
  activity of, 152-153
  between will aspect, mind, and brain, 255
  key, 194
  of lights, 196, 238, 270
  Technique of, 266-272

G

Gemini, symbolism, 271
Genius, production, 30
Germans, separativeness, 146-148
Germany, focus of world glamour, 163
Glamour—
  and illusion, distinction between, 83
  aspects, four, 40, 41
  breeders, 82
  causes, 84, 104-125, 200, 220
  contrast with illumination, 139-148
  contrast with maya, 149
  definition, false, 20
  definitions, 26, 94
  disappearance, results, 241
  dissipation—
    method, 36-37, 73, 83, 139-140, 252, 264
    powers needed, 201-202
    process, stages in individual, 204-205
    technique, 171-172, 193, 195-241
  elimination, seven keys, 24
  eradication, participants, qualifications, 207, 211-213, 214, 224-227
  extrication from and entrance into unity, 95
  forms on astral plane, 72
  freedom from, achievement, 100
  group, breaking, 15
  group, formula, 221
  growth, racial and individual, 94-104
  increased by breathing exercises, 258
  individual, dissipation, 202-221
  national, 71
  nature of, 26, 31, 32, 33, 73, 241
  of—
    authority, types, 45-53
    devotion, 73, 77-79
    family desire life, 71
    hatred of Jews, 146-148
    ideal of freedom, 46-48
    materiality, 73, 74-76
    pairs of opposites, 74, 79-80
    sentiment, 73, 76-77
    separateness, 145-146
  on—
    astral plane, 41, 69-84
    etherical levels, 84-90
    mental plane, 41, 53-68, 90-93
  penetration, 218
  personal, 71
  potency, 241
  problem, 21, 40-45
  racial, 71-72
  recognition, 44-46, 84
  seat, 149
  spiritual, 100
  stages, 95-103
  types, contrasts, 125-160
  understanding, 15
  whole, of entire plane, conflict with, 206-207
  world—
    attacking, beginning, 38
    causes producing, 104-125
    phases, 39
    removal, 167
    smashing, aid, 15, 68
    technique for group, 237-240
    three aspects expressed by three nations, 161
Glamours—
  choice for handling by group, 226
  differentiation, 117-118, 212
  higher and lower, contrasts, 125-160
  individual, five types of force, 116-117
  of Path, 74, 80
  of self, 80
  origin, 220-221
  psychological influences, 120
  regarding God, 243
Glands, consideration, 118
God—
  description, 244
  glamours regarding, 243
  idea, formulations, 130
  Immanent, 162, 176
  love of, 170
  mind, 131
  purpose, 244
  Transcendent, seen and known, means, 162

understanding, 135-136
Will, 170, 244
Goodwill, development, 244-245
Great Illusion, release of disciple from, 252
Group—
  Angel, 160
  glamour *See* Glamour, group.
  initiation, 271
  intuition. *See* Intuition, group.
  meditation for dissipation of glamour, 143-144
  members united as souls, 231-232
  of intuitively inclined people, demand, 189
  personal, 68
  personality, 160
  personnel, requirements, 224-225
  "pooling of the light", 226
  problem, 27
  realisation and work, 271
  revelation of cure, 188-189
  revelation of Presence, 160
  service, xiii-xiv, 216, 271
  soul, 160
  tension, revelations due to, 189
  united, 231
  work, esoteric, 1
  See also New Group of World Servers.
Groups—
  dissipating glamour, requirements, 201-202
  exchanging illusion for intuition, 136-139
  non-initiate, 225-226
Guru, problem, 255

H

Head—
  centre—
    highest, vehicle for soul, 250
    vibration, 7
  living in, 152
Healing, right methods, increase, 18
Heart—
  centre, light transferred to, 142
  centre, use to dispel glamour, 141-144
  living in, 152
  of disciple, intuition, 43
Hierarchy—
  aid to, 15
  Angel of Presence, 159
  Custodian of secondary revelations, 183
  freedom of, 137
  ideas, 130, 131
  knowledge of Plan, 131
  love of God, 170
  musical quality, 259
  placement of currents of energy, 61
  plan, 36
  problem, 33
  work, 213
Higher Way, relinquishing, 182
Hitler, power, source, 210
Human—
  progress, guarantee, 153
  values, change, 23
Humanity—
  advanced, on threshold of divinity, 159
  awaits coming revelation, 167
  Dweller, 152-153, 159
  education in distinctions, 164
  future, 160
  problem, immediate, 22, 158
  Rays governing, 156-157
  revelation imposed, 174
  today, 161-163
Humility—
  need for, 63
  value, 145

I

Idea—
  behind ideal, 132
  definition, 14
  distortion, 55-61
  divine, symbol of, 13
  fixed, 29, 119
  integration, wrong, 62-63, 65
  interpretation, wrong, 59-60, 65
  of God, formulations, 130
  perception, wrong, 57-59, 65
  whole, grasp, 131
Ideal—
  definition, 57
  rightly grasped and used, 133-134
Idealists, illusion, 97-98, 131-132
Ideals—
  growth, 133-134
  illusory, 135
Ideas—
  and ideals, 130-131
  application, wrong, 64-65
  appropriation, wrong, 60-62, 65
  as formulated into clear thought-forms, 256-257
  currents of energy on mental plane, 61

INDEX

descent from intuitional levels, 61
development, stages, 124
direction, wrong, 62, 65
embodiment, wrong, 63-64, 65
from buddhic plane, 131
misrepresentation, result, 36
new incoming, 167
sensed in interplay between disciples, 61
source, 54
stepped down into consciousness by Master, 61
types, 129-130
world of—
    awareness of, 54
    perceptions, 194
    working and living in, 14
Identification—
    reaction engineered by soul, 242
    with—
        all beings, 3
        form life, withdrawal from, 4
        integrated personality, 250
        the loved, 5
        Universal Mind, 4
Illumination—
    contrast with glamour, 139-148
    definitions, 140, 144, 145, 172
    directing physical action, 261
    effects, 241
    from soul, 55, 140, 193
    keynote to solution of problem, 40-41
    need for, 82
    of—
        astral plane, 43, 170
        intuition, 3-4
        mind, 252
    search for, 99-100
Illusion—
    and glamour, distinction between, 83
    and reality, distinction between, 101
    basis, 178
    breaking, means, 15
    Buddhist and Christian, 186
    built around intuition, 29-30
    comprehension and investigation, 18
    concern, primary, 172-173
    contrast with intuition, 128-139
    definition, false, 21
    definitions, 26, 54-55, 67, 128-130, 131, 173, 240
    dispelling agencies, 83
    dispelling, technique, 171, 190, 252, 264
    dissipation by Lord's Prayer, 24
    effects, 135
    facing and overcoming, 53-54
    in science and religion, 189
    of—
        doctrine and dogma, penetration through, 187
        power, 51-53, 187
        superiority, 187
    problem, 21
    submergence of new revelation, prevention, 190
    theological, of anthropomorphic Deity, 242
    world—
        problem, 173
        shattering, 16-17
Illusions—
    recognition, 45-46
    types, 57-65
Imagination, creative, use, 143, 211, 215, 217, 218, 234
Imperil, nature of, 151-152
India, people, characteristics, 255
Indifference—
    cosmic and divine, 242-244
    Technique of, 172, 193, 241-265
Individual—
    glamour, dissipation—
        formula, 215-221
        mode, 202-215
        Ray influence, 221-224
    man, study, 114-125
Individualisation of animals, 87
I-ness, 5
Infallible instrument, 101
Inferiority complex, 207
Initiate—
    consciousness, 205
    functioning, world, 195
    illusion dispelling, 65, 82
    insulation, 82
    life, inner, 196
    of first and second degrees, 101
    power, development, 192
    true, intuition, 81
    use of triangle, 250-251
    work from above down, 190
Initiates—
    dissipation of glamour, 202
    lives, Dweller in, 40
    of fourth degree, 254
    of third degree, 256

ranks, augmentation, 165
Initiation—
  definition, 88
  door, passing, 126, 127
  fifth, 103-104, 266
  first, 52-53, 54, 103, 172
  fourth, 103
  production, 88
  readiness for, indication, 126
  second, 103, 172, 200
  third, 3, 101, 103, 171, 173, 183, 203, 204
Initiations—
  five, results, 127, 206
  three, 268
Insanity, mental, production, 29
Inspiration—
  by soul, automatic response to, 150
  contrast with maya, 148-152
  definition, 259
  from meditation, exercise, 260
  intuitional, 31
  keynote to solution of problem, 40-41
  leading to, 241, 257, 259
  reservoirs, 259
  sources, 261
Insulation, right, result, 82
Integration—
  act, 216
  soul-mind-brain, 7
Interlude for constructive thinking, 182
Interpreters, mediating, 31
"Intruding agent of light", 182
Intuition—
  ability to break glamour and illusion, 15
  awakening, mode, 6
  concern, 181-182, 194
  contrast with illusion, 128-139
  cultivation, difficulty, 37
  definitions, 1, 2-6, 81, 171
  developed, 15
  development, 1, 184
  divine, inhibited, 241
  effect of Technique of Presence, 190
  effect on glamour, 23
  effect on illusion, 177-178
  evocation, vi
  free play, prevention, 135
  group, dispels world illusion, 184
  instrument, 101, 102
  keynote to problem of glamour, 40-41
  light of. See Light of intuition.
  plane, illumination by soul, 54
  plane. See also Buddhic plane.
  precipitation into human thought, 184
  production of understanding, 194
  relation to illumination, 7
  revelation, 241
  source of ideas, 54
  unfoldment, 8
Intuitive recognition of reality, 167
Intuitives—
  development, 184
  natural, 184
  presentation of next phase of truth, 176
  reaction to revelation, 176
  reaction to truth, 67
  training, 23, 184, 185
  work, 167, 178, 184
Invocation of spiritual will, 236, 239
Invocative decision of personality, 269
Involuntary process, 190
Irritation, nature of, 151-152
Isaiah, vision, 137
Isolated unity, 196
Isolation, right kind, result, 82
Italy, expression of world illusion, 163

J

Japan, maya, 163
Jesus, dispelling illusion, 65-66
Jews, separativeness, 146-148
John the Baptist, quotation, 270
John the Beloved, vision, 137

K

Kama-manas—
  definition, 21
  disappearance, 66
Kingdoms of nature, objectives, 90
Knowledge—
  and wisdom, distinction between, 101
  light of See Light.
  nature of, 194-195
  of how to dispel glamour, 191
Koot-Hoomi, Master, aid to, v
Kurukshetra, occurrence, 87-88

L

Law of—
  correspondences, vi
  rebirth, 179
Lemuria—
  freedom from glamour and illusion, 32, 40
  maya, 40

INDEX

Life—
  of three worlds, nature of, 195
  ordered purpose, production, 256

Light—
  activity, world-wide, 165
  and—
    love in disciple, 168
    soul, synonyms, 194
    substance, synonyms, 194
    uses, comprehension, 194
  appropriation, power, 201
  beam—
    fades out, 236
    use, 202, 204, 218, 219
    withdrawal, 219, 220
  bearer, 196
  bodies of all forms, 3
  breaks in on astral plane, 214
  definition, 193
  dual, focussing, 230, 235-238
  emanating center, 177
  energy, handling and projecting, 226
  false, 209
  focus. *See* Focus; Focussed; Focussing.
  increasing, revelations, 205-206
  in head, 3, 203, 208
  inherent, 208
  inner, use, 208
  into dark places, process, 191-192
  intuition, 3
  means of dissipating glamour, 206
  of—
    Ages, 3
    aura, 35
    body cells, 5
    brain, 209
    intellect, 3
    intuition, 3, 5, 43, 181-182, 206
    knowledge, 144, 145, 191, 192, 194-195
    matter, 208, 209, 210, 215, 219
    mental body, blending, 208
    mind, 191, 206, 208-209, 210, 215, 219
    personality, 192, 208, 219
    reason, 167
    soul. *See* Soul, light.
    substance, 208
    wisdom, 191, 192
    world, 3
  One, 49, 192, 231
  point behind all appearance, 180
  point in every atom of body, 196
  pouring into dark places, 204
  power, use, 218
  projection into world of glamour, 201-202
  projection onto astral plans, 264
  recognised, appropriated, and used, 196
  seen in light, 168
  stand in, between opposites, 100
  stream, 142
  substance of things hoped for, 193
  Technique of, 171-172, 190-241
  transfer, 142, 143
  triple, 210, 217, 220, 237, 238
  unified, 220
  united, 233
  use, conscious, 140
  within all forms, 191
  See also Searchlight.

Lighted centre within, 191
Lighted Way. *See* Way.
Lights—
  focussing, 235
  various types, 205-206
Light-substance, 191
Logos—
  Planetary, form-building activity, 241-242
  Planetary, life expression, 242
  relation of man to key, 192
Lord of the World. *See* Sanat Kumara.
Lord's Prayer, use, 24-25
Love—
  and light in disciple, 168
  definition, 5
  emanating from soul, 261
  from intuition, traits, 4-5
  need for, 224
  universal, 3

M

Magician, black, production, 209-210
Man—
  identification with transient creation, 242
  relation to Logos, 192
  soul-mind-brain, 66
  See also Ray; Rays.
Manas, eye, 251
Manasic force, use, 251
Manifestation, nature of, 94, 221
Mantrams, 229, 231, 232, 233, 234, 236, 238
Masonic ritual, 228

INDEX

Master—
  becoming, 42
  capacities, new, 266-267
  liberated, dual functioning, 266
  problems, 33
  spiritual attention, shift, 266
  Tibetan—
    call to service, 271-272
    contact with, 16-17
    use of telepathy with disciple, 61
Masters, dissipation of glamour, 202
Matter—
  control, 128
  energies, ancient, 86
  light of, 196, 210
Maya—
  causation, 33
  contrast with glamour, 149
  contrast with inspiration, 148-152
  deceptive power, 86
  definition, false, 20
  definitions, 26, 148, 241-242
  devitalisation, 252
  ending, clue, 245
  increased by breathing exercises, 258
  in emotional form, 149
  non-identification with, 264
  overcoming, technique, 241, 265
  problem, 22, 84-89, 148, 150
  relation to forces pouring in through centres, 85
  seat, 149
  subhuman kingdoms, 40
  terminated, 172
  world, de-vitalising, 88
Meaning, penetration to, value, 13
Meditation—
  activation of head centre, 250
  alignment in, 89
  clue to success, 204-205
  effect on illusion, 22
  for control of glamour, 204, 208, 215
  group, x, 143-144
  means of mental control, 209
  method of Technique of Presence, 178-183
  on soul contact, 238
  process, 67, 209
  work, 13
Mental—
  control, 209
  energy distribution, 251
  levels, point of tension for disciple, 264
  plane—
    distortion on, 30-31
    irradiation, 170
    pair of opposites, 91
    soul upon, 231
    Technique of Presence effective, 193
  polarisation, 197
  vehicle, focus of light in, attempt, 208-209
Messenger of revelation—
  group, 188-189
  individual, 188-189
Mind—
  awareness, 54-55
  control, technique, effect, 22
  dispelling agency, 100
  higher, production of transfiguration, 175
  holding steady in light, 81, 204-205, 217, 231, 236
  human, development, 184
  illumined, 171
  light. *See* Light of mind.
  lower, thoughtform-building activity, 178
  lower, use by masses, 178
  plane, illumination by soul, 54
  power, illuminating, 145
  rationalising activity, 192
  relation to will, 256
  relation to worlds of experience, 194
  revelation of existence of desire, 202
  subduer of emotion, 144
  Technique of Light, related, 193
  thoughtform-making properties, 67
  training, 15, 62
  universal, *See* Universal mind.
  use as reflector of soul light, 82
  use by Masters, 192-193
Minds of men, veiled and clouded, 183-184
Monad—
  focus for point of tension, 267
  in command, 251-252
  life of, result, 195
  link with personality, 261
  reaching toward, 2-3
  relation to etheric force, 97
Monadic influence, 256
Moon, full—
  contact with Master, 16-17
  time for dispelling glamour, 17, 19
Morya, Master, aid to, v

Motives, study and understanding, 149
Music of—
    Hierarchy, 259, 260
    soul, 259
    spheres, 260
Mystical—
    vision, transfer to higher levels, 180
    way, 180
Mysticism, Eastern, 180
Mystics, practical, subject to revelation, 138-139

N

New Age—
    characteristics, 197
    inauguration, 166
    revelation, 189
    work, 27-28, 213
    See also Aquarian Age.
New Group of World Servers—
    blow at world glamour, 40
    project, 38
    work, xi, 48
Noble Eightfold Path, 59
Noble Middle Way, 100, 101

O

Obliteration, occult, 269, 271
Observer—
    attitude, 17, 190
    divine, 243
    mental, 253
Observers, trained, 15, 38
Occidental, characteristics, 255
Occult obedience, 49
Occultism—
    practical, field, 245
    Western, 180
Occultist, work, 243-244
Occultists, practical, subject to revelation, 138-139
Old Commentary, quoted, 150-151, 153
OM, use, 217, 218, 231, 234, 236, 239, 254, 262
Omnipotence, development, 267
Omnipresence and omniscience, gifts, 266
One and other, relation, 221
Oneness, universal, sense of, 5
Opposites—
    first pair, 96-97, 99
    pairs—
        battle between, 84, 85-86, 87, 91, 126-127
        battlefield, 141
        final fight, 203
        on astral plane, 98
        resolved, 241
        standing in light between, 100
Oriental, characteristics, 254-255
Orthodoxy, trammels, release of truth from, 184
Over-stimulation. *See* Stimulation, undue.

P

Pairs of opposites. *See* Opposites.
Patanjali—
    teaching, 9, 83, 135, 195-196, 217, 221
    See also Yoga, Raja.
Path—
    of—
        discipleship, 42, 91, 99, 100, 165, 172
        Evolution, 205
        Higher Evolution, 178, 181
        initiation, 42, 91
        Probation, 42, 91, 165, 172
        Purification, 42, 91, 97, 99, 100
    six rules, 50-51
Pattern of things on trestle board, 243-244
Pattern-forms, production, 2
Penetration of light into darkness, 234
Perception becoming accurate, 101
Personality—
    agent of spirit, 252
    confronting by Angel, 267
    cooperation with soul purpose, 249
    direction by soul, vehicles, 250
    illumined, reaction to tendency of Triad, 195
    integrated, 4, 33, 152, 250, 251-252
    life, latent impulses, 86
    link with Monad, 261
    magnetic, 5
    orientation, 2
    purified shell, 269-270
    splits, 118-119
    will, 209
Personality-soul unification, 4
Physical—
    body, galvanising, 253
    body, nature of, 247, 260-261
    coordination, need for, 89-90
    culture and sports, benefit, 89
    plane—
        forces and energies worked out on, 42
        influence, free from, 84

pairs of opposites, 91
personality direction on, 250
Pineal gland, area of brain, 1, 5
Piscean Age, 157
Plan—
    agent, attitude, 190
    awareness of, 244
    cooperator with, efficient, 191
    service of, 195
    work with, 13, 131
Plutarch, quotation, 14
Power of—
    direction, work with, 250
    transfiguration, 171
    transformation, 172
    transmission, 172
Prana, world of, energies emanating, 85
Pranic fluids, 86
Prayer from *Upanishad*, 198
Presence, the—
    attention shift to, 266
    definition, 162, 176
    emanation via Shamballa, 159
    energy transmission, 160
    functioning, 183
    intuiting, 152
    living unity, 102
    overshadowing, 172
    relation of integrated Self to, 127
    revelation, 172
    sensing, 180, 181
    Technique of the, 171, 172-190, 192-193, 198, 241
    today, 159
    vision of, stupendous, 180
    voice of, heard, 183
Pride—
    false, 145
    of mental type, 60
Priests, true, line of, 137-138
Principle—
    Christ, indwelling, 4
    of universality, 3
Prophets, line of, 137
Protection from glamour, 226, 227
Protective Formula, 229-230, 237-238
Psychological—
    influence, 120
    understanding, true, 1
Psychology of future, 118
Pure reason, power, 81
Purpose—
    ascertainment, 181
    divine, revelation, 195

Q
Questions put to oneself, 35

R
Raincloud of knowable things, 135
Ray—
    Destroyer, 6
    factor in dissipation of glamour, 199, 201, 204
    fifth—
        glamours, 122
        methods, use, 64
        people, characteristics, 223
    first—
        glamours, 120-121
        people, traits, 4, 6, 222
        people, work, 6
    focus, 199
    fourth—
        glamours, 122
        governing fourth Creative hierarchy, 157
        initiates, 225
        people, 199, 223-224
        personality, effect on Dweller, 156
    influence, 118
    quality, determination of glamour, 117
    second—
        characteristics, 224
        glamours, 121
        people, work, 5, 199
        problem, 222-223
    seventh—
        glamours, 123
        people, difficulty, 222
    sixth—
        glamours, 123
        people, 199, 222, 225
    soul, activity, 117, 156
    third—
        glamours, 121-122
        materialistic personality, 160
        person, difficulty, 37, 222
        type, factor in distortion of ideas, 56
Rays—
    governing three bodies, 92
    knowledge of, need for, 248-249
    personality, glamours, 120-123
    seven, channel of ideas, 131
Razor-edged path, 49-50
Real, the—
    contact with, 82
    identification with, 204

INDEX

seeing, 204
Realisation of Being, 241
Reality—
   and illusion, distinction between, 101
   approach to, control, 240
   awareness of, 200
   definition, 221
   intuiting, 15
   inward and spiritual, symbols of, 190
   nature of, conception and recognition, 198
   precipitation, 200
Recognitions, five, of disciple, 270
Records, keeping, 19, 25
Reflection, value, 81
Religion—
   new world, 214
   situation, today, 162
Renunciation, keynote, 166
Reorientation of race, production, 97
Resolution of duality into unity, 97
Revealing Agency—
   recognition, 189
   task, 176
Revelation—
   by intuition, 174
   combined efforts of Buddha and Christ, 167-168
   embodiment, 182
   of glamour by focussed light, 209
   of glamour by soul, 139
   one unified unfoldment, 206
   process, theme of technique, 175-176
   source, 135-136
   subject to, types of people, 136-139
   substance, material, form of energy, 187
   succumbing to illusion and descent into glamour, 183
   total, 183
   true, 9, 187
Revelations—
   basic, presentation, 186
   primary and secondary, 183-184
Rhythm—
   established, recipients, 251
   importance, 225, 246
   of sound, 260
Rhythmic control, 252
Rules of the Road, 49-51

S

Sanat Kumara—
   divine indifference, 244
   planetary symphony, 260
   task, 266
   See also Lord of the World.
Saviours, world, 136-137
Schools of esotericism, future, 259
Science—
   of Breath, 241, 245, 253-260
   revelation in, 187, 188-189
Scientific—
   approach to problem of glamour, 197
   work, 210-211
Searchlight—
   creation, 219
   of—
      blended light, 231-232
      mind, 197, 217-218, 219, 220, 233, 235, 236, 237
      soul, 34, 140, 239
   visualisation of, 220, 232
Self, integrated, 127
Sensitives, groups, achievements, 19
Sensitivity—
   development, indication, 158
   psychic, 195-196
   to divine ideas, 184
   to psychic gift waves, 61
Separateness—
   glamour of, 145-146
   sense of, loss, 3
Server regards oneself as radiating light, 196
Service—
   act, 235
   aid to, 13
   new fields, 192
   of Plan, development, 195
   result of training, 23-24
   world, definite, 197
Shamballa—
   Custodian of primary revelations, 183
   freedom of, 137
   will of God, 170
Silence, minutes of, 228, 232, 234, 239
Singers, effects of breathing exercises, 259
Singing, new type, 259
Soul—
   activity, 231
   alignment, 54
   and light, synonyms, 194
   characteristic, major, 140
   contact with, 141
   contemplation, 67
   control over personality, 1, 266

direction by, 250, 252
dispelling illusion, method, 83
energies, distinction, 42
energy—
    activation, 250
    distinction from forces, 42
    evoked, 43
    misuse, 42
    vehicle, 250
    work with, 42
evidence of life, 193
eye, 250
force, distribution on physical plane, 241
group-conscious, 2
identification with, 104
in command, 251-252
inspiration by, automatic response, 150
inspiration of centres, 150
instruments, 250-251
integrated, 3
levels, 43
life, spontaneity, 80
light—
    and personality light, bringing together, 208
    awareness of, 208
    basically group conscious, 48
    blended, 210, 230, 238
    distortion, 53
    functions, 194
    irradiation, 193
    knowledge of, 208
    nature, 191, 196
    qualities, 139
    rays from, 81
    recognition, 230, 237
    return to astral body and heart, 141
    transfer, 141-145
    unification with light of matter, 219
    use, 140, 144, 191
love, 261
music of, 259
nature of, 143, 193, 243
point of tension within, 264
pre-rogative, 2
pull offsetting pull of glamour, 207
purpose through personality cooperation, 249
reaching in two directions, 2-3
re-focussing in, 182
relation to astral plane, establishment, 141
searchlight *See* Searchlight seeing and hearing, 217
source of reaction of identification, 242
    See also Angel.
Sound, permeation of all forms, 260
Sounding OM. *See* OM.
Spiritual—
    consciousness, trestle-board, 244
    perception, faculty, use and control, 178
    reading, 8-9
    Triad. *See* Triad.
    values, world of, apprehension, 175
Stand in spiritual being, 245
Stimulation, undue, avoidance, 17, 142
Subhuman kingdoms, maya, 40
Substance—
    and light, synonyms, 194
    control of spirit, 128
    hold over life of spirit ineffective, 193
    light, 208
    material, form of energy, revelation, 187
Suicide, cause, 207
Sun—
    central spiritual, 143, 192
    heart, 143, 192
    physical, 192
Swamis from India, 254
Symbol—
    analysis, stages, 10-11
    cross, 230
    meaning, penetration, results, 8-9
Symbolic reading, 6-10
Symbolism of forms, 190
Symbols—
    seeing, explanation, 2
    study, 1, 6-15
Symphony, planetary, 260
Synthesis, threefold, 159
Synthesising experience, 42
Synthetic recognition, 9-10

T

Technique of Fusion, 266-272
Technique of Indifference, 172, 193, 241-265
Technique of Light, 171-172, 190-241
Technique of the Presence, 171, 172-190, 192-193, 198, 241
Telepathic—
    Communicators, service, 18-19
    sensitivity, objective, 18-19
    work, growth and understanding, 18
Telepathy, use by Master, 61

Tension—
   point—
      for disciple, 264
      for incarnating man, 261
      for initiate, 264
      for Master, 267
      in center of burning-ground, 269
      in dissipating glamour, 218, 231
      needed, production, 269
      spiritual, points involved in inspiration, 261
      stage of meditation, 178, 179
Tests of—
   aspirants, 51-53, 201
   disciples, 201
Theological—
   interpretations, 177
   systems built up, 186
Theosophical groups, 183-184
Things, definition, 241
Thinking—
   hard straight, value, 83
   world, response to presented truth, 177
Thought—
   built-up, illusory, 177
   idealistic background for breathing, 257-258
   power, use, 217-218
   right, impact, 18
   substance, magnetic, field, 235
Thoughtform building activity, 178
Thoughtforms—
   Aryan Race, 32-33
   created by man, 58
   formulation for embodying revelation, 182
   human, 220-221
   illusive, 240
   nature of, 72
   potency, 29
Tibetan Master—
   call to service, 23-24
   contact with, 16-17
   my work, statement, v-vi
Training—
   for dissipation of glamour, 36-37
   for life of intuitive perception, 195
   of disciples, objective, 33
   of group, objectives, 38
Transfer of forces, 150, 152
Transfiguration—
   initiation. *See* Initiation, third.
   meaning, 168
   of the personality, 198
   secret revelation, 187
Transformation, secret, revelation, 187
Transmutation—
   of emotional devotion, vi
   secret, revelation, 187
Triad, Spiritual—
   expression, 195
   faculty, intuition, 81
   identification, tendency, 195
   perceptions, intuitive, 194, 195
   point of tension for initiate, 264
   will aspect, relation with brain and mind, 256
   will of, activity, 256
Triangles of forces, 250-252, 253
Truth—
   and truths, distinction between, 101
   concrete, perception, 145
   definition, 240
   mental perception, misinterpreted and misapplied, 175, 177
   new, appreciation and appropriation, 176
   old, new light upon, 184
   presented, response to, 177
Truths—
   new, revelation, 170
   taught by Buddha and Christ, 165
2025, until progress, theme, 170-171

U

Understanding-
   result of intuition, 1, 4,
   synthetic, 2
Unification, consummation, 3
United Nations coalition-
   demonstration of spiritual values, 165
   on side of Angel, 163
Unity—
   and life more abundantly, achieved, 203
   isolated, 196
   secret of disillusionment, 94
Universal—
   love, 3
   Mind, 2, 13, 244
Universality, principle, 3
Upanishad, quotation, 198

V

Veil—
   astral, 141
   of illusion, 82

Vision, eye of, 250
Visualisation—
  importance, 231
  power, development, 15
  use in dissipating glamour, 217, 231, 232, 234, 239
Vital body, control and activation of physical, 96

W

War, World, interpretation, 88
Way—
  everlasting, 267
  irradiation, 3
  Lighted, seen ahead, 101
  Lighted, walking by group, 38
  of—
    disciple, 25, 43
    Higher Evolution, 178, 181, 266
    Raja Yoga, 100
    opening before man on Path, 271
Will—
  act of, 218, 232, 269
  activity, need for, 255-256
  activity, scientific, 267
  aspect, 244
  directed, effects, 256
  divine, 269
  employment by disciple, 270-271
  factor absent in East, 255
  focussed, 233
  individual, relation to divine will, 206
  of God, 244
  of Spiritual Triad, 256
  soul-personality, use, 217
  spiritual—
    aspects, 268-269
    destructive, 233
    invocation, 236, 239
  synonymous with breath, 245
  use, 202, 268
Will-to-good, 244
Wisdom—
  ageless, teaching, v
  and knowledge, distinction between, 101
  cloud, 135
Withdrawal—
  from identification with form life, 4
  process, 219, 220
Word of power, sacred. *See* OM.
Words of power, saying, 233, 239

World—
  crisis, present, 159
  glamour, dissipation, 221-235
  inner, meaning, 232
  of—
    conflict between real and unreal, 206
    desire, 206
    divine revelation, 195
    divinity, 206
    energies, 243
    feeling, 175
    forces, 243, 245
    form and forms, 206
    formless, 206
    human experience, 206
    ideals, 206
    ideas, 14, 206
    instinct, 206
    intuition, 184
    matter, 206
    meaning, 190, 194, 231
    mind, 206
    phenomena, transfiguration, 175
    psychic meaning, 191
    reality, 175, 191
    spiritual values, apprehension, 175
    subjective spiritual activity, 231
  servers, 159
  servers. *See also* New Group of World Servers.
  tension today, cause, 97
Worlds, three, of phenomena, 175, 206

Y

Yoga—
  Agni, 171, 178-179, 183
  Karma, 172, 183
  Raja—
    discipline, 81, 205
    related to Technique of Light, 172
    rules for Technique of Light, 195
    study, necessity, 81
    system, 195
    teaching, 196
    technique, cure of glamour, 59
    way of, 100
    See also Patanjali.

Z

Zodiac, cycles, incarnations, 157